The Triumphant Holy Spirit!

*His Power, Works, and Wonders
for
This Final Generation*

In Dedication to my grandchildren who will see the greatest outpouring of the Holy Spirit that the world has ever seen. They will be used in signs, wonders, and miracles to the glory of the Lord.

In their birth order:

Malachi, Hazel, Jackson, Jacob

and the two twins, Rogan and Rinley .

❧❦

"And it shall come to pass in the last days, says God, that I will pour out My Spirit on all flesh; your sons and your daughters shall prophesy, your young men shall see visions, your old men shall dream dreams. And on My menservants and on My maidservants I will pour out My Spirit in those days and they shall prophesy." (Joel 2:28-29)

❧❦

All rights reserved solely by the author. The author guarantees all contents are original and do not infringe upon the legal rights of any other person or work. No part of this book may be reproduced in any form without the permission of the author. The views expressed in this book are not necessarily those of the publisher. Unless otherwise indicated, "Scripture taken from the NEW AMERICAN STANDARD BIBLE®, Copyright ©1960,1962,1963,1968,1971,1972,1973,1975,1977,1995 by The Lockman Foundation. Used by permission."

Copyright © 2024 by Don Kremer

Table of Contents

Forward by	Mel Tari	1
Introduction	A Critical Reality	3
Chapter 1	In All That God Is	9
Chapter 2	Five Cycles of Evil	14
Chapter 3	Seven Prophetic Church Periods	23
Chapter 4	The Ephesus Church	26
Chapter 5	The Smyrna Church	30
Chapter 6	The Pergamum Church	32
Chapter 7	The Thyatira Church	34
Chapter 8	The Sardis Church	37
Chapter 9	The Philadelphia Church	44
Chapter 10	The Laodicea Church	47
Chapter 11	The Neo-Pentecostals	53
Chapter 12	Cessationism and the Holy Spirit	64
Chapter 13	Arminism	77
Chapter 14	In Consideration of It All	79
Chapter 15	The Holy Spirit Was Not Yet Given	92
Chapter 16	Jesus Sends the Holy Spirit	97
Chapter 17	The Final Words of Jesus	103
Chapter 18	The Promise of the Spirit's Baptism	105
Chapter 19	The Spirit's Gift is For God's Children	110
Chapter 20	Tongues is The Proof	114
Chapter 21	Salvation But No Baptism of the Spirit	117
Chapter 22	What Is Normal Christianity	120
Chapter 23	The Holy Spirit Comes to Cornelius	127
Chapter 24	Peter Testifies of the Spirit's Baptism	131
Chapter 25	Believers in Ephesus Are Baptized	134
Chapter 26	Five Operations of Tongues	137
Chapter 27	The Unregenerated Soul	155
Chapter 28	The Corinthians Church Confusion	162
Chapter 29	Receiving His Baptism	169
Chapter 30	The Gifts of the Holy Spirit	181
Chapter 31	The Gift of Tongues	193
Chapter 32	The Doorway To The Eight Gifts	200
Chapter 33	The Last Days	209

Forward by Mel Tari
Author of *Like a Mighty Wind*

Starting as a young man in my late teens and now well into my adulthood, I have been privileged to be part of the great moves and revivals of the Holy Spirit that happened in my lifetime. My first experience happened Sunday, September 26, 1965 on the island of Timor, Indonesia, when the Holy Spirit came as He did on Pentecost with a mighty wind and cloven tongues of fire that rested on the heads of about two hundred people in the Presbyterian church where I attended. We had received POWER to be witnesses of Jesus Christ and we were Baptized in the Holy Spirit.

The news of the Indonesian revival spread like fire around the world. Stanley Mooneyham, vice president of international relations for the Billy Graham Evangelistic Association said, "What the Holy Spirit is doing in Indonesia today is more like another chapter added to the Book of Acts than anything else."

Hundreds of thousands of people came rushing to Jesus during this revival. The numbers of salvations were happing so rapidly that it exceeded the capacity of those trying to record them.

During this revival, I personally experienced the same working of miracles as in the Book of Acts including water turned into wine; people raised from the dead; accidently eating poison that brought no harm to us; walking on water; fire coming down from Heaven destroying idols; healings, miracles, deliverances—and all for one purpose: the saving of souls. We did not seek miracles, signs, and wonders. The display of such power that came from our Heavenly Father followed the words we preached as we reached out to lost souls needing salvation in Jesus Christ. I wrote the full testimony of this account in my book, *Like a Mighty Wind* which became a best seller across the Body of Christ.

God took me as a young island missionary from my country and sent me to every nation in the world except for two nations. Today, with great anticipation, I am excited about the coming world-wide revival. I will once again see the marvelous works of the Holy Spirit that will race across every nation and around the world in this final generation. It will be even greater than the fires of revival that I saw in Indonesia—greater than any revival that has ever occurred on earth since Adam.

This book, *The Triumphant Holy Spirit*, is insightful and helpful to all of us who want to partner with Jesus in the last great harvest of souls of our generation. It describes, as best as anyone can, the size and power released upon this generation. After all, we are the generation that must reach over six billion souls in a short period of time before the soon return of Jesus Christ.

By the efforts of man, this task is absolutely impossible. It is staggering beyond comprehension. It can only be accomplished by the Holy Spirit. There is no other way except by His power. As this book describes, the current number of lost souls needing salvation, healing, deliverance, and miracles would form a line 1,193,181 miles long that circles the earth forty-eight times, plus an additional line of people stretching 6,225 miles long from Los Angeles to Corsica, Italy! This is difficult to grasp. So the next time you are standing in the night, look up at the sky. The number of lost souls would form over six lines of people stretching from the earth to the moon.

Our hope cannot be in any system of religion or by the great and noble efforts that we use today. It will only be possible by the glorious Triumphant Holy Spirit.

I encourage you to spread the news and be a part of what the Lord Jesus, in His great mercy and love for humanity, is about to pour out upon all of mankind. By God's grace, this book convey an insight of our Heavenly Father's last great move for the salvation of souls. I wholeheartedly endorse this book.

A Critical Reality

The Critical Reality of Our Times
"A Prophetic Introduction"

On April 7, 32 AD,[1] Jesus Christ sat on the Mount of Olives overlooking Jerusalem. His disciples asked Him three question folded into one statement: "When will these things be (the destruction of the temple); what will be the sign of Your coming; and the end of the age."

Starting from Matthew 24:3 through the end of chapter twenty-five, Jesus answers their questions. His explanation mirrors the words found in Revelation chapters six and seven which would be written sixty-four years later. By that time, all the Foundation Apostles were martyred with the exception of John—the last living Foundation Apostle. By divine destiny, according to the unfathomable wisdom of our gracious Heavenly Father, John is divinely preserved to write the final book which is specifically assigned to THIS generation—The Book of Revelation.

Reaching from 32 AD, Jesus explains the events that are about to occur during our life. Sadly, few people realize that we are the grand finale, the *final* generation, the *select* generation throughout all of humanity. It is *our* generation that sees the enthronement of Antichrist *and* the return of Jesus Christ—in that order. And while it sounds exciting, what lies before us is both tragedy and triumph.

In faithfulness to Jesus, two billion Christians[2] will be martyred for refusing to take the Mark of the Beast. Therein lies the testimony of the victorious triumphant church at the end of the age. The tragedy, however, is the remaining six billion three hundred million souls currently on the rolls of the eternally damned. Because of this, the Father's heart grieves. Even for them, He gave His only begotten Son, Jesus Christ. But unless they accept Jesus Christ as the ONLY answer, they will die an eternal death for refusing Him.

---

[1] The precise date of this even when Jesus explains the endtimes, is accredited to Royal Observatory at the Greenwich Time laboratory.

[2] The actual number is equal to ¼ of mankind starting from the 4th Seal of Revelation through the 6th Seal at the time of Jesus' return. Currently, there are slightly over eight billion people on the earth. In concept numbers, ¼ of mankind is two billion.

A Critical Reality

It is nearly impossible to comprehend a global population of eight billion three hundred million (8,300,000,000) people. Therefore, let me offer another way to grasp the enormity of so many souls: If a person started counting one second per number, twenty-four hours a day, non-stop, from 1 to one billion (1,000,000,000), it would take thirty-one years and six month to reach the final number. Counting to six billion (6,000,000,000) would take one hundred eighty-nine (189) years.

Visually, if one billion souls stood shoulder to shoulder (using an average sized shoulder span of sixteen inches), the line would stretch 252,525 miles in length. This is equal to a line that circles the earth ten times, plus a 3,469 mile line-segment of people stretching from Philadelphia to Portugal!

Based on today's population of eight billion three hundred million people (8,300,000,000), when Antichrist kills one fourth of mankind (Revelation 6:8), two billion seventy-five million (2,075,000,000) souls will be slaughtered. The number of martyrs would form a line 523,990 miles long that circles the earth twenty-one times, plus a 6,748 mile line-segment of people stretching from Los Angeles to France!

Currently, there are six billion three hundred million (6,300,000,000) unsaved souls heading into the torment of eternal damnation. Their number would form a line 1,590,909 (one million five hundred ninety thousand nine hundred nine) miles long that circles the earth sixty-three times, plus a 6,225 mile line-segment of people stretching from Los Angeles to Corsica, Italy!

Hard to imagine? Consider this: The number of unsaved people would form slightly over six lines from earth to the moon plus a 15,767 mile line segment.

For this reason, Jesus said:

> "Enter through the narrow gate; for the gate is wide and the way is broad that leads to destruction, and there are many who enter through it. 14 For the gate is small and the way is narrow that leads to life, <u>and there are few who find it</u>. "(Matthew 7:13-14. Underline by author for added emphasis.)

A Critical Reality

The Holy Spirit's final outpouring upon this generation is measured against the enormous and incomprehensible task of reaching six billion three hundred million souls (6,300,000,000) *before* Jesus returns. It cannot be done using a "word-only" Gospel message such as we see today throughout the Body of Christ. We must have the power of the Holy Spirit to reach our world right now with more souls that are unsaved than at any time in the history of mankind.

We are in a time compression of the last minutes of this generation. Therefore, the intense outpouring of the Holy Spirit upon the Christians of today is proportionate to reaching six billion three hundred million people (6,300,000,000) in a short time *before* God pours out His wrath in judgment against those who refuse Jesus Christ.

Based on the compression of time and the enormous task set before us, we have a reasonable idea of how powerful and intense the Holy Spirit's outpouring will be upon His people. We are the Ambassadors of Jesus (2 Corinthians 5:20)—His servants that bear the testimony of His salvation for today's global masses. This can only be accomplished by the Holy Spirit!

Because of the Father's great love, mercy, and compassion, His power is about to be poured out upon His people as never before seen. A massive number of souls will be harvested before the coming great day of God's judgment as written in the Book of Revelation.

This Endtime army of Spirit-filled Christians are poised to cover the earth and testify of Jesus Christ. Being filled with the Holy Spirit's power, their words about Jesus Christ will be proven by indisputable signs, wonders, and miracles to six billion three hundred million people (6,300,000,000). These same Spirit-filled-Christians are an army of more than two billion (2,000,000,000), people who will not bend knee to Antichrist or receive his mark.

When Jesus created His church, it was born in power, armed, and ready to assault the gates of Hell. Then, as now, she is commissioned to go throughout the world and preach the Gospel. She is no longer on the *defense*. She fights with an overwhelming *attacking* charge against the ever-increasing tides of demonic hosts, political barriers, financial greed, religious strongholds, changing social values, and military blockades.

A Critical Reality

Nothing can stop her. The gates of Hell have no power against her. She cannot fail. She fights not *for* victory, but *in* victory, a victory already won by Jesus when He defeated Satan on the cross.

Satan's long anticipated fear is about to go exponential. Knowing the invincible power of the Holy Spirit, history records his relentless attacks upon the true church of Jesus Christ. Nonetheless, the gates of Hell can never prevail against her.

Born in power, God's people will go up in power. The Rapture will not come at an hour of weakness, but at the hour of our greatest glory in God.

When our Father receives His saints at the moment of Jesus' return, they will be spotless, powerful, majestic, glorious, and fearless—a reflection of the Groom that returns for her. They will shine as Ambassadors of Jesus—citizens of a Heavenly Kingdom. They have long been divorced from the entanglements of this age.

A 4th dimensional surge is swelling at this moment. It is not tangible—it is spiritual. It is nothing less than an incredible Spirit-filled invasion that overwhelms the natural world.

Where the slip-knots of man's religious dogma have stifled the Lord's people, this coming Pentecostal visitation will be different. It will not be a localized revival or even a regional renewal. People will not travel from afar to visit the place of His presence.

This visitation comes as a powerful mighty supersonic wind coursing throughout the world. Miracles of unusual manifestation will be its signature. The dead, carried in one door, will leave walking through another. The seams of church buildings and meeting halls will burst with God's glory—the manifest presence of His Holy Spirit. All denominational labels, titles, celebrity personalities, and acrimonious doctrines will fall to the dirt. This Endtime army will be one people under one name, Jesus Christ, the King of kings and the Lord of lords.

No religious ritual, philosophy of man, or pious clergy will quench the Holy Spirit. He comes with a ravenous unstoppable cleansing fire. Even now, the forces of Satan shutter at the thought of this imminent holy assault.

A Critical Reality

At this very moment, there are dynamos of Spirit-filled congregations strategically positioned and prepared by Jesus. They are poised to accomplish His purpose. All over the earth, entire regions of people will be transformed by God's Holy Spirit. They will network in the power of the Holy Spirit until the whole earth is covered with the testimony of the Living God.

In every place where the name of Jesus Christ is preached, healings, miracles, and salvations will manifest. Religious wailing, formulas, and spiritual manipulations will be a thing of the past. The Lord Jesus will be glorified and the cross will be preached without shame. Triumphant victories of salvation and demonstrations of the Holy Spirit will be everyday events. A new wave of revelational faith, a knowing Him by covenant in the power of His resurrection will be the catalyst of deeper dimensions.

Scrambling to the forefront, denominational oppositionists will resist the Holy Spirit's works. However, their dogmatic stubbornness will melt like wax in the fire of His miracle working power as God's love burns through their confusion.

Those cultured in the brine of religious antagonism will kneel before God as their religious chains and shackles turn to powder. Hardcore Cessationists will molt outside God's presence until their prideful skins can no longer endure the undeniable evidence of His love and power.

Who are these oppositionists? They are the modern Pharisees draped in the same spirit that withstood Jesus. What they cannot produce, they ridicule. Within the confines of their religious order, they persistently oppose the Holy Spirit's gift—the Baptism of the Holy Spirit. In jealousy and pride, they resist His works in order to protect their doctrinal error. This, however, will not stop the Lord. Denominationalism did not die for the sins of the world—Jesus did. All souls are His and He comes to make claim.

What you are about to read is the instruction Jesus gave His church in order to walk in *power*—the power that comes exclusively through the Baptism of the Holy Spirit. This is the prescription given by Jesus so that we can powerfully minister the Gospel exactly as the Apostles—exactly as the early church.

Throughout the ages, many have opposed the Holy Spirit's power under the presumption of logic-based philosophical teachings. However,

A Critical Reality

God's Word is immutable. His Written Word still points directly to the Holy Spirit's Baptism to accomplish what Jesus assigned the church.

This book might challenge your doctrines and traditions. It might even offend you. Truth often does that sort of thing. But if you are willing, shift from all patterns of mental-reflex and objectively consider the Scriptures for what they plainly state.

My prayer for you is the same prayer as the Apostle Paul:

> "That the God of our Lord Jesus Christ, the Father of glory, may give to you a spirit of wisdom and of revelation in the knowledge of Him." (Ephesians 1:17)

Ready? Let us begin the journey.

CHAPTER 1
In All That God Is
"Every Ministry Must Reflect God's Character"

"If I have the gift of prophecy, and know all mysteries and all knowledge; and if I have all faith, so as to remove mountains, but do not have love, I am nothing." (1 Corinthians 13:2)

♦ ♦ ♦ ♦

Almighty God, our Heavenly Father, never changes. He is the same yesterday, today, and forever (Hebrews 13:8). He is infinite in all His virtues. He is perfect. His wisdom, knowledge, and understanding through which He does all things is beyond the ability of man to fathom or quantify.

Our Father does not seek counsel to improve, nor does He experiment with trial and error. He makes no mistakes. He knows the end from the beginning of all things.

He stands outside of time, space, and matter by which all things exist. Everything is subject to Him. He is preeminently before all things and in Him, by Him, and for Him, all things exist and are held together (Colossians 1:15-16).

His glory is defined as everything He is and everything He possesses. By His own Words, His character is described in three fundamental infinite, incalculable, and unsearchable virtues: love, light, and truth.

- **He is love:** His character is love. Everything He does flows from the virtue of Himself. He does not increase or decrease in love. He does not improve in love. He does not adjust His character to a greater love. He does not "put on love". He IS love. His love cannot be quantified. His love is so great and unending that it supersedes the ability of man to fully comprehend.

In All that God Is

- **He is truth:** He does not increase or decrease in truth. In everything He speaks and does, it is truth-based. There is no uncertainty in Him. His truths are not adjustable, negotiable, or wavering. They are not subject to social trends or the changing opinions of man. His truth is pure and righteous. His ways are eternal and ABSOLUTE.

- **He is light:** There is no darkness or shadow in our Heavenly Father. He is the well-spring of light. His judgments are PERFECT and beyond man's ability to comprehend. All things are laid open and bare before Him. Nothing is hidden from the glory of His light. Every soul is known by Him. He knows every detail, every pain, every facet of each person's life and He loves the souls of mankind.

From His Written Word, the Bible, a million volumes of information, testimonies, and commentaries have been written about Him. Yet, quantitively speaking, the sum total of knowledge that we have of our eternal Heavenly Father equals to but a grain of sand in the Sahara desert.

He is hope to the hopeless; the Father to the fatherless; He gives purpose to the wanderer; and success to the grieving who have failed in life. He is health to the sick and peace to troubled hearts; His love endures to the second chance, third chance, fourth chance, and through the unending depths of brokenness for whoever calls on Him. He is freedom to the imprisoned and joy to the downtrodden. He is light to those who sit in the confusion of darkness. For those in the pit that are snared by sin, He is the *rope-of-hope*. He picks up and renews the life of those with shattered dreams. For those clothed in shame, He is glory and light. He is the key to every prison door; the answer to every person's future, regardless of who they are, where they are, or how deep they stand in sin. If they call upon the name of Jesus, He will save them.

In everything our Father does, in all His ways, in all His Words, in all His instruction, and in everything He expresses—it passes through the character of His love. He heals in love; He restores in love; He guides in love; He forgives in love; He judges in love; He does miracles in love. And...He *disciplines* in love so that we might attain greater success.

> "Bless the LORD, O my soul, and forget not all His benefits: 3 Who forgives all your iniquities, who heals all your diseases, 4 who redeems your life from destruction, who

In All that God Is

crowns you with lovingkindness and tender mercies, 5 who satisfies your mouth with good things, so that your youth is renewed like the eagle's…10 He has not dealt with us according to our sins, nor punished us according to our iniquities. 11 For as the heavens are high above the earth, so great is His mercy toward those who fear Him; 12 As far as the east is from the west, so far has He removed our transgressions from us." (Psalm 103: 2-5; 10-12)

The most violent overwhelming force in the universe is love. We don't think in those terms. But because of our Father's immeasurable undefeatable love, He sent Jesus to take away the sins of the whole world. By this level of sacrifice, we get a glimpse of how dark and deadly sin actually is. It took the violent sacrifice of His Son's life to destroy the violent power of death and darkness. In love, Jesus died an agonizing death to annihilate the works of Satan so that we can walk in the newness of life—no matter who you are.

Within Satan, there is no love, light, or truth. He is darkness—the cursed one, the accuser of God's people (Revelation 12:10). Despite his efforts, schemes, plans, and ways, He cannot defeat the love that our Father has for us. Satan's only option, therefore, is to accuse God's love in our hearts by distorting truth in our minds. Yet, even in this, the Holy Spirit guides us out of our confusion and into the glorious light of our Father where His perfect love casts out all fear (1 John 4:18).

Jesus Christ is the mirror-perfect reflection of our Father's glory. Our Father gave His only Son as the ultimate and final sacrifice to break down the dividing wall between us and Him.

Our Father withholds nothing from His children. Through Jesus, He gives YOU everything YOU need for complete and total victory.

> "And He [Jesus] is the radiance of His [the Father's] glory and the exact representation of His [the Father's] nature, and upholds all things by the word of His [Jesus'] power."
> (Hebrews 1:3a. Square brackets by author for added clarity.)

To emphasize the point: Because of our Father's unfathomable love, He sent His only Unique Son, Jesus Christ. Jesus took away our sins, disease, fear, doubt, shame, and confusion. He took away our poverty; gave us His mind; freed us from mental and physical diseases; filled us

In All that God Is

with His Holy Spirit; and gave us His POWER to change our lives _and_ our generation. Through Jesus, all condemnation is removed!

> "The glory [Father] which You have given Me [Jesus]I have given to them, that they may be one, just as We are one." (John 17:21. Square brackets by author for added clarity.)

> "For His [the Father's] divine power has bestowed on us [absolutely] everything necessary for [a dynamic spiritual] life and godliness, through true and personal knowledge of Him who called us by His own glory and excellence." (2 Peter 1:3. Amplified Bible)

> "The thief comes only in order to steal and kill and destroy. I, [Jesus Christ] came that they may have life, and have it in abundance [to the full, till it overflows]." (John 10:10. Amplified Bible)

If you want this life that comes through Jesus Christ, it is yours. You can have it abundantly by asking Jesus into your life right now! If you are backslidden, then RIGHT NOW recommit your life to Him. Call on Him. He is ready to forgive, restore, and renew! By accepting and receiving Him, you have complete forgiveness. No sin formed against you is greater than the power of Jesus' blood! _Life_ triumphs over failure, sin, death, sickness, and defeat!

> "Jesus said, 'I am the way, and the truth, and the life; no one comes to the Father but through Me.'" (John 14:6)

He offers eternal life to all who ask Him! Through Jesus, our Father gives you His divine power by the indwelling presence of His Holy Spirit that permanently abides in you and will never leave you.

In this book, you will learn about the Triumphant Holy Spirit; the Bright One; the Holy Spirit of God; The Spirit of Revelation and Truth; The Miracle Worker; The Comforter; the Teacher; and The Revelator. He is the One who indwells every Christian. Specifically, you will learn about His power and how His power can flow through you so that you can _credibly_ testify about Jesus Christ with proving signs, wonders, and miracles.

This power is available to you RIGHT NOW through the Holy Spirit's gift called, "The Baptism of the Holy Spirit". It is His power that makes

In All that God Is

you an effective Ambassador of Jesus Christ to share the Father's love with over six billion three hundred million (6,300,000,000) lost souls on their way to eternal damnation. It is YOU He has chosen to be His arms, His eyes, and His heart. As you walk with Him, He will pour His hope through you unto everyone you meet— a hope everyone seeks. Nothing can stop you! Nothing!

CHAPTER 2
THE FIVE CYCLES OF EVIL
"Why the Holy Spirit Baptism is Critical for Today"

Chronicled throughout Scripture is the scattered evidence of five distinct cycles of evil, or conversely, Satan's five major attempts to establish his dominion on the earth and be worshipped as God Almighty. Despite his best effort, three of the five cycles have collapsed in dismal failure. One is currently in process, the 4th. It is the worst of all five cycles. The 5th cycle does not occur until *after* the 1,000-year rule of Jesus on earth.

When Satan fell from his exalted position, Isaiah records the depth of pride that toppled this glorious arch angel whom our Father loved as one of His sons:

> "How you have fallen from heaven, O star of the morning, son of the dawn! You have been cut down to the earth, you who have weakened the nations! 13 But you said in your heart, 'I will ascend to heaven; I will raise my throne above the stars of God, and I will sit on the mount of assembly in the recesses of the north. 14 I will ascend above the heights of the clouds; I will make myself like the Most High.'" (Isaiah 14:12-14)

Ezekiel describes Satan's glory before Satan fell:

> "You were in Eden, the garden of God; every precious stone was your covering: the ruby, the topaz and the diamond; the beryl, the onyx and the jasper; the lapis lazuli, the turquoise and the emerald; and the gold, the workmanship of your settings and sockets, was in you. On the day that you were created they were prepared. 14 You were the anointed cherub who covers, and I placed you {there.} You were on the holy mountain of God; you walked in the midst of the stones of fire. 15 You were

Five Cycles of Evil

blameless in your ways from the day you were created until unrighteousness was found in you." (Ezekiel 28:13-15)

Satan is obsessed with two relentless goals: (1) to rule the world and (2) be worshipped as God. As he pursues those objectives, each time his plan reaches a certain point, God suddenly destroys it. The global flood of Noah's day is one such example. Satan endeavored to corrupt the human race through hybridization with fallen angels. His motive was to destroy the human pedigree lineage, specifically a young virgin through which the hope of humanity, the Messiah, would come according to God's prophecy (Genesis 3:15; Isaiah 7:14).

The Words of Jesus that encapsulate the Endtimes, (as recorded in Matthew's Gospel, chapters 24 and 25), occur during the 4th cycle of evil which is the times of Revelation.[3] Consequently, when Antichrist strolls into the newly built temple between the 3rd and 4th Seal of Revelation and declares himself to be God, the 4th cycle of evil reaches a pseudo-climactic moment. It is short lived, precisely 1,290 days in duration and filled with the judgments of God.[4]

Let's Start With The First Cycle of Evil

In the first failed attempt, Satan sought God's glory. Moreover, he wanted God's authority and staged a rebellion in Heaven. In response, God cast him to the earth as a bolt of lightning. He then became a wandering disenfranchised spirit. This cycle runs from the moment of Satan's fall and leads to the Garden of Eden.

> "He [Jesus] said to them, "I watched Satan fall from heaven like [a flash of] lightning." (Luke 10:18)

---

[3] The actual number of days starting from the 1st Seal of Revelation to the first day of Jesus' 1000-year rule, is 2,595 days. There is 1,260 day from Seals 1through 3 + 1,260 days from the 4th Seal to the 6th Trumpet Judgment + 30 days from the 1st Bowl Judgment to the end of the 7th Bowl Judgement + 45 days of global reconstruction after the judgments of God = 2,595 days in all.

[4] From the actual time of the 4th Seal of Revelation when Antichrist comes into the newly build temple in Jerusalem, he stops all sacrifice and declares himself to be God Almighty. This is called the "Abomination of Desolation" (Daniel 12:11-12; Matthew 24:15). From that moment until the 7th Bowl Judgment, Daniel says there will 1,290 days.

Five Cycles of Evil

In the Second Cycle of Evil

After Satan is cast out of Heaven, he roamed the earth as a wandering spirit having no domain or place of authority (Matthew 12:43). Hence, he is called the god of the air (Ephesians 2:2). He took note of Adam whom God had given global dominion and authority over the earth (Genesis 1:26). It was this authority that Satan targeted in order to gain a starting point for his ultimate conquest to rule the world.

As we all know, Adam defaulted to sin; took on Satan's nature; and Satan stole Adam's dominion. As a result of Adam's failure, all of creation was corrupted. This cycle runs from the Garden of Eden to the time of the global flood (Romans 8:22).

In the Third Cycle of Evil

Satan began modifying the pedigree genetic human design through which the Messiah was prophesied to come. He assigned select fallen angels to engage in sexual intercourse with the daughters of men in order to produce a hybrid society of people called the Nephilim (Genesis 6:1-4; Jude 1:6).

Because of the supernatural interplay between darkness and humanity, this subject is almost never taught in church. Of no surprise, few Christians realize the difference between the characteristics of fallen angels and demons. For instance, God created angels with an innate ability to change from a spiritual substance to a tangible form and back again (Genesis 19:1-5). Even fallen angels retained this innate ability.

However, fallen angels are uniquely different from demons. Demons are disembodied spirits of which the Bible does not explain their origin. Nonetheless, according to various biblical examples, they do not possess the same characteristics as angels. Consequently, to express themselves they need the physical form of another life—a container. Their first choice, of course, is people, or, in the case of the demon possessed man of Gadara, they will also inhabit the body of an animal (Mark 5:1-13).

Except for eight righteous pedigree humans, Noah and his family, the earth was saturated in wickedness. Ultimately, the Messiah would come through one of Noah's three sons, specifically Shem. Consequently, the global society of wicked people, which also included the hybrids, were destroyed in the flood. This cycle runs from the time of the flood until the Tower of Babel when people began repopulating the earth.

In the Fourth Cycle of Evil

We are currently in the 4th Cycle of evil. This cycle runs from the Tower of Babel to the final judgment of God's wrath in the Book of Revelation which is the 7th Bowl Judgment.

Starting with Nimrod, the people of Mystery Babylon (Revelation 17:5) were Baal sun worshippers. During this time, everyone spoke the same language. In the pride of their humanism, they declared independence from their Creator. Consequently, God confounded Satan's humanist move by confusing the languages and scattering the people across the earth. This started the development of nations. When the people scattered, a plethora of religious beliefs dispersed throughout the world. Consequently, the doctrines of demons remain rooted among the various populations such as we see in India, Asian nations, and the indigenous tribal people.

During this cycle, Satan temporarily achieves his objective to be globally worshipped. Regardless of his quasi-victory, his rule through Antichrist only lasts for 1,290 days before Jesus casts Antichrist and the False Prophet into the Lake of Fire. Approximately forty-six days later, Satan is locked into the Abyss for 1,000 years.[5]

> "They fell down and worshiped the dragon [Satan] because he gave his authority to the beast; they also worshiped the beast, saying, 'Who is like (as great as) the beast, and who is able to wage war against him?'" (Revelation 13:4. Square brackets by author for added clarity.)

Today, we are perched on the precipice of the opening of Revelation—the final days of the 4th cycle of evil—the most cataclysmic period of all time. It is a time unlike humanity has ever faced and will never experience again. For this reason, we MUST have the Holy Spirit's power to be witnesses of Jesus in His final sweep for billions of lost souls.

---

[5] The chronology for Endtime events are precisely laid out in my book entitled "The Chronological Order of the Endtimes which is available through Christian book stores and on Amazon.

Five Cycles of Evil

A Closer Look At The Fourth Cycle

The most brazen displays of shameless evil occur during the 4th cycle. Even now, at the time of this writing, global masses are duped into social philosophical perspectives that embrace evil as the new standard of truth. Today's WOKE generation proves this point. How did an entire generation lose the simplicity of gender identity as being either male or female? What swirls in the minds of people who cover themselves in tattoos, inordinate piercings of metal, irreversible mutilations of the body, or transgender mutilation surgery?

Right now, the depths of darkness is steadily increasing. We are rushing toward the moment when the False Prophet, Antichrist's cohort, will call down a sustained turning pillar of fire from the sky to prove his spiritual authority. It will be Antichrist's pseudo-climactic event when he strolls into the newly built Jewish temple and declares that he (Antichrist) is Almighty God.

When sin first violated God's creation, immediately our Heavenly Father set the boundary, limits, and time of evil. According to His timing, plan, and purpose and by His mercy, grace, and wisdom, He will once and for all put away sin. We are the generation to see God's justice against Satan and his evil.

Throughout the world, each of Antichrist's enamored followers will worship an image of him. Furthermore, demonic personalities will be assigned to each image that speak in an audible voice. Conversations with demonic spirits that masquerade as the voice of Antichrist will be the new norm—something completely supernatural.

Today, the church faces an unprecedented contrast between darkness and light. Now more than ever, we MUST have God's POWER operating in us.

In the Fifth Cycle of Evil

At the time of the 5th cycle, the Bride of Christ will have been in her glorious state of perfection for over 1,000 years. However, the people born during Jesus' Millennial Reign on earth will not have been proven and refined. This is because Satan is locked in the Abyss starting on the first day of Jesus' 1,000-year rule on earth.

Five Cycles of Evil

At the end of 1,000 years, Satan is released from the Abyss for a short time. Exactly how long, the Scriptures do not say. Nonetheless, he quickly gathers an army against the Lord from among the Magogic lineage of people that were born during the Millennium (Revelation 20:7-9). Mysteriously, for some reason, many will choose to follow him. This brief but final war ends with Satan and his minions being cast into the Lake of Fire along with the wicked souls in Hell.

The Only Prescription for Power

The only prescription Jesus gave for power comes exclusively through the Baptism of the Holy Spirit. For this reason, He told His disciples to "wait" for the promise of the Father", specifically the Baptism of the Holy Spirit *before* they commenced their ministry.

> "And behold, I am sending the promise of My Father upon you; but you are to stay in the city until you are clothed with power from on high." (Luke 24:29)

But Did Not the Apostles Have Power?

To emphasize this point, consider that Jesus intensely developed His disciples over the course of forty-two months. Every question they had concerning the Kingdom of God was answered by Him. In brief, they lived with God who taught them!

> "...and He did not speak to them [the general public] without a parable; but He was explaining everything privately to His own disciples." (Mark 4:34. Square brackets by author for added clarity.)

> "And there are also many other things which Jesus did, which if they were written in detail, I suppose that even the world itself would not contain the books that would be written." (John 21:25)

These men, with the exception of Judas, were moral, righteous, and upstanding. Furthermore, they were indwelt with the Holy Spirit's presence starting on the 3rd day *after* Jesus' resurrection, specifically *after* Jesus was re-glorified.

> "And when He had said this, He breathed on them and said to them, 'Receive the Holy Spirit.'" (John 20:22)

Five Cycles of Evil

The narrative of that event is found in the 20th chapter of John's Gospel. On Sunday morning before the sun came up, Mary and her companions met Jesus at the tomb (John 20:1). Ecstatic with joy, Mary Magdalene kept hugging Him upon which Jesus said, "Stop clinging to Me, for I have not yet ascended to the Father." (John 20:17).

Later that same day, Jesus ascended into Heaven and was re-glorified with the glory He had before the world existed (John 17:5). In the evening of the *same day after* His re-glorification, He came back, met with His Apostles, breathed on them and said, "Receive the Holy Spirit." At that moment, the omni-presence of the Holy Spirit went into all Believers throughout the earth. This is an immensely significant event that commences the New Testament church![6] It is the defining moment when the Holy Spirit was originally sent to *permanently* indwell every Believer. It is distinguished from the event of Pentecost which occurred forty-seven days later when they received *power*, namely, the Holy Spirit's Baptism.

What? They Needed Power!

But wait, why would Jesus' disciples need power? They were taught by Him directly; they were in good moral standing; they had insight and understanding about the Kingdom of God that no one else possessed, especially since they were taught by God, not by man. Moreover, they already had field experience in the working of signs, wonders, and miracles (Matthew 10:7-8)!

Based on the above, we must realize three specific facts regarding the power which Jesus told them to wait for—namely, the Holy Spirit's Baptism of power—specifically, the Holy Spirit's gift.

- **Knowledge:** Regardless of how much academic-knowledge a person possesses about God's Word, knowledge of itself does not produce power.

---

[6] Many have assumed that when the Holy Spirit came in power on the day of Pentecost, it was the beginning of the church. However, the church is not defined by the power, but by those who belong to Jesus proven by the permanent indwelling presence of the Holy Spirit. Romans 8:9b clearly states, "But if anyone does not have the Spirit of Christ, he does not belong to Him." Hence, anyone who has His Spirit, belongs to Jesus, which in the universal sense, is His church on the earth. By contrast, on the day of Pentecost, the Holy Spirit came in power through those who already had His permanent indwelling presence which occurred 47 days earlier.[6]

- **Moral obedience:** While holiness cannot be over-emphasized, power is not the result of righteous living. However, a righteous life is a life the Lord can *trust* with power.

- **Man's appointed positions and ordinations:** Ordinations, degrees, positions, titles, appointments to offices, and certificates of accomplishments do not produce power. In fact, depending on one's affiliation under which people are licensed or credentialed, these sometimes teach error in contrast to God's Word.

As will be repetitively emphasized throughout this book, the only place through which power comes is by the Baptism of the Holy Spirit. This is not to suggest that God does not use a person in an incident of power who is *not* Baptized in the Spirit. He does at times. However, having the resident-gift of the Holy Spirit's power is dramatically different than being used in a single incident of power.

Even though the handpicked Apostles of Jesus received the Holy Spirit who permanently indwelt them on the 3rd day after Jesus was resurrected, Jesus said they still needed *power* before they commenced their ministry.[7]

We Need His Power Now More Than Ever Before

We are the exit generation, the grand finale that faces off against evil in its greatest manifestation. Especially before the coming of Antichrist, the need for the Holy Spirit's POWER is the greatest ever since the fall of Adam. In that regard, we are fast approaching a time unlike the world has ever seen before or will ever see again (Matthew 24:21).

Despite this coming reality, many denominations ignorantly reject the *only* means Jesus prescribed for POWER to be His witness. Mistakenly, they assume that knowledge is power.

> "For our gospel did not come to you in word only, but also in power, and in the Holy Spirit and in much assurance, as you know what kind of men we were among you for your sake." (1 Thessalonians 1:5)

---

[7] See the entire 20th chapter of John's Gospel.

Five Cycles of Evil

This is precisely what Satan wants the church to believe. Should we be surprised, therefore, that many *Christians* will depart from the truth and give heed to seducing spirits (1 Timothy 4:1)?

CHAPTER 3
SEVEN CHURCHES—SEVEN PROPHETIC TIME PERIODS
"Satan's Attack on the Baptism of the Holy Spirit"

Today, a vast majority of church denominations completely reject the Baptism of the Holy Spirit. That, however, will soon change. When the inarguable glory of the Holy Spirit's presence manifests throughout the world in the greatest revival of all time, they will see that there is no better way to win souls than through the Holy Spirit's power.

As it currently stands, without the Holy Spirit's power that *proves* the testimony of Jesus, much of Christianity trundles along in a labyrinth of troublesome doctrines and traditions. This leaves them as less than effective witnesses of Jesus Christ. As a consequence of not following Jesus' instructions regarding the Baptism of the Holy Spirit, over six billion three hundred million people (6,300,000,000) remain unpersuaded about Jesus and have no salvation. In a different way of stating it, seventy-five percent of the world's population is presently unsaved. For that, we look at the failure of Christians trying to win souls without the Holy Spirit's power. And yet, if such Christians knew they were missing what Jesus prescribed, they would rush to receive His power.

Seven Eras of the Church—Then and Now

In the following overview of seven prophetic eras of the church age, we shall see how the Holy Spirit's Baptism is Satan's most targeted concern. If he can keep the church weak, confused, and void of the Holy Spirit's power, he doesn't care what kind of information is preached from their pulpits, including the reading of Scripture.

There are Seven Churches mentioned in the Book of Revelation: Ephesus, Smyrna, Pergamum, Thyatira, Sardis, Philadelphia, and Laodicea. All seven churches existed at the same time when John wrote the Book of Revelation. Being listed in a prophetic book, each church also represents a prophetic time period starting from the time of the New Covenant to the very end of the age in which we currently live.

Seven Churches of Revelation

It is important to understand how their church-type still speak to us regarding God's divine power, specifically the Baptism of the Holy Spirit.

For the purposes of this review, I have confined the focus of each prophetic church era to the subject of the Holy Spirit's Baptism. Certainly a great deal can be stated about each church, however, that is not the intention of this book. Accordingly, you'll see how the Baptism of the Holy Spirit was an essential tool of the early church until His gift was cast aside for over 1000 years and then regained in our generation.

Of these seven church-types, three of them passionately embrace the Holy Spirit's Baptism: Ephesus, Smyrna, and Philadelphia. Three of them are tepid: Pergamum, Thyatira, and Laodicea. Of the one remaining church-type, Sardis, their doctrine aggressively opposes the Holy Spirit's gift under the teachings of Calvin's Cessationist Theology, a term used throughout this book.[8] Today, Calvinism is the primary nemesis of the Holy Spirit's Baptism of power.

There are seven individual messages, one for each church, and they are recorded in the Book of Revelation from chapter 2:1 to 3:14.

1. To the angel of the church in Ephesus, write:
2. To the angel of the church in Smyrna, write:
3. To the angel of the church in Pergamum, write:
4. To the angel of the church in Thyatira, write:
5. To the angel of the church in Sardis, write:
6. To the angel of the church in Philadelphia, write:
7. To the angel of the church in Laodicea write:

---

[8] "Cessationists" is a word that describes those whose doctrine comes from the Reformation period under John Calvin and Jacobus Arminius. They hold to the belief that the Baptism of the Holy Spirit was only valid during the early church in order to help establish it. Further, they believe that since we now have the printed Bible, the Baptism of the Holy Spirit is no longer needed. This doctrine is contrary to the teachings of the Apostles. It is logic-based, void of spiritual insight, and without Scriptural support. Many of their *other* doctrines are laden with anti-biblical beliefs for today's church. They believe that some people are predestined to salvation while other are predestined to eternal damnation. Again, this teaching is contrary to the Foundational Apostles and stands in opposition to multiple areas of Scripture.

Seven Churches of Revelation

John is told to write to the angel of each of the Seven Churches. But first, we must identify what the angel of each church is. After all, it seems a bit strange that John, an evanescent man, is asked to write to sinless eternal angels.

Regarding the *angel* of each church, there is a common misunderstanding on this very point. Since holy angels stand in the presence of God on a daily basis (Matthew 18:10), it makes no sense that John should write anything to them on spiritual matters.

The word "angel" means "messenger". As it applies to each of the seven churches, it is a metaphor referring to the *pastor*. He is the messenger of God's Word to the local church. In this context, John was instructed to write to the *pastor* of each of the Seven Churches.

Specifically, what we want to know is how each church-type in its prophetic representation regarded the Baptism of the Holy Spirit. Further, we want to know how each church-type influences Christianity today. By knowing their individual history, it explains the fierce opposition against the Holy Spirit's Baptism that extends into the era of the modern church.

Look and see.

CHAPTER 4
THE EPHESUS CHURCH
"The Apostolic Pure Doctrine"

The prophetic age of this church ranges from 33 AD to 100 AD and is known as the "Apostolic Church". Through the Holy Spirit's inspiration, the Foundation Apostles were the doctrinal architects that set the blueprint for all churches. Their teachings should have remained without modification until the Lord's return.

The Apostolic Church period ended with the death of John—the last living Apostle who died by natural causes in 100 AD. The other eleven Foundation Apostles were martyred.

God inspired His Foundation Apostles to establish concise and completed doctrines for all Christian churches to follow. Because their teachings were given by the Holy Spirit, the doctrines were to remain untouched, unmodified, and unchanged—nothing added and nothing taken away.

Of key importance is the pure Apostolic doctrine of the Ephesus church. Nothing within the teachings of this church denied any aspect of the Holy Spirit's operation, including His Baptism of power.

The Ephesus church doctrines is the blueprint-church for all churches throughout the entire church age until the return of Jesus. Christians of this prophetic period considered the Baptism of the Holy Spirit as a *fundamental necessity* in order to credibly and persuasively testify about Jesus Christ. They believed Jesus' instructions where He said:

> *"But you will receive power and ability when the Holy Spirit comes upon you; and you will be My witnesses [to tell people about Me] both in Jerusalem and in all Judea, and Samaria, and even to the ends of the earth." (Acts 1:8. Square brackets by author for added clarity.)*

The Ephesus Church

They zealously embraced the Holy Spirit's gifts including: **Prophecy, The Gift of Tongues, Interpretation of Tongues, The Word of Knowledge, The Word of Wisdom, Miracles, Faith, Gifts of Healing,** and **The Discerning of Spirits**. Such gifts commonly manifested in each service according to the Holy Spirit's wisdom.

Signs, wonders, miracles, and salvation were the norm of the Ephesus church period. All this and more came through the power of the Holy Spirit. Members of this church expected the supernatural. Of no surprise, the church was the miracle center where the testimony of Jesus Christ was proven by the works of the Holy Spirit.

The Ephesus Church was not an *information-based academic church*. It functioned and flowed in the *revelation* of God's Word each time they met. They were not marooned on the historical narrations of God's works that were centuries previous to Christ. Rather, they enjoyed the very active presence of the Lord in their gatherings. In everything, they were contemporary with the Holy Spirit's leading. By the working of His power, they stormed the earth with the Gospel. In their day, it was believed that every person had a chance to hear the Gospel message. They accomplished this task from person to person. Miracles, signs, wonders, salvations, and healings was the signature of this church.

As previously stated, their leaders preached a *revelation-based* doctrine—a *right now God of signs, wonders, and miracles* in the covenant of Jesus Christ! Nothing of His truths were dummied-down to an information-based Gospel absent of God's power.

Without the demonstration of His glorious presence in the operation of the Holy Spirit's gifts, their Christian testimony and the working of their faith would have been just another philosophy of religion. However, their message was different. They proved Jesus Christ by the power of the Holy Spirit. When they preached the truths of His covenant, people were saved, healed, delivered, and brought back from the dead.

Their services were not stagnant, sedentary, and boring. There were no empty lectures, no review of Bible stories where line by line and chapter by chapter they trudged along through the history of the Old Testament. They were not stuck in the *ancient analysis* of God in the days of yore. Rather, the assembly of Believers came together expecting the Holy Spirit's demonstrations of power as He confirmed the words they preached. Accordingly, Jesus was in the *present tense of their fellowship*.

As the Apostle Paul said:

> "For our gospel did not come to you in <u>word only</u>, but also <u>in power and in the Holy Spirit</u> and <u>with full conviction</u>; just as you know what kind of men we proved to be among you for your sake." (1 Thessalonians 1:5. Underline by author for added emphasis.)

They preached and ministered in the Holy Spirit's *power* with indisputable evidence through His Baptism. Signs and wonders followed what they said (Mark 16:20). Without the Baptism of the Holy Spirit, they could not have reached the known world of their day.

> "And the disciples went everywhere preaching, and the Lord was with them and confirmed what they said by the miracles that followed their messages." (Mark 16:20. TLB)

By the time John died in 100 AD, Christianity's immutable doctrines was firmly established. As such, the teachings of the Foundation Apostles (including the Apostle Paul) were intended to remain unchanged. It was one truth, one faith, one Spirit, one glorious Heavenly Father, one Lord, one water baptism, one Holy Spirit Baptism, and one unchanging Gospel for all time.

Their doctrines were fully established as the standard throughout all time. Unfortunately, because of the Holy Spirit's absence of power in our modern denominations, today's preaching has defaulted to intellectualism and logic-based philosophical theology. Sadly, multiple generations of Christians have grown up with a powerless Gospel. Some have never seen a single miracle, healing, or deliverance.

> "And my message and my preaching were not in persuasive words of wisdom [using man's academic opinion], but [they were delivered] in demonstration of the [Holy] Spirit [operating through me] and of [His] power [stirring the minds of the listeners and persuading them], 5 so that your faith would not rest on the wisdom *and* rhetoric of men, but on the power of God. 6 Yet we do speak wisdom among those *spiritually* mature [believers who have teachable hearts and a greater understanding]; but [it is a higher] wisdom not [the wisdom] of this *present* age nor

The Ephesus Church

of the rulers *and* leaders of this age, who are passing away; 7 but we speak God's wisdom in a mystery, the *wisdom* once hidden [from man, but now revealed to us by God, that wisdom] which God predestined before the ages to our glory [to lift us into the glory of His presence]". (1 Corinthians 1:4-7. The Amplified Bible.)

Today, the majority of our modern churches reminisce about the Holy Spirit's power as something *historical.* They believe the day of miracles has passed; that the gifts of the Holy Spirit are no longer relevant for the church; and that the offices of the apostle[9] and prophet are non-existent.

The Ephesians clearly understood the difference between the Holy Spirit's permanent indwelling presence that every Believer has within them, and the separate event of the Holy Spirit's Baptism that gave them power. As we shall see, this cornerstone-belief would be modified as the church age progressed, especially if you belonged to the church-types of Pergamum, Thyatira, or Sardis.

---

[9] There are four classes of apostles in the Bible: (1) Jesus Christ, the apostle of our faith; (2) The original eleven Foundation Apostles (not counting Judas) that became apostles "before" the ascension of Jesus Christ; (3) the Paul who became a Foundation Apostle "after" the ascension of Jesus Christ; (4) all others apostles such as Timothy and even those of today, who are post-ascension, <u>Non-foundation</u>, apostles that build upon the works of Jesus, the eleven, and Paul.

CHAPTER 5
THE SMYRNA CHURCH
"The Suffering Church"

This prophetic era is represented by the church in Smyrna and is known as the "Suffering Church". It covers a period of time from 100 AD to 314 AD. They were the first generation of Christians *after* all the Foundation Apostles died.

They closely followed the Apostle's teachings and clung to the Holy Spirit's Baptism as a critical part of their faith-walk and testimony. Consequently, they knew Jesus in the intimacy of His power, resurrection, and love.

When Jesus addressed each of the Seven Churches in the Book of Revelation, it is noteworthy that the church of Smyrna was one of two churches for which He had nothing critical to say. Philadelphia, the church of our generation, was the other one.

Of key importance to us, the Christians of this era were persecuted unto death. They serve as models of faithfulness for us today. In the Philadelphian church age (which is our era), over two billion Christians will be persecuted. It will be a time unlike mankind has ever known before when over one-fourth of humanity is martyred for refusing to take the Mark of the Beast. Regarding such persecution, Jesus says:

> "Do not fear what you are about to suffer. Behold, the devil is about to cast some of you into prison, so that you will be tested, and you will have tribulation for ten days. Be faithful until death, and I will give you the crown of life." (Revelation 2:10)

> "For then there will be a great tribulation, such as has not occurred since the beginning of the world until now, nor ever will. 22 Unless those days had been cut short, no life

The Smyrna Church

would have been saved; but for the sake of the elect those days will be cut short." (Matthew 24:21-22)

Ten days of tribulation represented ten consecutive Roman emperors whom Satan used to relentlessly persecute Christians over the span of two hundred fourteen years. By the power of the Holy Spirit, they refused to compromise until more than five million Believers were crucified, tortured in various ways, and socially shunned.

The martyrdom of this era was so encompassing that the hillsides looked like branchless trees with Christians nailed to them—some as young as three years old.

In the Roman cities, hundreds were impaled on poles, dipped in tar and fat, and set on fire. The Roman Emperor, Nero, called them his human torches. In the coliseums, others were torn apart by starving lions and wild beasts to entertain the bloodthirsty crowds.

The unwavering testimony of the early Christians sends a message that still speaks to us after more than 1,800 years! Therefore, we must observe a very important fact about the Smyrna Church era that reaches into the very day we live: Jesus never routed His church *away* from persecution. Instead, He strengthened her *through* it as a testimony to all the world of their love and faithfulness to Him.

The church is never subservient to the intimidations of Satan or his demonic minions. History shows that Jesus made the church to persevere through all things and not shirk in fear.

The pure Apostolic doctrine of God's immutable Word was the powerplace of the Smyrna Church. Their hearts were strong and the power of the Holy Spirit was actively present among them. On the cause of these two characteristics, (1) doctrinal accuracy, and (2) the power of the Holy Spirit's Baptism, they remained faithful unto death. They knew Him by revelational intimacy, something much deeper and exceedingly more powerful than academic head-knowledge.

CHAPTER 6
THE PERGAMUM CHURCH
"The Compromising Church"

This era of the church is known as the "Compromising Church" and spans across time from 314 AD to 590 AD. It was a period when the fundamental doctrines of the Apostles were gradually abandoned, including the Baptism of the Holy Spirit.

The church became polluted under the secular government of Constantine—a Roman emperor. He was first a sun worshipper who claimed he saw a vision of a cross superimposed against the sun with the words, "'In Hoc Singo Vinces' ('with this sign, you shall win')." As the account is told, supposedly he had a dream that Jesus Christ appeared to him and confirmed what he saw. Soon thereafter he was recognized as the leader of the entire known world.

As a Roman emperor that converted to Christianity, he used his government authority to set policy for the church and zealously declared Christianity as the official religion of Rome. With passion and presumption, but certainly *without* God's wisdom, his methods of evangelism were anything but led by the Holy Spirit. He offered anyone who joined the church—converted or otherwise, a new white robe and thirty pieces of gold. As a result of his open-door policy, paganism polluted the Apostolic doctrines in the church.

His intentions, noble as they seemed, were carnal. But, Jesus was not interested in the physical presence of people sitting in church without any intention of being converted. As a result, the pagans saw Constantine's gesture as nothing more than a financial opportunity. Being unsaved, they brought demonic beliefs into the church and adulterated the Apostle's teachings with cultic and occultic beliefs. Thus Christ spoke to this church and said:

> "But I have a few things against you, because you have there some who hold the teaching of Balaam, who kept

The Pergamum Church

teaching Balak to put a stumbling block before the sons of Israel, to eat things sacrificed to idols and to commit acts of immorality. So you also have some who in the same way hold the teaching of the Nicolaitans." (Revelation 2:14-15)

Even though the Christians tenaciously held to the Apostle's doctrines, eventually their devout numbers waned by attrition from one generation to the next.

Soon, the Holy Spirit's Baptism was considered as nonessential and altogether neglected. The pagans opted for different avenues of power—dark powers—powers of Satan.

Today, we see the same adulterating process. Social and philosophical ideologies now flood the church. The Woke generation's new standard of social equality strikes against the very oracles of God's righteousness. Even worse, multiple denominations are trapped in heretical teachings.

The stage was set for a deeper downward cycle that lasted to the end of the Thyatira church period until 1517 AD.

The Thyatira Church

CHAPTER 7
THE THYATIRA CHURCH
"The Roman Catholic Church"

This period in the church lasts from 590 AD to 1517 AD and is known as the "Romanist Catholic Church". It was a time when Christianity enters the most challenging time—a time appropriately called, "The Dark Ages."

During this period, the Believer's relationship and intimacy with the Holy Spirit was stifled by ritual and formality through manmade doctrines never before practiced. This church-type is void of Apostolic doctrinal guidance.

The Romanist Catholic Church believes she is the only true church. Her newly invented doctrines gradually evolved over the centuries to enhance the priests' authority in a new system of religion. Such doctrines, as they claim, were given by the inspiration of God.

Under this church type, it's leader, the pope, is considered infallible when he speaks from the seat of his office. In fact, the Romanist Catholic priests consider the pope's words equal to the authority of God's Written Word—the Bible.

In their mind, their oral traditions pre-date the Written Word of God. This audacious claim is entirely without proof, especially since this church-type did not exist until 590 AD—a full four hundred ninety years *after* the last foundation Apostle died.

Both the Pergamum and Thyatira churches were bonded to secular government. But under the Thyatira's Romanist's Church, the church grew even more corrupt. The power of civil government gave this church-type both spiritual and legal authority over the people. Thus, as history records, the populace faced a woeful priesthood, a priesthood that imposed capital punishment upon those deemed as

The Thyatira Church

dissenters—specifically those who refused to swear allegiance to the pope and the Romanist Catholic Church.

From generation to generation over the next nine hundred twenty-seven years, the people were shackled to the Catholic Romanist system through ignorance and duress. Consequently, they looked to man and his system of priests instead of the priesthood granted to each Believer through Jesus Christ.

> "And He has made us [Christians] to be a kingdom, priests to His God and Father–to Him be the glory and the dominion forever and ever. Amen." (Revelation 1:6. Square brackets by author for added clarity.)

In the Catholic Romanist system, consecutive generations of Christians were indoctrinated with unscriptural teachings. This included their adoration of the pope and his quasi-spiritual authority. In all the glitter and gold of this religious *system*, including its pomp and formality, the Holy Spirit's power and revelation were set aside.

This isn't to say that every Christian followed the Romanist system. Nonetheless, every Christian was certainly subject to the government authority of the Romanist Church.

Under the papal government authority, services were spoken in Latin. Their manmade doctrines included such things as confession of sins to a priest, paying to have sins forgiven, the rosary, purgatory, the worship of Mary, praying to dead saints, and hosts of other rules, traditions, and various ungodly regulations.

In the later stages of this ever-worsening system, murderous schemes were implemented against anyone who refused allegiance to the church or its clergy. Based on that cause, the horrendous Inquisition was imposed. Over 800,000 Christians were tortured and killed for refusing fidelity to the pope and his system. To this church period, Jesus says:

> "Behold, I will throw her [the leaders] on a bed of sickness and those who commit adultery with her into great tribulation, unless they repent of her deeds. 23 And I will kill her children with pestilence, and all the churches will know that I am He who searches the minds and hearts; and I will give to each one of you according to your

The Thyatira Church

deeds." (Revelation 2:22-23. Square brackets by author for added clarity.)

The Baptism of the Holy Spirit was altogether ignored by this new order of priests. Was it because they had no revelation of His purpose? Was it because they didn't understand what He offered? The answer, of course, is this: systems of religion are always substituted when God's presence is absent. Consequently, in the absence of truth, man creates his own system of approach to God.

The Holy Spirit exalts Jesus above all rule and authority of man. If the Romanist Catholic system had discovered the power of the Holy Spirit, doubtless, the Catholic Romanist system would have crumbled.

Even today, their priests do not permit the manifest power of the Holy Spirit to operate in their services during general mass.

Jesus does not see His children under the labels of denominations. In the end, the Triumphant Holy Spirit will bring God's family into one truth, one power, and one agreement in faith. He will raise us up together as a mighty army to reach the greatest number of lost souls in the history of mankind.

Despite the centuries of attack upon God's *true church*, the truth could not be extinguished. Her light dimmed, but never went out. At the cost of many lives and against the tide of sweeping persecution, the Holy Spirit broke the tyrannical bonds of Romanist Catholicism in what is described as the *Reformation*.

Unfortunately, leaders of the Reformation Church failed to complete the works that God called them to accomplish. They considered the Holy's Spirit's Baptism as irrelevant. Sadly, the Reformation was largely an *intellectual pursuit* instead of a spiritual one. But, for the first time in hundreds of years, the glowing light of Scripture was shared in the language of the common people rather than spoken in Latin.

Finally, new winds began to blow.

CHAPTER 8
THE SARDIS CHURCH
"The Reformation Church"

This period of the church runs from 1517 AD to 1800 AD and is known as the "Reformation Church". Most notably, it gained speed under a Catholic monk named Martin Luther.

Luther listed ninety-five points of disagreement that he had with the Romanist Catholic doctrines. Initially, he had no intentions of leaving the Catholic Church. His primary purpose was simply to correct a few of their unbiblical positions.

Essentially, the Holy Spirit revealed to him that the just shall live by faith, something strangely different from the liturgical formality imposed by the papal government. At the peril of his own life (which could only be accredited to the power of the Holy Spirit), Luther staunchly defied the Romanist Catholic's political/religious system. As a result of his insistence, the Reformation gained a strategic position.

Several factors empowered the Reformation period. First, strongholds of Romanist Catholicism were substantially weakened under Luther's courage.

Second, the printing press came into greater prominence. It was first invented in 1450 AD during the time of John Wycliffe and John Hus, early voices of the Reformation. However, nearly a half a century later, it gained substantial popularity during the time of Luther.

Previous to the Reformation, Roman Catholicism forbid anyone to own or possess a Bible except for the clergy. According to them, only the clergy had the right to interpret Scripture. However, during the Reformation, Bibles were produced in greater quantities at a much more affordable cost than the handwritten copies. Still, the poorer people could not afford one. Nonetheless, they were printed in the common language of the people, not in Latin.

The Sardis Church

Third, free education became the norm of society. The illiterate and under-privileged people learned to read. Peasants and common people could now hope for a future and the means to improve their lives through education.

The combination of all these in one confluence broke the spiritual influence of Roman Catholicism. Those who dissented and joined the ranks of Martin Luther and others like him, became part of the *Protestant Movement*, meaning to "protest".

As history shows, the basic corps of Reformers deviated from the Foundation Apostle's teachings in key fundamental areas. They created new twists of doctrine related to salvation, predestination, election, grace, and the Baptism of the Holy Spirit, to name just a few.

Thus, on the heels of free education, the publication of the Bible in the people's language, and the preaching of God's Word in the common grammar of the people, the true church of Jesus broke free of her constraints after 1,200 years of spiritual darkness that started during the Pergamum era.

Among the many Reformers, two figures prominently stand out: John Calvin (1509-1564 AD), and Jacobus Arminius (1560-1609 AD).

Calvin was a French humanist[10], lawyer, and biblical polemic. The teachings of Calvin and Arminius evolved from the platform of *logic-based-reasoning* of the Scriptures rather than through the Holy Spirit who *imparts revelation-based understanding*.

Under the pretense of human logic, the Reformers teachings were easy to understand for the common people. As a result, the Reformers gained rapid popularity among the uneducated populace that found their new Bible teachers refreshing. What they taught, however, was unlike the teachings of the Foundation Apostles.

---

[10] The Renaissance overlapped with the Reformation and included an intellectual movement known as "Humanism"–the primary influence in Calvin's life. Humanism is the pride of man's intellect which advances the idea that humans are at the center of their own universe and should embrace the edicts of evolving intellect, logic, achievements in education, classical arts, literature and science. Humanism was the core of Babel when God scattered the people and confounded their languages.

The Sardis Church

"There is a way *which seems* right to a man *and* appears straight before him, but its end is the way of death." (Proverbs 14:12)

God's divine assignment for the Reformation Church was to return to the teachings of the Foundation Apostles—not modify their doctrines to fit a new era. Regrettably, the Reformers, each influenced by the other during the Renaissance era, created new logic-based doctrines that were never before taught in the church over the previous 1,500 years.

For this reason, the doctrines of John Calvin and Jacobus Arminius were fittingly named after themselves. If the Reformers were teaching the *same* doctrines as the original Foundation Apostles, why were such teachings named after the Reformers?

The answer is quite obvious: they were NOT the same doctrines as the Foundational Apostles. Rather, the Reformers taught Scripture according to their logic-based academic perspective. Further, their teachings were permeated by the influence of humanism which was prolific during the Renaissance Period that overlaid with the Reformation Period.

As previously stated, the teachings of the Reformation Church were fresh and new to the people. Such teachings, being intellectually-driven, in many cases, was not entirely wrong, but wrong enough to produce error.

According to the Reformers, if any part of Scripture seemed illogical, especially in the New Testament writings, then its meaning was modified to meet the standard of logic. Consequently, their teachings completely disregarded any revelation of biblical truth which only comes through the Holy Spirit. Thus, according to the Reformers, reason and intellect are the guiding influences for interpreting Scripture rather than drawing from the Holy Spirit's inspiration.

According to David M. Whitford of Claflin University, USA:

> "Given Luther's critique of philosophy and his famous phrase that philosophy is the "devil's whore," it would be easy to assume that Luther had only contempt for philosophy and reason. Nothing could be further from the truth. Luther believed, rather, that philosophy and reason had important roles to play in our lives and in the life of the community. However, he also felt that it was

important to remember what those roles were and not to confuse the proper use of philosophy with an improper one.

"Properly understood and used, philosophy and reason are a great aid to individuals and society. Improperly used, they become a great threat to both. Likewise, revelation and the gospel when used properly are an aid to society, but when misused also have sad and profound implications."[11]

The Reformers promoted a philosophical logic-based doctrine known as *Cessationist Theology* which is still present in the church today.

In all fairness, it is important to mention that Luther was not the author of such doctrines. Rather, Cessationism evolved after his death in 1546 AD. Those who embrace the Reformers teachings, specifically that of Calvin and Arminius, are best known as the Baptists, Presbyterians, Episcopalians, Anglican, Methodists, Calvary Chapels, branches of the Vineyard Churches, Catholics, and many independent churches.

Cessationists hold to the belief that the gifts of the Holy Spirit such as speaking in **Tongues**, **Prophecy**, **Gifts of Healing**, working of **Miracles**, or any of the nine gifts, ended with the death of John, the last living Foundation Apostle.

Cessationists interpret multiple areas of God's Written Word differently than the intended meaning of the Foundation Apostles. Accordingly, Cessationists view Scripture through the lens of their logic-driven dispensational reasoning.

The Pergamum and Thyatira Church periods adulterated the purity of Apostolic doctrine which resulted in great spiritual darkness. Thus, the Reformer's new teachings came at a time when the general population was starving for any understanding of God's Word in their own language. Owning a Bible, therefore, was a highly valued possession.

---

[11] https://iep.utm.edu/luther/

The Sardis Church

Even though printing-press-copies were laboriously produced in number, very few Bibles were available at the beginning of the Reformation. Of those that existed, they were expensive.

In the course of such developments, the masses, hungry to understand the Gospel, were like chicks in a nest at feeding time. They opened wide and indiscriminately swallowed whatever was offered—every word of the Reformers. Thus, the Reformer's teachings rapidly developed roots which became the very doctrines anchored in major denominations of churches today.

The Reformers were sincere, but sincerity of itself does not eliminate error. They were expert linguists in Hebrew, Greek, Latin, and Aramaic, and...they were intellectually logic-based driven, all of which was sautéed in the spice of humanism. In the pride of their humanity, they completely rejected the Baptism of the Holy Spirit as relevant for the church from that time forward until the return of Jesus. As a result, they placed no emphasis upon the *revelation* of Scripture.

As we near the return of Jesus Christ, the Triumphant Holy Spirit will purge all that separates and divides the Father's children. We will be one people, one family, one faith, under one truth, in one agreement, and empowered by the might and glory of the Holy Spirit.

This cannot entirely be their fault. Many of the preachers and leaders, such as John Calvin, were first nurtured in the teaching of Roman Catholicism before entering the Reformation. Thus, they too had limited understanding. Absent of the Holy Spirit's revelational insights which they rejected, their doctrines were formulated according to the logic of "common sense deduction" which Luther disdained when improperly applied.

According to the Reformers, the printed Bible replaced the offices of the prophet and apostle among the five-fold ministry offices (Ephesians 4:8-13). Adding to this error, they assumed that since the church was now established in its doctrines ("their" doctrines), the Baptism of the Holy Spirit was no longer needed to prove Jesus Christ by signs, wonders, and miracles. Consequently, by rejecting the Holy Spirit's revelational influence, they were left to their own persuasions. This left them

The Sardis Church

floundering in the stew of their humanist pride. In contrast, Paul said this:

> "We also speak of these things, not in words taught *or* supplied by human wisdom, but in those taught by the Spirit, combining *and* interpreting spiritual *thoughts* with spiritual *words* [for those being guided by the Holy Spirit]." (1 Corinthians 2:13)

To the Sardis church era, which is the Reformation period of new doctrines, Jesus said:

> "To the angel of the church in Sardis write: He who has the seven Spirits of God and the seven stars, says this: I know your deeds, that you have a name that you are alive, but you are dead. 2 Wake up, and strengthen the things that remain, which were about to die; for I have not found your deeds completed in the sight of My God." (Revelation 3:1-2)

The Reformation churches were elated with their freedom as much as they were with their leaders. As previously mentioned, entire denominations that are present today evolved out of such teachings—teachings named after the leaders who created the doctrines.

The Reformers believed they had *regained* the fullness of the Gospel. However, it was branded with the trademarks of their intellectualism and was filled with error. Accordingly, they refused anything that did not line up with the logic of their views. Moreover, they withstood those who disagreed with them, especially on the subject of the Holy Spirit's Baptism. Nonetheless, the Holy Spirit of God would not rest. There was a world to win to Christ.

We are the final generation of mankind. Today, we number in the multiple billions of people as compared to the global population of Calvin's day which was about four hundred thirty-eight million (438,000,000) people. As it presently stands, the global population of our generation is over nineteen times larger than the world population during the time of the Reformation period.

It is worth noting that the leaders of the Reformation considered their world as the entire world. Furthermore, in THEIR world view, they had no idea that generations of mankind were yet to be discovered in other lands across the ocean where populations of people existed. To

The Sardis Church

that reality, John Calvin was fifteen years and six months of age when Christopher Columbus discovered new lands, specifically the Americas.

The task before us today is to reach a world population of people that is nineteen times larger than John Calvin's world. It is impossible without the Holy Spirit's Baptism of power as emphasized by Jesus Christ and taught by the Foundation Apostles.

The Reformers were sincere in wanting the truth. But, they rejected the Holy Spirit's power that only comes through His Baptism. Consequently, their academic approach was, and still is, void of power. However, the next church age, the Philadelphian Church era, would return to the Apostle's doctrines and complete the work Jesus initially assigned to the Sardis Church era.

CHAPTER 9
THE PHILADELPHIA CHURCH
"The Missionary Church"

The Philadelphian Church age ranges from 1800 AD to the time of the Rapture. It is known as the "Missionary Church". This church completes the assignment that the Reformation Church failed to accomplish.

Along with the Smyrna Church, Philadelphia is the only church of which Jesus had no criticism. And, it is the only church since Smyrna that fully embraces the Baptism of the Holy Spirit as an essential need in order to preach the Gospel.

Of this church period, none of their doctrines are named after their leaders. Rather, this church returns to the original teachings of the Foundation Apostles.

The characteristics of the Philadelphia Church era are unique. Like the Ephesus Church, she is dedicated to the pure doctrines of the Foundation Apostles; she is faithful unto death like the Smyrna Church; and she is quantitatively the most globally advancing of all Seven Church types. Additionally, like the Smyrna Church, the Christians of the Philadelphia Church are greatly persecuted.

Even now, the Philadelphia Christians unwaveringly carry the Gospel into all nations. This unceasing endeavor will continue right up to the time of the world's greatest persecution throughout all of humanity. Accordingly, the Book of Revelation very specifically applies to this church era.

Persecution against her consistently increases toward the time of Christ's return. Starting from the 4th Seal of Revelation until the 6th Seal, over two billion Christians will be martyred during this church era. Their combined number is exponentially more than all of God's righteous people who have been killed starting from the time that

The Philadelphia Church

Cain slew Able. Moreover, the number of martyrs during the Tribulation is 4.6 times more than the entire world population of John Calvin's day.[12] Even worse, the number of people going to Hell starting from the time of the 6th Seal to the very day of the Millennium is over nineteen times greater than the world population of the Reformers.

As previously stated, we are presently in the era of the Philadelphia Church period, however, not every person that claims to be Christian aligns with the Foundation Apostle's doctrines. Supporters of Calvinism, Arminism, Lutheranism, or Catholicism, are trapped in the fog of Cessationistic error. Nonetheless, when the Holy Spirit covers the earth with fire and power, those who are deceived by their doctrines will see the light and prove to be some of the greatest Endtime warriors. As it stands, they only lack the revelation of His Word in order to come into the Baptism of the Holy Spirit.

Jesus said of the Philadelphia Church:

> "I know your deeds. Behold, I have put before you an open door which no one can shut, because you have a little power, and have kept My word, and have not denied My name." (Revelation 3:8)

As previously mentioned, the Philadelphia Christians are acutely aware of the times and seasons of Jesus' soon return. Global evangelism, signs, wonders, miracles, and the gifts of the Holy Spirit are characteristic of their ministry in order to convince a condemned world about Jesus and the need for salvation.

Unfortunately, Cessationists describe Spirit-filled Christians as shallow; emotional; disorderly; laden with gross error; and largely deceived by the works of the devil. But the undeniable proofs of the Holy Spirit's nine gifts among the ranks of Philadelphia Christians stand in hard contrast against the lifeless still-born doctrines of Cessationists type churches that quantitively have little to show for their labors.

---

[12] The world population during Calvin's life was estimated at close to four hundred thirty-eight million (438,000,000) people. Today's population is now over nineteen times larger at eight billion three hundred million (8,300,000,000). Source: https://www.census.gov/data/tables/time-series/demo/international-programs/historical-est-worldpop.html.

The Philadelphia Church

Cessationists cannot explain the multiple thousands that are saved, healed, and delivered under the Philadelphian teachings. And because they do not understand the Holy Spirit's operation, they denounce His works as demonic or of the flesh. Such conclusions are directly from their doctrines but not necessarily because they have a malicious heart.

Cessationists are marooned on the island of their own theology. Their preaching is a *word-only* Gospel that is cluttered with error. In stubbornness, they stand in blind patriotic faith to their traditional doctrine. Yet, when the power of the Holy Spirit manifests in this generation, His Baptism of power will offset every doctrinal error.

> "For our gospel did not come to you in word only, but also in power and in the Holy Spirit, and with full conviction; just as you know what kind of men we proved to be among you for your sake." (1 Thessalonians 1:5)

> "And my message and my preaching were not in persuasive words of wisdom, but in demonstration of the Spirit and of power, 5 that your faith should not rest on the wisdom of men, but on the power of God." (1 Corinthians 2:4-5)

Meanwhile, the number of Philadelphian Christians are steadily increasing throughout the world while enjoying the power, presence, and the manifestations of the Holy Spirit.

It is important to know that Jesus calls out to all His people, even those suspended in the doctrines of Reformational teachings, or pickled in the brine of Cessationism, or blinded by religious traditions. As a result, many are coming out of their dead doctrines unto the Living Word that is filled with power.

Jesus *will* have a people in these last days that will do His bidding.

CHAPTER 10
THE LAODICEA CHURCH
"The Harlot Church"

This period of the church, (which overlays with the Philadelphia Church era), started around 1988 AD and continues to the close of the final judgment in the Book of Revelation. Unfortunately, Jesus has nothing good to say about Laodicea in His letter.

At this stage in the annals of Christendom, the characteristics of Philadelphia is a synergy of the Ephesus and Smyrna churches. At the same time, Laodicea is a synergy composed of the Pergamum, Thyatira, and Sardis type churches.

1988

Arguably, the Philadelphia Church emerged during the 1800s in Europe when the Holy Spirit's revival-fires raced across nations including America. During this time, the status of the Laodicean Church was dormant.

If we survey the various cycles of revival as far back as 1725, we find that in 1735, 1800, 1857, and 1904, revivals occurred in America and various other nations in a somewhat predicable timeframe. Incremental to such revivals, was the Healing Movement in 1940s; the Jesus Movement in the late 60s and early 70s; the Charismatic Movement that overlapped with the Jesus Movement in the late 60s and late 70s; the Teaching Movement in the mid 70s that overlapped with the Charismatic Movement; and ultimately the emphasis of the Five-fold Ministry Offices at the start of the late 70s into the early 80s.

Based on the Holy Spirit's pattern, predictably, we should have had another revival in 1988, or at least within close proximity of that time. However, there was no revival. Instead, church congregations exploded into mega-churches around the world. Hundreds grew to thousands; and thousands grew into multiple-thousands.

The Laodicea Church

Today, some of the world's largest congregations are located in Nigeria, Africa. For example, the Redeemed Christian Church of God has two million members; Mountain of Fire Miracle Ministry has five hundred fifty thousand members; Winner's Chapel has two hundred fifty thousand members—to name just a few. Each of these are Spirit-filled churches.

Generally speaking, (and certainly not in all large churches), during 1988 a shift in the preaching the Gospel message occurred. Under the pretense of "love and sociological acceptance", gradual degrees of compromise crept into the churches and gained fast-moving popularity. Liberal Seeker-Friendly churches such as Saddleback Community Church (pastored by men like Rick Warren) became the new model. They evolved with a tolerance for sin under the guise of love, mercy, and grace so that their Gospel message did not offend anyone with truth that required repentance. Consequently, today's generation is a field ripe for harvest and laden with tares among the wheat.

༄༅

In these last days, the Triumphant Holy Spirit will reach lost souls that are wandering in confusion. He will invade all religions with the power of His love and reveal to every man the glory and splendor of Jesus Christ.

༄༅

As the saying goes, "Not all that glitters is gold". While *large* seems good, what lurks under the surface of many Seeker-Friendly congregations is an untested and largely ill-informed body of Christians completely isolated from the refining fires of God's Holy Spirit. Today, we have massive congregations that blend the world and God's Kingdom in what seems loving, sensitive, equitable, and godly. Yet, on the standard of Scripture, it is an oil and water mixture—a Pergamum type of invasion.

Time and opportunity soon reveal a person's heart. As we near the return of Jesus Christ, Paul prophesied of a great falling away from the central truths of Scripture. It is a seduction in graduated degrees where truth is substituted with man's sociological equities. "Wokers" epitomize this reality. Most likely, this encompasses those who never developed deep roots of holiness unto the Lord.

The Laodicea Church

At the same time, there will be an ever-increasing persecution against those who refuse to compromise the truth. Consequently, to the Laodicean Christians, the Philadelphian Christians are inflexible, demanding, and somewhat bigoted.

Regardless of the church-type today, the Holy Spirit's consuming fire will burn through every congregation and bid His people to come out from among the ungodly. Unfortunately, many will choose not to walk in His righteousness. Rather, they will merge with the congregations of the Laodicean Church type.

> "They went out from us [seeming at first to be Christians], but they were not *really* of us [because they were not truly born again and spiritually transformed]; for if they had been of us, they would have remained with us; but *they went out* [teaching false doctrine], so that it would be clearly shown that none of them are of us." (1 John 2:19, The Amplified Bible.)

Laodicea bonds itself with the doctrines of New Age, including cultic and occultic religions. She blends with various social, philosophical, and religious beliefs in a format of what *seems* righteous and loving.

Even worse, Laodicean churches have raised an entire generation without allegiance to truth. This church-type is politically correct, lukewarm, and fronts a synthetic form of holiness while denying the genuine power of God. Their words sound loving, inclusive, embracing of all souls, and tolerant of all lifestyles. However, they do not require repentance according to the standard of God's righteousness.

Being a lukewarm church, Laodicea promotes inclusivism—a philosophy of acceptance for all faiths, credos, and lifestyles at the expense of Scriptural truth. The Lamas, Yogi, Shamans, "seeker-sensitive" Protestant leaders, New Age spiritisms, along with nearly all religions, commune from this blend of intoxicating drink.

The goal of the Laodicean Church is more political than spiritual. She wants numbers in attendance—not disciples of Jesus. She uses her social platform to enhance her political ambitions. As seen in the Book of Revelation, she is a habitation for Antichrist and the False Prophet.

The Laodicea Church

"She has become a dwelling place for demons, a dungeon haunted by every unclean spirit, and a prison for every unclean and loathsome bird."(Revelation 18:2b)

She does not go up in the Rapture with the Philadelphia Church, but in fact, she goes through the tribulation to the final end of the 7th Bowl Judgment as part of the godless masses of people. Descriptively, she is a blend of the Five Foolish Virgins and the wicked unsaved masses (Matthew 25).

Even though she gives mental ascent to the Baptism of the Spirit, to her it is nothing more than a pointless spiritual experience, an appeasement, exactly as it was with the Pergamum and Thyatira churches. For this reason, the Baptism of the Holy Spirit has no distinguished importance with her.

Specific to this church period, Paul prophesies ample warning in his letters as follows:

> "Let no one in any way deceive you, for it will not come unless <u>the apostasy comes first</u>, and the man of lawlessness is revealed, the son of destruction." (2 Thessalonians 2:3 Underline by author for added emphasis.)

> "But the Spirit explicitly says that in later times <u>some will fall away from the faith</u>, paying attention to deceitful spirits and doctrines of demons by means of the hypocrisy of liars seared in their own conscience as with a branding iron." (1Timothy 4:1-2 Underline by author for added emphasis.)

> "For the time will come when <u>they will not endure sound doctrine</u>; but wanting to have their ears tickled, they will accumulate for themselves teachers in accordance to their own desires." (2 Timothy 4:3 Underline by author for added emphasis.)

Thus we have Seven Churches, seven church periods, and the unique characteristics of each one. However, the point of focus in this book deals with the attitude of the church today regarding the Baptism of the Holy Spirit.

Common to most within Christendom, there are a few mutual points of agreement such as Jesus' virgin birth, the power of His shed blood

The Laodicea Church

for forgiveness of sin, and the commandment of water baptism. On these matters, the Reformation Christians share the same ground with the Philadelphian Christians. However, they are unquestionably split on the issue of the Holy Spirit's Baptism and the gifts of the Holy Spirit. As a result, a third camp of Christians emerged—the Neo-Pentecostals. They are a compromise between the Reformation Christians and on-fire Pentecostal Christians.

Part II

A Brief History of Neo-Pentecostalism, Calvinism, and Arminism.

☙❧

*Let us judge nothing before it is time.
If we are in Christ, then we are children of the Most High God.
Each of us in Jesus have His Holy Spirit. We are, therefore,
co-heirs of His salvation. This is the hour when the
Triumphant Holy Spirit will unify us as one body,
in one agreement, and standing as one in the power of
His divine, holy, and unstoppable love.*

☙❧

The Neo-Pentecostals

CHAPTER 11
THE NEO-PENTECOSTALS—HYBRID CALVINISTS
"Stifling the Holy Spirit"

The word "Neo-Pentecostal" is a compound word. According to Webster's dictionary, *neo* means, "A new and different period or form; in a new and different form or manner; new and abnormal."

Neo-Pentecostalism notably evolved during the "Jesus Movement" in the late 60s and early 70s when scores of thousands of young people and hippies came rushing to Christ.[13]

The Jesus Movement began under a man named Lonnie Frisbee whom God strongly used in the gifts of the Spirit including **Healing**, **Words of Knowledge**, **Word of Wisdom**, and **Prophecy**. Frisbee boldly witnessed about Jesus Christ in the power of the Holy Spirit. It was this very power that launched the Jesus Movement into prominence. Hundreds gathered on the beaches and were water baptized.

At the inception of the movement in California, Frisbee met a man named Chuck Smith, the pastor of a small struggling church called *Calvary Chapel* which was located in the Costa Mesa area of California. At the time, Smith's church was wanning, without vision, and near lifeless. It consisted of about twenty-five senior citizens.

God used Frisbee to fill Smith's church with enthusiastic new coverts in Christ. New Believers came flooding in and were clueless about traditional churchianity. Moreover, they were radically in love with Jesus

---

[13] Neo-Pentecostalism and the Jesus Moment are not to be confused as being one and the same. The Jesus Movement did not create Neo-Pentecostalism. Neo-Pentecostalism emerged as a result of those in the Jesus Movement that avoided the Holy Spirit's gifts in the church service. Most notably, Chuck Smith of Calvary Chapel, is the father of Neo-Pentecostalism.

and joyfully let others know! In a short time, largely due to Frisbee and the power of the Holy Spirit that operated through him, Calvary Chapel was inundated with several hundred new faces.

More On The Jesus Movement

Another moniker of the Jesus Movement was the "Blue-Jeans and T-shirt Crowd" that boldly invaded churches of nearly every denomination. They were new converts, anti-establishmentarian, and they sought the reality of truth, not the formality of religion. Unfortunately, many mainline churches rejected them on the superficial basis of their *unchurchie* dress appearance and bold demeanor.

The Jesus Movement overlapped with the Charismatic Movement. The combination of these two movements challenged a wide spectrum of churches. The Jesus People came with their attire of beads, long hair, bare feet, and five daisy patches that were crudely sewn to their daily-worn dirty jeans and bellbottom pants. Conventional Believers were befuddled. They did not know what to do with the radiant smiles of converted hippies that unabashedly greeted people with, "Hey, Jesus loves you!"

The rigidly formatted Spirit-filled churches were just as shocked as the Calvinist type churches. To see God's grace extend to such people in their manner of dress and lack of panache, shocked their theology. Would God really honor them if they came to church in blue jeans?

Churches were faced with choices. They could stiffen like oaks in the wind of the Holy Spirit and break, or bend like palms trees and adapt to what He was doing.

Setting aside their carefully formatted traditions, they learned to apply deeper levels of God's grace and mercy. This was not a compromise of biblical truth, rather just the opposite. As a result, many churches acknowledged what God was doing in mercy and grace.

In combination with the "Blue-Jeans-Jesus-People" and the Charismatic movement, there were three prominent positions of Christianity:

Hardline Calvinists.
Spirit-filled Christians.
Charismatic Christians.

The Neo-Pentecostals

Almost no one knew what to do or how to handle the new influx of life that flooded the congregations of churches. The reactions were different from one to another. Some were more flexible and resilient; some were staunch and unyielding.

The first ones to the firing line were traditional Calvinists. They fiercely rejected the Charismatic Movement and quickly judged it as emotionalism and works of the flesh. Any Spirit-filled Christian that appeared in their services was put under a watchful eye. To protect traditional church protocols and maintain doctrinal control, the Holy Spirit's gift were strictly prohibited. Anyone disturbing their services by raising hands during worship, or uttering spontaneous "Amens", or showing any facsimile of being Spirit-filled, was met with stern reprimands. Violators were quietly taken aside and instructed that such behavior was not acceptable.

Second, the Charismatic Movement crashed through the walls of nearly all denominations. Many sedentary churches were suddenly jolted with new life and the operation of the supernatural.

The Jesus people, especially those that were Spirit-filled, had no intention of surrendering their freedom to mulish traditions be they Calvinist types; wet-wood sleepy Pentecostal types; or hardline legalistic types. As a result, many new Spirit-filled Christians were given the cold shoulder of fellowship. For that reason, they found greater freedoms in home-settings which later became churches.

Despite all the changes, some churches recognized what the Holy Spirit was doing and accepted His works. They made their adjustments, taught the truth of His movement, and joined in cadence with the Lord. Of no surprise, their congregation numbers quickly swelled.

Conversely, churches that staunchly opposed the Charismatic Movement found an increasing number of empty seats in their house while sternly defending their traditional formats. To them it was a new and unexplored area for which many felt was a high risk venture.

Despite all the good coming from the Charismatic Movement, it had its problems. The church as a whole was not well taught on the Holy Spirit and His works. Trial and error sometimes produced more error and a lot of trial. For some people, it was an uneasy adjustment. Accordingly, they disassociated with Charismatic Christians and retreated to more familiar settings. After all, even the leaders within the

The Neo-Pentecostals

Charismatic Movement seemed to be groping their way through, learning and adjusting as they went.

> "But new wine must be put into fresh wineskins. 39 And no one, after drinking old wine wishes for new; for he says, 'The old is good enough.'" (Luke 5:38-39)

Overlaid with the Charismatic Movement, the *Teaching Movement* moved to the frontline. Teachers flooded the Body of Christ and brought balance and sensibility to both movements. They brought clarity on issues such as faith, character, prayer, fruits of the Holy Spirit, holiness, the Baptism of the Holy Spirit, grace, etc.

During the adjustment period, a hybrid group evolved which were appropriately dubbed as *Neo-Pentecostals*. They are best known today as "Calvary Chapel"—a blend between Calvinism and Pentecostalism. One could justly describe them as the religious arbitrators between hardline Calvinists and Spirit-filled Christians.

To achieve a détente between both groups, Calvary Chapels[14] delicately crafted a non-offensive doctrine. Their tenets appealed to the Calvinists who wanted more than their traditional teachings. At the same time, they appealed to Spirit-filled Christians, who, for whatever reason, had no ambition to be used in the Holy Spirit's power.

So What's The Deal?

In a general description, Neo-Pentecostals are the Calvary Chapel types of churches that acknowledge the Baptism of the Holy Spirit and His works. However, to avoid conflict, they do not allow the Holy Spirit's manifest presence to operate through people during their church services. Politically, this creates a neutral habitation for those defined as non-Spirit-filled Christians, while at the same time it

---

[14] To suggest that Calvary Chapels were not mightily used of God would be a complete mischaracterization of the great things the Lord did with them. Nothing is more valuable that salvation. And once a Christian is saved, they must be nurtured in the Word of God for maturity in Christ. Unfortunately, Calvary Chapels downplayed the importance of the Baptism of the Holy Spirit in their church services. By minimizing His works and stifling His power, they set an unscriptural president before their masses and shaped them according to a different belief of the Holy Spirit's gifts. In their church affiliation of some 1,400 Calvary Chapels worldwide, they foster a different model than the Foundation Apostles emphasized.

The Neo-Pentecostals

pacifies Spirit-filled Christians that have no interest in the power they possess by the Holy Spirit's Baptism.

Calvary Chapels do not deny the Holy Spirit's gifts, but they find that those who exercise them as being too risky, disruptive, sometimes offensive, and producing too much controversy. Therefore, in order to achieve their version of peaceful coexistence, the Holy Spirit's gifts are diplomatically stifled.

This was precisely the over-arching philosophy of Chuck Smith at midstream of the Jesus Movement. Doubtless, he witnessed disorder by over-zealous new Believers acting without wisdom. The answer, however, was not to prohibit the Holy Spirit's gifts, but to instruct and guide such new Believers in the correct use of them.

Chuck Smith did not seem to have much experience in being used by the gifts of the Holy Spirit. Perhaps this added to his uneasiness when it came to their manifest presence. Regardless of all reasons, he transitioned the services into a *word-only* format and suppressed the Holy Spirit's gifts into a state of inactivity. After all, in his thinking, thousands of people were flowing into the Calvary Chapel churches, so why did his churches need power? What the people needed, in his thinking, was an understanding of God's Word. Bluntly stated, he was right! But, his doctrinal perspective was not well balanced, especially concerning the open operation of the Holy Spirit's Baptism which he tactfully suppressed.

What a contrast as compared to the Foundation Apostles that considered the Holy Spirit's power as an essential need to prove the testimony of Jesus Christ as Healer, Deliverer, Savior, and Restorer.

> "And my message and my preaching were not in persuasive words of wisdom, but in demonstration of the Spirit and of power, 5 so that your faith would not rest on the wisdom of men, but on the power of God." (1 Corinthians 2:4-5)

Like the Calvinists, Calvary Chapel Christians have unquestionable love for Jesus. Nonetheless, one can sincerely love the Lord and still miss essential truths such as the Holy Spirit's gift.

The Neo-Pentecostals

Today, Calvary Chapels are largely unchanged. They merely *talk about the power* of God while at the same time avoiding the operation of the Holy Spirit's gifts in their general services.

Even though Chuck Smith's wanning church was revived, its new strength came through Lonnie Frisbee whom the Holy Spirit used in power.

Smith eventually modified his church to resemble something closer to the doctrines of the Reformers: a *once-saved-always-saved* theology without the need for the Holy Spirit's demonstration of power. As a result, the doctrine of Neo-Pentecostals is a patch-quilt theology of "a little from this and a little from that".

Breakthrough! The Road Divides

As previously mentioned, Lonnie Frisbee was the point leader that God used in the Jesus People Movement. Chuck Smith owned the barn, in a manner of speaking, but it was Lonnie Frisbee whom God used in the power of the Holy Spirit to bring in the souls.

Under Frisbee's anointing, Smith's church grew, not as a cause of Smith's ministry, but rather that of Frisbee's. On the other hand, one might say that Smith helped balance the over-zealous enthusiasm of the new Believers by teaching the Word. Unfortunately, Smith's teaching came at the expense of the Holy Spirit's power that would have operated throughout the Calvary Chapel churches.

It would be unjust to imply that God did not use Chuck Smith. As iron sharpens iron, Smith and Frisbee balanced each other. Frisbee needed Smith's experience of practical church management, and Smith needed Frisbee's zeal and experience in the Holy Spirit's working of signs and wonders.

After Smith adjusted his Calvary Chapel church to its multiple hundreds, the day came when Smith emphatically dialed down the gifts of the Holy Spirit that God used through Frisbee—very particularly in the **Word of Knowledge**, **Word of Wisdom**, and **Healing**. This led to a disagreement between Smith and Frisbee and they parted ways.

Oddly, Smith was a graduate of *Life Bible College* of the Four Square Church International. The motto of the Four Square Church denomination is symbolized by four points of emphasis: (1) Jesus as Savior;

(2) Jesus as Baptizer of the Holy Spirit; (3) Jesus as Healer; and (4) Jesus as the Soon-Coming King.

The Four Square Church International was forged in the Holy Spirit's fire through its founder, Aimee Semple McPherson. Under her Holy Spirit anointing, multiple thousands were saved, healed, delivered, and Baptized in the Holy Spirit. Even to this day, the miracles which God worked through McPherson remain as a powerful testimony in the chronicles of Christian healing.

However, Smith's original church, Calvary Chapel, which was a Four-square Church, did not enthusiastically embrace Jesus as the Baptizer of the Holy Spirit or as Healer. Even though Smith believed it, he constructively did not allow it. Aside from that, Smith personally did not operate in the Holy Spirit's gifts like Lonnie Frisbee. Consequently, the church was modeled around the subjective experiences of Chuck Smith when it came to the Holy Spirit's operation of power.

As previously mentioned, Smith was cautious about letting the Holy Spirit operate in a free and open display during the services. Was it because he did not flow in them? Was he insecure by contrast to Frisbee? Was he satisfied with a *word-only* ministry? Whatever the reason, Frisbee was sidelined to the status of *persona non grata*. By default, Smith maneuvered himself to the front of the Jesus Movement where his church overflowed with the new converts, largely by how God used Frisbee, not Smith.

Over the course of years, Smith's church raised up and sent out many pastors. Such pastors were not forged in the Holy Spirit's fire like that of Frisbee, instead, they modeled Smith's perspective of a "word-only" church without the demonstration of the Holy Spirit's power.

Smith's new corps of pastors, like himself, did not emphasize the importance of the Holy Spirit's Baptism in their churches. They acknowledged the Holy Spirit's gift, and perhaps even led people into the Baptism of the Holy Spirit, but they did not allow His operation during their services.

However, the Lord's plan for the Jesus Movement, as in His other revivals, always emphasized the Baptism of the Holy Spirit with salvation, healings, and deliverances. Sadly, however, healings, deliverances, and the gifts of the Holy Spirit were sidelined and then substituted for Chuck Smith's *word-only* format.

The Neo-Pentecostals

Break Through!

About ten years later in 1980, Frisbee visited a Calvary Chapel church in Yorba Linda, California where John Wimber was pastoring. Through a series of events that can only be credited to the Holy Spirit, God once again used Lonnie Frisbee.

Very quickly, just as it was in the beginning of Chuck Smith's church, John Wimber's church exploded with new life. News of this coursed throughout the Calvary Chapel pastors. They wanted to know why Wimber's church was surging and why their churches were only holding ground. Wimber credited it with allowing the Holy Spirit's presence of power, something Chuck Smith avoided in open display.

The contrast between Wimber's church that operated in the power of the Holy Spirit as compared to Chuck Smith's Calvary Chapels and their "word-only" formats, produced questions.

Ultimately, Chuck Smith called a meeting of his pastors in 1980. After a great deal of testimony and debate, Chuck Smith drew the dividing line. Whoever wanted to follow Wimber's model where the Holy Spirit's gifts were in open display with healings, prophecy, miracles, tongues, and the interpretation of tongues, could line up on one side of the room. And those who chose to remain with Smith's model of a word-only format of teaching, could line up on the other side of the room.

Smith followed his convictions, and Wimber followed his convictions. This was not a caustic bitter meeting, but one that followed along the lines of true Christian character. Chuck Smith and John Wimber were to be commended for their way of handling the issues.

The Vineyard Movement Is Born

Ken Gulliksen, a Calvary Chapel pastor under Chuck Smith, had three churches in Los Angeles named "The Vineyard". He saw the powerful works of the Holy Spirit in Wimber's church and decided to join up with him. Soon thereafter, Gulliksen felt led by the Lord to place his very successful churches under Wimber's headship. Ultimately, Wimber adopted the name that Gulliksen called his three churches: "The Vineyard". Thus, a new movement came to the forefront that was marked with salvations, miracles, the Baptism of the Holy Spirit, and healings—all of which became known as "The Vineyard Movement".

The Neo-Pentecostals

From that point forward, the directions were set: Calvary Chapels, which came out of the Jesus Movement, remained staunchly a *word-only* group that are classically defined as Neo-Pentecostals. While they would never deny the Holy Spirit in their churches, at the same time they purposefully prohibit His gifts from operating during their services. Again, as contradicting as it sounds, they do not discourage their members from receiving the Baptism of the Holy Spirit in a personal and quiet way. Thus it is acceptable as long as there is no operation of the Holy Spirit's gifts during the times when the church meets as a congregation.

By mere observation, the Calvary Chapels missed an incredible opportunity in the season of God's move. A massive number of spiritually hungry, willing, and able Believers were poised and ready to storm the world with the *power* of God's Spirit. All they needed was someone to instruct them, encourage them, and send them forth in the Holy Spirit's power.

If Chuck Smith had allowed the next step as Wimber did, Calvary Chapels would have been a nuclear tool in the hands of the Lord, immeasurably greater than today.

Furthermore, if the leaders of Calvary Chapel had followed the model of the Foundation Apostles, millions of new converts would have been endued with power from on high. After all, everything was poised for receiving. All the factors were there for a world-wide revival marked with signs, wonders, miracles, salvations, and deliverance. But, the Calvary Chapel's Neo-Pentecostal leaders had a different view of the Holy Spirit's Baptism.

Thankfully, the Vineyard Churches continued where the Calvary Chapel churches stopped. The Vineyard churches blazed with the fires of the Holy Spirit's Baptism. They saw miracles, healings, salvations, and deliverances. They surged forward in profound depths of worship with anointed songs birthed by the Holy Spirit that flooded the Body of Christ. In a short time, the Vineyard Churches quickly spread into multiple nations and were globally recognized for the power of God's presence.

Some Get Stuck

Cessationist Christians cry for more of God. However, they have great difficulty moving past their logic-based teachings about the Baptism of the Holy Spirit. For them, it is a quantum leap to join the ranks of Spirit-filled Christians. So, for the most part, they looked for a halfway house. The Neo-Pentecostals, largely the Calvary Chapels, and later on, some of the Vineyard Churches that digressed back to a word-only format, provided this venue.

Lethargic Spirit-Filled Christians

Sadly, lethargic, complacent, and indifferent Spirit-filled Christians are all too common, especially today. Being sedentary and apathetic, they have no ambition to be used by the Holy Spirit after receiving His power. Likely, they were never taught about the Holy Spirit's Baptism. Typically, such Christians has little to no burden for lost souls. Consequently, they preferred something less demanding, a digression from the fires of Pentecost. Again, the Calvary Chapels opened their doors for those that merely wanted to sit and listen—nothing more.

To this indifference, Jesus speaks by principle when He said:

> "For whoever has [faithfulness and stewardship], to him more shall be given; and whoever does not have [faithfulness and stewardship], even what he has shall be taken away from him." (Mark 4:25. Square brackets by author for added clarity.)

The followers of Jesus are to be *doers* of the Word, not just *listeners*. Each of His disciples is called to actively testify about Him, cast out devils, heal the sick, and harvest souls for the Kingdom (Mark 16:17-18). Christians were never called to be *do-nothing information-based head-stuffed people*.

Paul modeled an action-type of Christianity that was filled with the power of the Holy Spirit when he said:

> "For our gospel did not come to you in Word only, but also in power and in the Holy Spirit and with full conviction; just as you know what kind of men we proved to be among you for your sake." (1 Thessalonians 1:5)

Neo-Pentecostalism is an informational-based word-only Christian faith. Today, more than ever before, their churches are inclined toward the compromised seeker-sensitive formats that avoid offending anyone with the truth. When preaching the full counsel of God's Word, this is nearly impossible. Therefore, to achieve a peaceful détente, truth must be compromised in order to avoid its demand that produces offense. To achieve this, Neo-Pentecostal churches water-down

The Neo-Pentecostals

the doctrines of the Foundational Apostles, especially concerning the Baptism of the Holy Spirit. In most cases, one can barely tell Neo-Pentecostals apart from Calvinist and Cessationist type churches where the opinion concerning the Holy Spirit's Baptism is largely an historical perspective.

CHAPTER 12
CESSATIONISM—OPPOSITION TO THE SPIRIT-FILLED FAITH
"Shunning the Holy Spirit's Works"

This chapter, straightforward as it seems, is not a judgment against any Christian aligned with Calvinist doctrine. In fact, it might surprise many to know that the fervent fires of nearly all revivals since the 1700s came from the camp of Calvinist Christians—a tribute to the Holy Spirit's power that can burn through every limitation. And, as we shall see in the near few days, Calvinists will be used mightily by God as part of His 2,000,000,000 (two billion) army of Christians that storm the earth in the power of His Holy Spirit. For now, however, that is NOT the case.

Without hesitation, Cessationist Christians (which are largely Calvinistic and Arministic in doctrine) are blood-bought by Jesus and have His Holy Spirit in them. Their love for Jesus is unquestioned. However, their logic-based doctrines have steered them away from the very thing they desire! Even so, the day will come, and very soon, when they will fearlessly lead the front lines of revivals around the world.

In the manifest glory of God's Holy Spirit, every manmade religious law, tenet, and doctrine will be as nothing when He pours out His love in salvation, healing, miracles, and the gifts of His Holy Spirit. This includes the Cessationist Theology that was created about 1,500 years *after* the Apostles set their immutable doctrines. Conversely, Calvin's teachings came into existence about 485 years ago.

Regardless, anything and everything that stands in dissonance to the Holy Spirit's ways, wisdom, and works will be dismantled by the presence of His indisputable power. Don't be surprised, therefore, if Pentecostals also find themselves under the microscope of His holy scrutiny.

As repetitively stated, Calvinists and Arminists are the designers of Cessationist doctrines. In many areas of Scripture, such doctrines

Cessationism

erroneously apply brackets of time to define God's purposes and plans. For instance, according to Cessationism, two of the five-fold ministry offices no longer exist, specifically the offices of the apostle and prophet. Furthermore, they combine the office of the pastor and teacher into one office. This leaves only the office of the pastor-teacher and the evangelist. Such logic-driven assumptions are based on the "notion" that when the last Foundation Apostle died, the apostolic office ceased to exist. As will be explained later, Scripture contradicts this opinion.

According to Cessationism's logic-driven assumption, since the Bible is now canonized and printed, we no longer need the office of the prophet for illumination. Again, Scripture contradicts this false conclusion.

As previously stated, Cessationism is largely formulated from a deductive-based reasoning apart from the Holy Spirit's revelation of truth. As a result of over five centuries of cultivating such error, Cessationism is now widespread throughout Christendom.

> "There is a way *which seems* right to a man *and* appears straight before him, but its end is the way of death." (Proverbs 14:12)

In consideration of the above Scripture, it is wise to remember that not all truth is logical, and not all logic is truthful. However, according to Cessationism, that which is not logical is also not truthful. Sadly, in nearly all denominations, this mode of thinking is common throughout the Body of Christ. To that belief, Paul tells us:

> "And my message and my preaching were not in persuasive words of wisdom [using clever rhetoric], but [they were delivered] in demonstration of the [Holy] Spirit [operating through me] and of [His] power [stirring the minds of the listeners and persuading them], 5 <u>so that your faith would not rest on the wisdom *and* rhetoric of men</u>, but on the power of God." (1 Corinthians 2:4-5. Amplified Bible. Square brackets and underline by author for added clarity and emphasis.)

John Calvin—a Humanist, Lawyer, and Theologian

The Reformers were brilliant men. In fact, it was Luther's writings that turned John Calvin from Catholicism to Protestantism.

Cessationism

Calvin's earned a Master's of Divinity at age eighteen and then a law degree. In law school, he learned the fundamentals of deductive reasoning and debating skills. He then applied these to his studies of Scripture. However, the predominant overarching influence throughout his life was his humanist views common to the Renaissance period. From the confluence of these persuasions, Calvin developed a plethora of logic-based doctrines which is dissimilar to the Foundation Apostles. But, because his conclusions seemed logical and reasonable (which were often influenced by his personal subjective experiences), they seemed to him, and many others, as the original intended meaning of the Apostles.

By the time Calvin converted to Protestantism, Protestantism was already rooted among the populace in his part of the world. Furthermore, the Renaissance humanist pride was in full swing. This was a period in the annals of humanity when man's intelligence was exalted. New philosophy and precepts of deductive reasoning were the signatures of his time. And, because John Calvin was an accomplished scholar, his works, writings, degrees, and influence were strong persuasions in his day.

He was the head professor of theology at a school he founded where over a thousand people from all around Europe came for biblical instruction. Before long, his view of Scripture, as filtered through his deductive reasoning, became known as "Calvinism". It quickly spread throughout Europe as the cornerstone of the Christian faith. Even John Knox venerated Calvin's school as "the most perfect school of Christ that ever was in the earth since the days of the Apostles." [15]

---

[15] "Calvin's international influence was vast, not only by means of written correspondence, but also through visitors. Exiles came from France, England and Scotland; refugees fled to Geneva from Germany and Italy – they came seeking both safety and instruction. Among them was John Knox, who declared the church which Calvin established in Geneva as 'the most perfect school of Christ that ever was in the earth since the days of the Apostles.' In 1559 Calvin founded the Geneva Academy. He was its professor of theology, and more than a thousand students from across Europe sat to hear him and Theodore Beza declare God's truth. The Academy was known as 'Calvin's school of death' because so many of its alumni were put to death as a result of their witness for Christ [during the Catholic Inquisition]." (https://banneroftruth.org/us/about/banner-authors/john-calvin/)

Cessationism

Then, as today, patrons of Calvin venerate his teachings with such zeal that those who differ with his doctrine are met with an unsavory carnal response.

Despite such discordant reactions, let it be clearly understood that in many ways, Calvin's logic-based deductions of Scripture was equally influenced by his *subjective experiences*. Thus, his teachings about salvation, healing, miracles, ministry office gifts, predestination, foreknowledge, and the Baptism of the Holy Spirit were strikingly different than what the Foundation Apostles taught.

For example, Calvin redefined the Baptism of the Holy Spirit so that it harmonized with the standard of his doctrinal conclusions. He asserted that after the Holy Spirit came on Pentecost, when the last Apostle died, the Holy Spirit's Baptism now means being *baptized into the Body of Christ* and has nothing to do with power. The Foundation Apostles would have termed Calvin's teaching as heresy.

It can be justly surmised that Calvin did not know of a single person in his day who was Baptized in the Holy Spirit. Thus, by his subjective experiences, he applied deductive reasoning and asserted that the Baptism of the Holy Spirit was only relevant for the early church. This error was vigorously taught in his school which then spread throughout the world.

ଓଓ
Every Believer will carry the light of our Father's glory. Together we will celebrate one name—Jesus Christ. Therefore let us not see each other through the lens of doctrinal difference. Rather, let us move as one in the Holy Spirit's power.
ଓଓ

Calvin deductively concluded that *after* the death of the last Foundational Apostle, healing and miracles was no longer part of the covenant in Jesus Christ. This audacious interpretation of Scripture, being diametrically opposite to the teachings of the Apostles, should have halted Calvin with a cautionary alarm. But instead, he was more convinced by his deductive reasonings which were absent of the Holy Spirit's inspiration. As a consequence, doctrines were introduced in his school which were never before taught in the Body of Christ. Thus, adherents of Calvin's doctrine still preach his same message today. They assert that as the Gospel applies to the modern church, there are no longer any miracles and healings in the covenant of Jesus Christ;

that such events were merely used to prove the veracity of God's power in order to establish the church.

Calvin Got Exactly What He Believed

Calvin was miserably plagued with physical illness as well as his wife and children:

"From his early thirties, Calvin had begun to suffer physically and bore numerous afflictions. He had become a chronic sufferer from ague, catarrh, asthma, indigestion, and migraine headaches, which sometimes kept him awake all night. In 1558 he suffered at length from quartan fever (an intermittent malarial fever) from which he never fully recovered. He also suffered from close-to-crippling arthritis, gout, kidney stones, ulcerated hemorrhoids, gum disease, chronic indigestion, and pleurisy that finally led to malignant pulmonary tuberculosis. For years, so afflicted, Calvin had often coughed up blood on account of his public speaking. Though [his] married life was in many respects a great joy, it was tempered with profound griefs: Idelette miscarried once, lost a daughter at birth, and delivered a son who died after only two weeks."[16]

Calvin fought no less that nine different maladies in his body without being healed of any of them. Consequently, rather than subjecting his experience to the immutable Word of God, his subjective experiences shaped his doctrinal view of healing. Therefore, Calvin adamantly preached that miracles and healings were only for the early church. For this reason, he lived a situational-faith-based life in many ways. Of no surprise, he viewed the covenant benefits of Jesus Christ with great uncertainty. Sadly, Idelette, his wife, died at the age of 49 and Calvin died at the age of 54.

> "Bless *and* affectionately praise the LORD, O my soul, and do not forget any of His benefits; Who forgives all your sins, Who heals all your diseases..." (Psalms 103:2-3, Amplified Bible)

---

[16](https://banneroftruth.org/us/about/banner-authors/john-calvin/)

Cessationism

False Premises Yielding False Conclusions

In Calvin's reasoning, since both Old and New Testaments were fully canonized and accepted as the inspired Word of God, he believed that no further illumination from the prophet's office was needed. By mis-associating unrelated factors, it produced error in his deductive reasoning.

Absent of the Holy Spirit's illumination, Calvin's method of deductive reasoning produced numerous series of mistakes that were linked one to the other. His logic-based theology is a tapestry of personal subjective experiences, misapplied historical references, and deductive reasonings that are now accepted as *orthodox* Christian beliefs among the Calvinist ranks.

Like Calvinism, Arminism was also framed in the logic of classic *Cessationism*. Both systems deduce that the Baptism of the Holy Spirit was only used to establish the church at its beginning. But since the church is now fully founded, (according to their deductions), the Holy Spirit's Baptism is no longer needed.

Again, the biblical subject of the Holy Spirit's Baptism was **re**defined to mean "baptized into the Body of Christ"—a desperate far reaching interpretation that devalues the integrity of Scripture and elevates the importance of man's reasoning. Thus, Calvin and Arminius erroneously applied the following Scripture to mean "Baptized in the Holy Spirit".

> "For by one [Holy] Spirit we were all baptized into one body, [spiritually transformed–united together] whether Jews or Greeks [Gentiles], slaves or free, and we were all made to drink of one [Holy] Spirit [since the same Holy Spirit fills each life]." (1 Corinthians 12:14, Amplified Bible. Square brackets by author for added clarity.)

According to Cessationism, if the above verse of Scripture means the Baptism of the Holy Spirit, then the Apostles did not need to wait in Jerusalem as Jesus instructed them until the Holy Spirit's gift came upon them at Pentecost. Being in Christ, and having the Holy Spirit in them after the third day of Jesus' resurrection (John 20), they would have already been baptized into the Body according to the thinking of Cessationism. However, Scripture definitively records when the Baptism of the Holy Spirit occurred with the promise given to all who are in Christ—on the day of Pentecost.

Cessationism

As it currently stands, Cessationists think that the Holy Spirit's permanent indwelling residence in every Christian (which occurs at the moment of salvation), and His outpouring of power (which came on Pentecost), are one and the same. Again, this is a far reaching desperate attempt that twists the meaning of Scripture in order to patronize their doctrinal position.

We must carefully consider the full counsel of God's Word in its proper context. Thus, in repetitive places throughout Scripture, we discover that the Baptism of the Holy Spirit—the Holy Spirit's gift—was for POWER. His gift did NOT serve as being baptized into the Body of Christ. However, the Holy Spirit's permanent indwelling presence at the instant of salvation DOES baptize us into the Body of Christ.

It is true that signs, wonders, and miracles helped establish the testimony of early Christians. Such proofs indisputably *verified* the words they preached concerning Jesus Christ and His blood covenant. Today, the same need exists among billions of people that are trapped in darkness with false teachings throughout the world. The unsaved of EVERY generation need the same *proof* of Christ that comes from the Holy Spirit's power by His Baptism.

An Example of False Premises

Cessationism's logic is commonly derived by using false premises without questioning the premise itself. Allow me to offer an elementary example of deductive reasoning (logic) that yield a false conclusion:

False premise: Water kills people because within ten days of a person dying, the deceased has drank water. Therefore, water is the one common factor of all who die.

Truth: Drinking water and people dying is a misassociation that yields a false conclusion. Why? Because a person dies without water in less than five days. But since every person who dies had drank water within ten days, the correlation is a false assumption because the premise is faulty.

The "misassociation" of one "unrelated factor" being connected to another "unrelated factor" produces the false conclusion.

Cessationists misapply the Holy Spirit's Baptism; the printed Bible; and the death of the last Foundation Apostle as time-related factors which

Cessationism

render false conclusions that in turn produce the false premises of Cessationism.

This error is even more obvious when we consider that there are over 6,000 non-English languages today that have no printed Bible.

In the 1500s, the world population was four hundred thirty-eight million people. It would have been difficult, if not impossible, for Calvin and his disciples to comprehend a world population that would be over nineteen times larger at eight billion three hundred million; or an unsaved world population that is fourteen times larger than the world population of their day with over six billion people on the roles of the damned. Consequently, now, more than ever, the power of the Holy Spirit is needed to *prove* Christ!

Consider the tenets of Cessationism as it applies to a remote African village where the people do not speak English and have never heard the name of Jesus. In such villages, their spiritual beliefs are based on longstanding pagan traditions involving witch-doctors, idol worship, and *supernatural demonstrations of the occult*.

Calvin's doctrine has no effect against such demonic powers. This is because Cessationists (Calvinists and Arminists) believe that God's supernatural displays of power was limited to the early church. Yet in the hidden villages of Africa, witchdoctors *demonstrate* the power of Satan and his demons. How then can a word-only preaching with no outward proofs stand up against the demonstrations of the occult?

༶

John the Baptist said, "A man can receive nothing except it has been given to him from Heaven." Therefore, who can brag upon any truth as if it came from himself? Except for what the Triumphant Holy Spirit, has given us, we know nothing.

༶

I can personally testify about the Holy Spirit's power in signs, wonders, and miracles that prove the credibility of Jesus in breaking occultic strongholds over villages that are riveted in pagan beliefs and practices. When preaching about Jesus under the power of the Holy Spirit, in the span of less than two hours, I have seen entire villages forsake multiple generations of spiritual beliefs and accept Jesus Christ. For such remote people, the Holy Spirit's demonstration of power was the

Cessationism

proof needed to persuade them. They saw the polio victims walk, deafmutes hearing, cancer victims healed, and various other miracles and healings.

Because Cessationists reject the Baptism of the Holy Spirit, they conclude that any Christian speaking in **The Gift of Tongues** either speaks meaningless gibberish, or speaks by a demon spirit.

Cessationists believe that **Miracles** and **Healings** are not part of Christ's covenant today. They believe such works, rare as they might be, (if they occur at all), is when God occasionally breaks pattern with His established norms. Therefore, Cessationists believe it is vain to pray for **Miracles** and **Healings**. In fact, many Christians believe God gives sickness to teach patience and faith. Therefore, with or without prayer, Cessationists believe that God may or may not perform a miracle or healing. This is because, in their view, He also gives sickness. To such Christians, I often advise them not to seek medical relief if they think it is God's will for them to be sick. While my answer sounds ridiculous, it is even more ridiculous to think that God gives His righteous ones sickness.

> "And He Himself bore our sins in His body on the cross, so that we might die to sin and live to righteousness; for by His wounds you were healed." (1 Peter 2:24)

Many Christians sit under the teaching of Cessationism and completely dismiss God's healing promises that are written throughout multiple areas of the Bible. Most certainly this was Calvin's subjective experience who suffered continual sicknesses and deaths in his family. We can only suppose that he entreated God (although in unbelief) for healing on behalf of his wife, children, and himself until he and his family were wiped out.

Should we be surprised that none of John Calvin's prayers for healing and miracles were answered? Forty-one times throughout the Gospels, Jesus referred to faith as "Your faith...", or "Let it be according to your faith...", or "Your faith has saved you...", or "Great is your faith...". By the error of Calvin's dispensationalism, he disavowed any belief in healing and miracles. Is it any wonder, therefore, that he did not receive healing? Bluntly stated, he received exactly as he believed.

> "But where there is no faith it is impossible truly to please Him; for the man who draws near to God must

believe that there is a God and that He proves Himself a rewarder of those who earnestly try to find Him." (Hebrews 11:6. Weymouth New Testament)

To a Cessationist, the Gospel is little more than a historical record of God, who today, is minimally interactive with His church. They have mistakenly chipped away at the four-fold[17] covenant that Jesus gave us. However, they left the crown jewel of eternal life. But by stripping away essential parts of the covenant, in their thinking, the Lord does little for us in this present life.

Again, and with great limitation to the church, Cessationists believe that the five-fold ministry offices of the apostle, prophet, evangelist, pastor, and teacher are different today. Based on their logic-driven interpretation of Scripture, the apostolic office[18] ceased after the death of John. They somehow miss the Scripture which affirms the ministry offices *until* we all come to the *unity of faith* in Christ (Ephesians 4:11-13). This would apply to our world today just as much.

> "And [His gifts to the church were varied and] He Himself appointed some as apostles [special messengers, representatives], some as prophets [who speak a new message from God to the people], some as evangelists [who spread the good news of salvation], and some as pastors and teachers [to shepherd and guide and instruct], 12 [and He did this] to fully equip *and* perfect the saints (God's people) for works of service, to build up the body of Christ [the church]; 13 until we all reach oneness in the faith and in the knowledge of the Son of God, [growing spiritually] to become a mature believer, reaching to the measure of the fullness of Christ [manifesting His spiritual completeness and exercising our spiritual gifts in unity]." (Hebrews 11:12-13. Square brackets by author for added clarity.)

---

[17] The covenant of Jesus Christ that is given to us in our salvation, encompasses the material realm, the mind, body, and spirit.

[18] There are four classes of apostles found in Scripture: (1) Jesus Christ who is the Apostle of our faith. He alone stand in this class. (2) The original eleven Foundation Apostles (excluding Judas). The were apostles "before" the ascension of Jesus Christ who set Foundation doctrines for the church. (3) The Apostle Paul stands in a class of his own being a Foundation Apostle "after" Jesus ascended. (4) Non-foundation apostles do not set foundation, but build upon the foundation of Jesus, the eleven, and Paul.

Cessationism

Again, Cessationists believe the office of the prophet is no longer valid today because we now have the Written Bible. This is a logic-based conclusion by misassociated pairing. Furthermore, they reject the Holy Spirit's gifts of **Prophecy**, **The Word of Wisdom**, **The Word of Knowledge**, **The Gift of Tongues**, **Interpretation of Tongues**, **Miracles**, **Healings**, and **The Discerning Of Spirits**.

While the teachings of Cessationism boldly assert such claims, on the basis of Scripture there is nothing to support their position. Accordingly, they must use fallacious deductive reasoning, logic, and philosophy to defend their position.

Because the Holy Spirit's Baptism is implied throughout Scripture, the subject cannot altogether be ignored. This presents an awkward problem for them. While trying to make their Cessationist doctrines fit the continuity of Scripture, they stumble over God's unchanging Word.

What do they do with over six hundred seventy-five million (675,000,000) Christians that form 33.75% of the Body of Christ which are Baptized in the Holy Spirit? Do they suppose that over a third of the Body of Christ is misled and not hearing the voice of the Chief Shepherd, Jesus Christ? What should be done with today's massive numbers of miracles, healings, and salvation that are accomplished through the Holy Spirit-filled Christians? Do they attribute their works to God, or Satan?

Well, quite obviously, God's house is not divided. If 675,000,000 Christians are Baptized in the Holy Spirit and fulfilling Scripture according to what Jesus instructed, then we have no choice but to agree with Scripture rather than the Cessationist's labyrinth of error.

It is ludicrous to believe that those who reject the Holy Spirit's Baptism have any argument against the weight of Scripture. Such critics, at best, use a *natural mindset* rather than a spiritual mindset according to the Holy Spirit's illumination and revelation (1 Corinthians 2:13).

While Cessationism has many more atypical positions in the framework of their theology, the point here is not to bash or audaciously criticize any *individual Christian* and their love for Jesus. Rather, it is to point out various contradictions within Calvinist doctrines which are used to dissuade Christians from receiving the Holy Spirit's power.

Cessationism

The time is coming when the Holy Spirit will burst His revelation and glory into the Body of Christ and break through every barrier. At that time, the Lord's people will be empowered as a mighty army for the final sweep of souls before the coming of Jesus. Therefore, it is wise to remember the words of Paul when he said:

> "So do not go on passing judgment before the appointed time, *but wait* until the Lord comes, for He will both bring to light the [secret] things that are hidden in darkness and disclose the motives of the hearts. Then each one's praise will come from God." (1 Corinthians 4:5)

God's Word...The Final Judge

No subjective experience stands in its own right without validation by Scripture. By the same principle, in the absence of supporting Scripture, no doctrine can be endorsed by philosophy and logic alone. Logic of itself is not the final criteria for defining God's Word.

The question we must ask ourselves is this: How much doctrinal error should be tolerated until it is heresy?

What would the Foundation Apostles call the teachings of Calvinism and Catholicism when both systems claim absolute truth but disagree one with the other? The contrasting doctrines of Cessationism, Catholicism, and even Neo-Pentecostalism is either right or wrong—they cannot be both.

As for the purity of truth, there is no middle ground, no multiple-choice-option, and no inconsequential outcome. All error is damaging. Only pure truth can set one free. The Holy Spirit only endorses "pure" truth. He is NOT joined to any degree of error.

John Calvin suffered immeasurably because he denied God's healing benefit along with the power that comes through the Baptism of the Holy Spirit. And while he was a man who apparently loved Jesus and unquestionably attained eternal life, yet, in this life, his error and doctrine has done great damage to himself and untold millions of others after him.

What do we say to screaming souls in the agony of eternal damnation as they echo Calvin's teaching that they could never lose their salvation? What will Calvin tell them about his "Once Saved Always Saved" teaching?

Cessationism

> "Not many [of you] should become teachers [serving in an official teaching capacity], my brothers and sisters, for you know that we [who are teachers] will be judged by a higher standard [because we have assumed greater accountability and more condemnation if we teach incorrectly]." (James 3:1. The Amplified Bible)

Again, if Cessationist doctrines are the same as the doctrines of the Foundational Apostles, why do Cessationists name their doctrines after their inventors? If they are the same teachings, why not leave them as the "Apostle's Doctrines"?

Despite all the doctrinal confusion throughout the Body of Christ, the Triumphant Holy Spirit will soon bring His people into the unity of truth and knit the Body of Christ in agreement under one truth, one Savior, one Father, and one Spirit.

> "But even if we, or an angel from heaven, should preach to you a gospel contrary to that which we [originally] preached to you, let him be condemned to destruction!" (Galatians 1:8. The Amplified Bible.)

As we shall see in the very near future, people of all denominations, doctrines, creeds, perspectives, offices, and persuasions will stand together by one truth in the power of the Holy Spirit. This final revival will cover the entire earth. The people of Christ will be as one in His Holy Spirit—an army of powerful witnesses to reach over 6,000,000,000 (six billion) unsaved people who will see indisputable works that prove Jesus Christ is the only answer to salvation.

Arminism

CHAPTER 13
ARMINISM--OPPOSITIONISTS OF SPIRIT-FILLED FAITH
"A Faith without Power"

Jacobus Arminius, a Dutch reformer, was an passionate follower of Calvin's theology. In fact, he was taught by one of Calvin's key disciples, Theodore Beza.

Arminius was only four years old when Calvin died. Yet, despite his careful mentoring from Beza, Arminius concluded that Calvin was wrong on several points of Scripture.

Briefly, Arminius rejected Calvin's predestination belief. However, he shared the same position as Calvin regarding the Holy Spirit's Baptism.

Calvin believed that those predestinated for salvation could not refuse God's grace—that it was not their choice, but God's choice. Arminius had a different opinion. Arminius believed man could choose to reject salvation, but if one accepted salvation, a Christian had to live mindfully of God's Word. While Arminius' doctrine initially seems Scriptural, he emphasized a works or performance-based relationship with God and thereby minimized God's grace nearly altogether. According to Arminius, what God began in salvation, the individual would complete.

Arminius' theology relied on legalism as contrasted against Calvin's hyper-grace doctrines which removes any accountability of sin for the Christian. While Calvin crashed on one side of the road, Arminius crashed on the other side. Both teachings are logic-based extremes.

Both Calvinism and Arminism assume that the Holy Spirit's Baptism was confined to the era of the Foundation Apostles. Therefore, both believe that the Baptism of the Holy Spirit ended after the last Foundation Apostle died.

Arminism

For this reason, they both rejected **Healings** and **Miracles** for the church today.[19]

As children of the Most High God, each of us are in the process of ever increasing illumination as the Spirit of Truth brings us into the revelations of God's glorious Word.

Rather than reading Scripture from an objective view and believing God's Word on its own credit, they filtered the Written Word through the lens of their own Cessationist logic rather than by revelation of the Holy Spirit.

Despite all the doctrinal confusion throughout the Body of Christ, in this generation, the Triumphant Holy Spirit will bring all men into the unity of truth and knit the Body of Christ under one truthful agreement, one Savior, one Father, and one Spirit.

---

[19] It is interesting that Calvin and Arminius lived over four hundred sixty-five years ago and yet their doctrines are spoken in the context of the "modern church". Specifically, however, they address the church's existence "after" the death of the last living Foundation Apostle, John. They designed entirely too much of their doctrines around the Bible being printed. These become misassociated factors rendering a wrong conclusion.

A Composition and Mixture

CHAPTER 14
IN CONSIDERATION OF IT ALL
"A Recap of Today's Churches and the Holy Spirit"

To recap, the church age of today (Philadelphia) stands unique as compared to any church age before us or after us. Yet within our day, the teachings of Calvinism, Catholicism, Neo-Pentecostalism, Arminism, and Laodiceanism mutually exist. Individually, they oppose the Baptism of the Holy Spirit, or as in the case of the Neo-Pentecostals such as Calvary Chapels, they rhetorically accept Him but make no allowance for His gifts during their church services.

Calvinism and Arminism emerged from the Sardis Church era over four hundred fifty years ago. Their doctrines are relatively new as compared to the teachings of the Apostles. Calvinism and Arminism believe that the Baptism of the Holy Spirit was only for the early church; that the Baptism of the Holy Spirit was no longer given after the death of the Apostle John in 100 AD. This opinion is entirely without any Scriptural basis.

Catholicism holds a slightly different position with regard to the Baptism of the Holy Spirit. In fact, during the Charismatic Movement in the late 60s and early 70s, many Catholics received the Baptism of the Holy Spirit without objection by the Catholic hierarchy. Nonetheless, the Holy Spirit's gifts are never part of the Catholic mass.

Neo-Pentecostalism is the lukewarm mixture between cold Calvinism and hot Pentecostalism. Neo-Pentecostals are the religious politicians that blend Calvinism and Pentecostalism into a seeker-sensitive format in order to avoid offending either group.

The largest majority of Neo-Pentecostals is better known as the Calvary Chapel churches along with many of the Vineyard churches. They preach an informational-based historical view of the Gospel as compared to a revelational-based right-now presence of God that moves in cadence with the Holy Spirit's leading. In truth, the Calvary Chapel

A Composition and Mixture

churches are remarkably more Calvinist in their view of Scripture than the doctrines of the Foundational Apostles.

Charismatic Christians and Spirit-filled Christians

Even though both Charismatic Christians and Spirit-filled Christians are Baptized in the Holy Spirit, there is a distinct difference between them.

A Charismatic Christian is one, who, after receiving the Baptism of the Holy Spirit, chooses to remain in a church where the Holy Spirit's gifts are altogether prohibited or suppressed. Thus, one can be a Charismatic Christian who is a Lutheran, Baptist, Presbyterian, Methodist, Episcopalian, Catholic, or Calvary Chapel—all of which make no allowance for the Holy Spirit's manifest glory. For this reason, the Baptism of the Holy Spirit is nothing more than a token experience to many Charismatic Christians.

A typical Charismatic Christian is untaught about the gifts of the Holy Spirit. For the most part, he or she has no understanding of their use, nor do they comprehend what they were given when they received the Holy Spirit's Baptism. They merely acknowledge the experience but have no ambition to be used in power.

In stark contrast, a Holy Spirit Baptized Christian is one, who, after receiving the Baptism of the Holy Spirit, attends church where the Holy Spirit and His gifts unreservedly operate without suppressive controls. In this context, Spirit-filled Christians are free to pursue the gifts and be used in the anointing of His power.

Despite all these contrasts, somewhere there must be a thread of truth. Accordingly, how shall we view the relevance of the Holy Spirit's Baptism in Christendom today? What rules of consideration should be applied for accurate and Scriptural conclusions with regard to His gifts?

Scriptural Balance

First, the final authority on anything related to God is Scripture—God's Written Word. Any philosophy, opinion, subjective experience, or doctrine must pass through the acid test of Scripture in its full consideration of context and complementary verses throughout the entire Bible. If philosophy, opinion, experience, or church doctrine cannot meet the *contextual* standard of God's Word, it is disqualified.

A Composition and Mixture

Second, we must carefully examine the Scriptures. What are the Scriptures that refer to the Baptism of the Holy Spirit that are relevant to the church today? Objectively, we must ask how long the Lord intended the Holy Spirit's Baptism to be part of His church. Further, what Scriptures are used that formulate doctrine related to the Holy Spirit and His works? Are such Scriptures properly applied? Or, are they manipulated by philosophy and deductive reasoning? Was the Holy Spirit's Baptism to continue until the return of Jesus Christ, or was it dispensational and limited to the time of the Apostles?

Third, as previously mentioned, Scripture must be considered in its contextual setting and mutual agreement with the whole of biblical truth. No singular verse of Scripture should be used apart from its context, or overlaid with the logic of man's prejudice. The Word of God must be rightly divided (2 Timothy 2:15). The "whole" counsel of God's Word must be considered, not just selective verses.

Fourth, we must be willing to set aside any preconceived notions, ideals, experiences, prejudices, and doctrinal views in order to objectively understand God's Word. We must not be so arrogant as to twist the Scripture in order to defend personal doctrine. Rather, we must subject our opinion and doctrine to the unbiased standard of God's Word.

Fifth, we must not read more into the Scripture than what it says. The Bible says exactly what it means. Adding to or taking away from the truth of Scripture creates an appendix of beliefs that are unsupported by the consistency of God's Written Word.

Basic Rules of Dispensationalism

As it relates to God's Word, a dispensation is a bracket of time where specific rules and orders apply until new rules and orders replace the existing ones. For instance, the Old Testament dispensation required the use of animal sacrifice to cover the sins of man. But after Jesus was crucified, a new dispensation was inaugurated by His blood which replaced the former dispensation.

In the present dispensation, God deals with sin through the shed blood of His Son that removes it, not just covers it such as the animal sacrifices of the former dispensation in the Old Testament.

In the Bible, when one dispensation is replaced with another, it is dramatically introduced with correlating events that unquestionably ends the old and begins the new. Thus, when dispensations change,

A Composition and Mixture

Scripture carefully records the changes in order to eliminate any ambiguity. For example, when our Heavenly Father sent His Son, the birth of Jesus was marked with *dramatic events* involving the angelic hosts and a glorious light that shone all about the shepherds in the field:

> "And an angel of the Lord suddenly stood before them, and the glory of the Lord flashed *and* shone around them, and they were terribly frightened. 13 Then suddenly there appeared with the angel a multitude of the heavenly host (angelic army) praising God and saying, 14 "Glory to God in the highest [heaven], And on earth peace among men with whom He is well-pleased."15 When the angels had gone away from them into heaven, the shepherds *began* saying one to another, "Let us go straight to Bethlehem, and see this [wonderful] thing that has happened which the Lord has made known to us." (Luke 2:9,13-15)

In another example, during the final hours of Jesus *before* and *after* He died, a series of dramatic events took place:

> "It was now about the sixth hour, and darkness fell over the whole land until the ninth hour, 45 because the sun was obscured; and the veil of the temple was torn in two. 46 And Jesus, crying out with a loud voice, said, "Father, into Your hands I commit My spirit." Having said this, He breathed His last." (Luke 23:44-46)

In still another example, when Jesus sent the Holy Spirit to permanently indwell those who believed in and accepted Jesus as their Savior, Jesus *dramatically breathed* on them and told them to receive the Holy Spirit:

> "Then Jesus said to them again, "Peace to you; as the Father has sent Me, I also send you [as My representatives]."22 And when He said this, He breathed on them and said to them, "Receive the Holy Spirit." (John 20-21-22)

When the Holy Spirit gave His gift, the Baptism, it too was marked with a dramatic demonstration:

> "When the day of Pentecost had come, they [one hundred twenty people] were all together in one place, 2 and suddenly a sound came from heaven like a rushing violent

wind, and it filled the whole house where they were sitting. 3There appeared to them Tongues resembling fire, which were being distributed [among them], and they rested on each one of them [as each person received the Holy Spirit]. 4 And they were all filled [that is, diffused throughout their being] with the Holy Spirit and began to speak in other Tongues (different languages), as the Spirit was giving them the ability to speak out [clearly and appropriately]." (Acts 2:1-4. Square brackets by author for added clarity.)

Revelation Knowledge vs Academic Knowledge

Without the Holy Spirit's impartation of revelation, man cannot access God's Word through mere academia. As a result, logic-based deductions are often substituted for revelation and assumed as truth. But when the Holy Spirit reveals God's Word and gives understanding, He illuminates the truths of our Heavenly Father's Word.

The Book of Hebrews, for instance, explains the difference between the old covenant and new covenant dispensations—that is, before and after Jesus shed His blood.

The Book of Acts explains the works of the Apostles as they ministered *in* the Holy Spirit's power after He dramatically gave His gift with fire and the sound of a mighty torrential wind.

The Book of Romans is the revelation which explains the finished works of Jesus in the New Covenant. Paul's teachings, (as inspired by the Holy Spirit) detail the New Covenant according to faith and not by works.

The Book of 1st Corinthians explains the Baptism of the Holy Spirit, His gifts, and their proper use during church services.

Galatians and **Colossians** explains our departure from the old law and how we should live by the Holy Spirit under the New Covenant.

As repetitively stated throughout this book, a natural mind that embraces the mere academia of God's Word cannot produce the revelation of truth. It takes the Holy Spirit to reveal the revelation of God's Word. Conversely, man, in his prideful intellect, cannot access the spiritual domain. This was precisely the problem with the Reformers. They academically approached the Scriptures without the Holy Spirit. As a

A Composition and Mixture

result, they were left to their own conclusions which invariably was discordant with the Apostle's teachings.

> "We also speak of these things, not in words taught or supplied by human wisdom, but in those taught by the Spirit, combining and interpreting spiritual thoughts with spiritual words [for those being guided by the Holy Spirit].(1 Corinthians 2:13)

From generation to generation, the Holy Spirit's power and revelation is available to any Believer who desires to be a witness of Jesus. The Holy Spirit's gift was never given as a substitute for God's Written Word, but in fact He complements, proves, and attests to God's Word. In this regard, the Baptism is not limited to the early church, and especially now where over six billion people are without salvation.

> "And they went out and preached everywhere, the Lord working with *them* and confirming the word through the accompanying signs. Amen." (Mark 16:20)

While Christians today stand in the common bond of Jesus Christ, most of them reject the power of the Holy Spirit. By default, they have a *word-only* testimony of Jesus in their preaching. They are substantially less effective without the Holy Spirit's power. The truth is, what distinguishes God's Word apart from other religions is the Holy Spirit's power that gives credibility to a Christian's testimony with proving signs and wonders, including **Healings**, **Miracles**, and **Deliverances**.

STORY:
A missionary living on an island-nation grew weary and frustrated with seeing no result for his labors. Largely, this was because the villagers feared the witch-doctors and fetish-doctors who operated in the supernatural powers of the occult. By contrast, the missionary's message carried no persuasion because it was a *word-only* testimony without power. Accordingly, the missionary prayed for God to show him what to do.

There was a notorious demon-possessed man on the island who was confined in a large bamboo cage and fed like an animal. He was so dangerous that his food and water were pushed toward him by a long pole. Day and night, he lived naked in the cage. The ground was covered in feces and urine, and no one dared come near him.

A Composition and Mixture

The Lord told the missionary to go inside the cage and set the man free. The missionary debated with the Lord by using various excuses until he finally surrendered to the Lord's command.

The missionary went to the keeper of the cage and asked him to open the door and let him in. The keeper strenuously objected and told the missionary that the demon-crazed man would kill anyone entering the cage. But, because the missionary had received a Rhema Word from the Lord, he was convinced that God would protect him. Based on that, he insisted that he be allowed entry. First, however, the keeper of the cage had to get permission from the village king and the witch-doctor.

News of the missionary's plan quickly spread throughout the villages. People gathered to see if his claims that Jesus could deliver the man in the cage were true. Everyone wanted to see the power of Jesus Christ according to the missionary's testimony.

The day finally came. The crowds gathered. The king and the witch-doctors stood at the front of the crowd. Several men stood ready. When the door was opened, they quickly shoved the missionary inside and then reset the latch.

The crowd watched.

Immediately the demoniac charged the missionary. When the demoniac came within reach of the missionary, the missionary threw his arms and legs around him. The missionary vociferously declared the name of Jesus Christ and commanded the spirits to leave the man. In but a few minutes, the demoniac relaxed and everything was quiet. The missionary, covered in urine and feces, stood up and then helped the man to his feet. The demon-possessed man was completely set free and given back his right mind. Everyone was in awe of the power that the missionary possessed in Jesus, a power that the witch-doctors could not match.

The missionary led the man out of the cage and testified to everyone about Jesus Christ and the power of the Holy Spirit. He told them they too could have God's blessing and power if they received Jesus as their Lord and Savior. It was, in fact, this very demonstration of power that testified of Jesus which resulted in the surrounding villages becoming Christian, including the witch-doctors.

◆ ◆ ◆ ◆

A Composition and Mixture

Lacking the Holy Spirit's power, Christians without the Baptism of the Holy Spirit often retreat in the face of such challenges. Being unacquainted with the Holy Spirit's power, they have no confidence to face the manifest authority of the supernatural that challenges them.

Because logic and reason is soul-driven and not Holy Spirit led, the natural mind of man opposes the Holy Spirit's Baptism. As repetitively stated, according to man's logic, Cessationists believe His gift is no longer needed as a witness of Jesus Christ. And, even though we have the Bible written in all *major* languages, over 6,000 languages are not translated into the Bible. Some of the languages have no written formats. For this reason alone, we must have the Holy Spirit's Baptism that gives us power to be an effective witness of Jesus Christ.

Those who teach against the Baptism of the Holy Spirit for today's Christian are spiritually just as blind as the Sadducees that were confused about the resurrection. They were reputed as "experts of the law". But Jesus corrected them when He said:

> "Jesus said to them, "Is this not the reason you are mistaken, that you do not understand the Scriptures or the power of God?" (Mark 12:24)

No one can *disprove* the Baptism of the Holy Spirit for today's Christians by the use of Scripture. Consequently, those who oppose the Baptism of the Holy Spirit must *add to or take away* from God's Word by infusing it with subjective experiences, logic-based false premises, and philosophical views that stand contrary to multiple areas of Scripture. Listen to their arguments. In every case, it is entirely logic-based deductions and distorted usages of Scripture out of its context.

The Spirit's Baptism Is Often Confused With Infilling

A common error among those who refuse the Baptism of the Holy Spirit, is the confusion between the Holy Spirit's Baptism of power and the initial permanent indwelling presence of the Holy Spirit at the moment of salvation. But, as the Bible proves, they are distinctly different in purpose and application.

To be sure, every Christian has the Holy Spirit living in them, but not every Christian is Baptized in the Holy Spirit. This also will be discussed in greater detail.

A Composition and Mixture

The Purpose Was Power To Be A Witness

Our need to be an effective convincing witness of Jesus Christ by the proofs of God's divine power has only intensified in these final days. To affirm this fact, Jesus said the season of His return would be marked with the characteristics of the days of Noah and the days of Lot (Luke 17:26-30).

> "And just as it was in the days of Noah, so it will be in the time of [the second coming of] the Son of Man: 27 the people were eating, they were drinking, they were marrying, they were being given in marriage, [they were indifferent to God] until the day that Noah went into the ark, and the flood came and destroyed them all. 28 It was the same as it was in the days of Lot. People were eating, they were drinking, they were buying, they were selling, they were planting, they were building [carrying on business as usual, without regard for their sins]; 29 but on the [very] day that Lot left Sodom it rained fire and brimstone (burning sulfur) from heaven and destroyed them all. 30 It will be just the same on the day that the Son of Man is revealed." (Luke 17:26-30 The Amplified Bible. Square brackets by author for added clarity.)

Noah's days depict a global saturation of wickedness (Genesis 6:6). The days of Lot were five hundred years later and depict a global saturation of sexual perversion. But when the characteristics of both eras come together in one stream, then we know it is the time—the season of the Lord's return.

Darkness, sin, lawlessness, perversions, false Christs, false teachers, false prophets, false apostles, false signs and wonders; apostacy within the church, heretical teachings; the enthronement of Antichrist, and the return of Jesus Christ are all factors and events that occur within *this* final generation.

If there was ever a need for the Holy Spirit's power in the church, it is NOW. In the midst of our increasing global turmoil and the soon enthronement of Antichrist, the burden to reach over 6,000,000,000 (six billion) people is IMPOSSIBLE without the Holy Spirit's power. There is simply no other way without His power that comes from His Baptism in order to accomplish the task set before us.

A Composition and Mixture

The Need for Power is 28 Times Greater!

In the time of Jesus, the world population was estimated to be around three hundred million people (300,000,000). Today, there are eight billion three hundred million (8,300,000,000) or twenty-eight times more people in the world than when the church began. Of that number, over six billion are registered on the rolls of the eternally damned, or, stated in another way: there are twenty times more people going to Hell than the entire world population than when Jesus ministered on the earth.

In consideration of this ever worsening darkness, should any Christian be so assuming that we can reach the unsaved without the Holy Spirit's divine power? Are we to believe that the power of sin is weaker today than it was 2000 years ago? Further, should we be so naïve as to think that man has reached such sophisticated refinement that his carnal nature is now tamed? Keep in mind, it is THIS generation that worships Antichrist and Satan!

> "They fell down *and* worshiped the dragon [Satan] because he gave his authority to the beast [Antichrist]; they also worshiped the beast [Antichrist], saying, "Who is like (as great as) the beast [antichrist], and who is able to wage war against him?" (Revelation 13:4. Square brackets by author for added clarity.)

Jesus instructed us that we need the Holy Spirit's power to be His witnesses. The ONLY prescription Jesus gave for us to receive His power was through the Baptism of the Holy Spirit—nothing else! Moreover, the challenge today is enormously greater than the days of the original Apostles. If they needed His power then, how much more do we need His power now in a world with twenty-eight times more people?

As long as Jesus' church is on the earth, His power-prescription will never change. And, if His people are to prevail against the opposition of unabashed darkness, we need the Holy Spirit's power in the face of incalculable evil as we near the time of Antichrist.

Look At The Proof

There is no question that just under two-thirds of all Christians openly denounce the Baptism of the Holy Spirit or have never heard of His Baptism. Yet, as we examine the results of those who have received the Holy Spirit's Baptism, why would any Believer attend a church that opposes, suppresses, or refuses His power?

A Composition and Mixture

Consider the statistical proofs of Christians that are Baptized in the Holy Spirit today:

- In the 1900s just after the Azusa Street Revival, there were very few Holy Spirit Baptized Christians on the earth.

- After the Charismatic movement in 1970, there were seventy-four million (74,000,000) Holy Spirit Baptized Christians.

- In 1996, there were four hundred seventy-five million (475,000,000) Holy Spirit Baptized Christians.

- By 2000, there were over five hundred fifty million (550,000,000) Holy Spirit Baptized Christians.

- In 2020, there are over six hundred seventy-five million (675,000,000) Holy Spirit Baptized Christian.

- Today, there is an estimated seven hundred twenty million (720,000,000) Holy Spirit Baptized Christians.

- 36% of all Christians today are Holy Spirit Baptized and the number increases every day.

- Holy Spirit-Baptized Christians conduct the largest evangelistic campaigns today.

- Holy Spirit-Baptized Christians operate the largest Christian TV/radio programs in the world.

- Holy Spirit Baptized Christians have the fastest growing number of newly planted churches in the world.

- Christian churches that embrace the Holy Spirit's Baptism have the fastest growing membership in the world.

- Holy Spirit-Baptized Christians have the largest churches in the world.

- Holy Spirit-Baptized Christians gather the largest crowds to hear the Gospel.

A Composition and Mixture

- Holy Spirit-Baptized Christians have the most consistent proofs of signs, wonders, and miracles.

- Holy Spirit Baptized Christians have consistently the largest number of converts to Christ.

It is no wonder that Satan fears the Baptism of the Holy Spirit. It is the weapon of his greatest undoing. For this reason, he spreads false doctrines that cultivate confusion within Christianity to persuade millions of Christians into rejecting or suppressing the most formidable weapon used against him—the Holy Spirit's power.

Satan's most woeful enemies are fire-breathing, devil stomping, tongue-talking, miracle-working, power-preaching Christians who are Baptized in the Holy Spirit!

The truth is, such powerful works among Spirit-Baptized Christians are NOT found in denominations that suppress, reject, oppose, or deny the Holy Spirit's power.

As we shall see in the very near future, people of all denominations, doctrines, creeds, perspectives, offices, and persuasions will stand together in one truth by the power of the Holy Spirit. This last and final revival will cover the entire earth. Christians will stand as one in the Holy Spirit as powerful witnesses in order to reach over six billion (6,000,000,000) unsaved people. The unsaved will see indisputable proofs that Jesus Christ is the only answer to salvation.

A Composition and Mixture

Part III

Twelve Key Observations About the Baptism of the Holy Spirit.

☙❧
No man is completed by the efforts of himself. It is the Lord who began the good work in us, and it is the Lord who finishes us. Our duty is to submit to the Triumphant Holy Spirit who teaches us by the illumination and revelation of His Word. Therefore let no man lock the door to any truth.
☙❧

The Holy Spirit Was Not Yet Given

CHAPTER 15
THE HOLY SPIRIT WAS NOT YET GIVEN
Key Observation #1

OBJECT SCRIPTURE

"He who believes in Me, as the Scripture said, from his innermost being will flow rivers of living water.'" 39 But this He spoke of the Spirit, whom those who believed in Him were to receive; <u>for the Spirit was not yet given</u>, <u>because Jesus was not yet glorified</u>." (John 7:38-39)

◆ ◆ ◆ ◆

If the Holy Spirit was not yet given, who was speaking through the prophets of old? What of those who worked **Miracles** and **Healings**? What about John the Baptist who was filled with the Holy Spirit while yet in his mother's womb (Luke 1:15)? Further, what do we do with the Apostles and the seventy disciples of Christ whom He sent out to preach the Kingdom of God with signs, wonders, and miracles (Luke 10:1-17)? What was the source of power in them that produced such great works? If the Holy Spirit was not yet given, then how did these people work the works of God?

To answer that question, we must first consider the Holy Spirit's mode of operation in both the Old and New Testaments.

The Presence of the Holy Spirit In The Old and New Testament
Many assume Jesus' ministry functioned in the New Testament dispensation. In fact, it did not. Jesus bridges the two covenants—the Old Testament to the New Testament. Nonetheless, multiple prophecies within the Old Testament still apply to THIS generation. Therefore, to assert that the Old Testament has no relevance in the New Covenant is an opinion founded upon great ignorance. Accordingly, we must remember that all of God's Word is to be received and rightly divided in its application.

Until the sacrifice of Jesus was completed, Jesus ministered under the Old Testament dispensation as did His disciples, including the last Old

The Holy Spirit Was Not Yet Given

Testament prophet, John the Baptist. Accordingly, the New Testament, or New Covenant, as it is sometimes called, did not commence until three things occurred: (1) Jesus ascended into Heaven after His crucifixion; (2) He was "re-glorified" with the glory He had before the world existed; and (3) His sending of the Holy Spirit.

By the evidence of Scripture, the Holy Spirit operated in, through, and upon chosen vessels of God in the Old Testament. *However,* He did not permanently indwell anyone's physical body and designate them as His temple until three things were completed: (1) His sacrificial blood on the cross, (2) the removal of sin, and (3) His *re-glorifcation*. Only then could the bodies of Believers be the Holy Spirit's temple.

> "For we are the temple of the Living God; just as God said, "I will dwell in them and walk among them; and I will be their God, and they shall be My people." (2 Corinthians 6:17)

Under the Old Testament law, the blood of bulls and goats could not remove the stain of sin. Like a suit jacket that covers a stain on a white shirt, the blood sacrifice of animals merely hid the sin but could never remove it. It was a ceremonial covering, not a legal cleansing. If the blood of bulls and goats were sufficient to *remove* sin, then the blood of Christ would never have been shed.

> "For it is impossible for the blood of bulls and goats to <u>take away</u> sins." (Hebrews 10:4. Underline by author for added emphasis.)

After Jesus shed His blood, He ascended to the Father and was re-glorified. The New Covenant, however, could not be inaugurated until Jesus sent the Holy Spirit. When He did, the Holy Spirit permanently indwelt every Believer. From that moment forward, our Father looks upon His children as cleansed by the sacrificial blood of Jesus Christ. And even though we sin daily, the blood of His Son keeps us in covenant relationship with God. This is because Jesus' blood is continual and constant in its cleansing power.

Referring to John 7:39 where it says that the Holy Spirit was not yet given, it meant that the Holy Spirit could not be sent as a *permanent indwelling Resident* until "after" Jesus was re-glorified.

Accordingly, after Jesus Christ put on the limitation of human flesh, He had to be fully restored to His glory—the glory He had before the

The Holy Spirit Was Not Yet Given

world came into existence. When that event was completed, Jesus sent the Holy Spirit to continue Jesus' mission through every Believer on earth.

> "But I tell you the truth, it is to your advantage that I go away; for if I do not go away, the Helper will not come to you; but if I go, <u>I will send Him to you</u>. 8 And He, when He comes, will convict the world concerning sin and righteousness and judgment; 9 concerning sin, because they do not believe in Me; 10 and concerning righteousness, because I go to the Father and you no longer see Me; 11 and concerning judgment, because the ruler of this world has been judged." (John 16:7-11. Underline by author for added emphasis.)

When Jesus clothed Himself in the limitation of humanity, He was made in all points as any human, yet without sin. His one significant difference was that He did not have a sin nature such as we have at the moment of our conception.

His commission as the unique "Son of God" was performed as the unique "Son of Man". Everything He did: His miracles, words, and works were under the direct inspiration and guidance of the Holy Spirit. His ministry and direction came through the Holy Spirit's power and presence.

> "Have this attitude in yourselves which was also in Christ Jesus, 6 who, although He existed in the form of God, did not regard equality with God a thing to be grasped, 7 but emptied Himself, taking the form of a bond-servant, and being made in the likeness of men. 8 Being found in appearance as a man, He humbled Himself by becoming obedient to the point of death, even death on a cross." (Philippians 2:5-8)

> "Therefore, He had to be made like His brethren in all things, so that He might become a merciful and faithful high priest in things pertaining to God, to make propitiation for the sins of the people. 18 For since He Himself was tempted in that which He has suffered, He is able to come to the aid of those who are tempted." (Heb 2:17-18)

The Holy Spirit Was Not Yet Given

> "And Jesus kept increasing in wisdom and stature, and in favor with God and men." (Luke 2:52)

At a certain point during Jesus' ministry, specifically near the end before the time of His crucifixion, He cried out to the Father and said:

> "Now, Father, glorify Me together with Yourself, with the glory which I had with You before the world was." (John 17:5)

As already stated, Jesus' re-glorification was mandatory. It had to be completed before the Holy Spirit could be sent to permanently indwell each Believer. Accordingly, starting from the time of Jesus' miraculous conception and all the way to His re-glorification, everything had to be completed *before* He could send the Holy Spirit.

> "I will ask the Father, and <u>He will give you another Helper</u>, that He may be with you forever; 17 that is the Spirit of truth, whom the world cannot receive, because it does not see Him or know Him, but you know Him because He abides with you and will be in you. 18 <u>I will not leave you as orphans</u>; I will come to you." (John 14:16-18. Underline by author for added emphasis.)

Jesus said He would not leave His apostles as orphans; He would come to them. But how and in what form? In verse sixteen, He said He would give them "another Helper." In the original language of the Scripture, it meant He would sent them an exact representation of Himself in the same way that Jesus Christ is the perfect representation of the Father.

> "Jesus said to him, 'Have I been with you for so long a time, and you do not know Me yet, Philip, *nor* recognize clearly who I am? Anyone who has seen Me has seen the Father. How can you say, 'Show us the Father?'" (John 14:9)

Just as Jesus gave the disciples authority to preach the Kingdom and work miracles *before His ascension*, the Holy Spirit does the same for Believers today through the same gift Jesus possessed: the Holy Spirit's Baptism of power.

> "And Jesus returned to Galilee <u>in the power of the Spirit</u>, and news about Him spread through all the surrounding district." (Luke 14:4. Underline by author for added emphasis.)

The Holy Spirit Was Not Yet Given

The purpose of Jesus being re-glorified with the glory He had before putting on humanity was simply that each person of the Godhead, the Father, Son, and Holy Spirit, would be in divine position to one another.

The Holy Spirit who indwells every Believer, is not limited in time, place, and location as Jesus was during His earthly ministry. The Holy Spirit is everywhere present at the same time and in every Believer throughout the world.

The indwelling permanent resident of the Holy Spirit is the seal of our redemption. Unless one has the *permanent indwelling presence of the Holy Spirit*, they do not belong to Jesus. Consequently, one cannot be part of Jesus Christ unless he or she has the Holy Spirit living within them. Thanks be to our Heavenly Father, at the instant of salvation, the Holy Spirit permanently indwells every Believer!

> "However, you are not in the flesh but in the Spirit, if indeed the Spirit of God dwells in you. But if anyone does not have the Spirit of Christ, he does not belong to Him."
> (Romans **8:9**)

After Jesus was re-glorified, He sent the Holy Spirit who instantly went into every Believer throughout all the world at the same time. This marked the beginning of the New Covenant which also started the New Testament church.

◆◆◆◆
Key Facts

1. Jesus Christ's ministry operated in the Old Testament dispensation.

2. After Jesus was re-glorified, on the third day after H, He sent the Holy Spirit.

3. Every prophet, disciple, follower, and Apostle *prior* to the time of Jesus' re-glorification functioned under the Old Covenant. The Holy Spirit worked in them and through them, but never as an indwelling permanent Resident within them.

4. The Holy Spirit operated *through* people in the Old Covenant, but He did not take *permanent indwelling residence* with anyone *until* they were legally cleansed of their sins by the blood of Jesus.

Jesus Sends the Holy Spirit

CHAPTER 16
JESUS SENDS THE HOLY SPIRIT
Key Observation #2

OBJECT SCRIPTURE

"But Mary was standing outside the tomb weeping; and so, as she wept, she stooped and looked into the tomb; 12 and she saw two angels in white sitting, one at the head and one at the feet, where the body of Jesus had been lying. 13 And they said to her, "Woman, why are you weeping?" She said to them, "Because they have taken away my Lord, and I do not know where they have laid Him." 14 When she had said this, she turned around and saw Jesus standing {there} and did not know that it was Jesus. 15 Jesus said to her, "Woman, why are you weeping? Whom are you seeking?" Supposing Him to be the gardener, she said to Him, "Sir, if you have carried Him away, tell me where you have laid Him, and I will take Him away." 16 Jesus said to her, "Mary!" She turned and said to Him in Hebrew, "Rabboni!" (which means, Teacher). 17 Jesus said to her, "Stop clinging to Me, for I have not yet ascended to the Father; but go to My brethren and say to them, "I ascend to My Father and your Father, and My God and your God."' 18 Mary Magdalene came, announcing to the disciples, "I have seen the Lord," and that He had said these things to her. 19 So when it was evening on that day, the first day of the week, and when the doors were shut where the disciples were, for fear of the Jews, Jesus came and stood in their midst and said to them, "Peace be with you." 20 And when He had said this, He showed them both His hands and His side. The disciples then rejoiced when they saw the Lord. 21 So Jesus said to them again, "Peace be with you; as the Father has sent Me, I also send you." 22 And when He had said this, He breathed on them and said to them, "Receive the Holy Spirit."
(John 20:11-22)

◆◆◆◆

Jesus Sends the Holy Spirit

In consideration of the above verses of Scripture, there are four notable observations:

(1) When Jesus met Mary Magdalene at the tomb, He had just returned from Hades[20], specifically, Paradise (Luke 23:43). All righteous Believers starting from Adam, who, by faith, believed in the promise of the coming Messiah, were waiting in Paradise for two essential factors: (a) the blood of Jesus to take away their sin, and (b) the Holy Spirit's permanent indwelling presence so they could occupy Heaven. Accordingly, Jesus spent part of Friday, all of Saturday, and less than six hours of Sunday in the center of the earth, specifically Hades, among the Righteous.

After proving His salvation to them, He returned from the heart of the earth (Matthew 12:40) and encountered Mary Madelene and her companions at the tomb. Mary, being ecstatic with joy, clung to Him.[21] What she did not know was that Jesus was on a precisely timed mission which included yet more divinely appointed encounters *before* He ascended to the Father for His re-glorification. Therefore, He told her to stop clinging to Him. This meant that He had not yet been re-glorified. Until that part of His mission was completed (John 7:38-39), He could not send the Holy Spirit.

(2) Within the same day that Jesus met Mary and her companions (verses 17 and 18), there was a change in time and setting *before* He met His Apostles (verses 19 and 20). Within that approximate twelve-hour period, Jesus ascended to the Father and was re-glorified.

(3) At evening time of the same day that Jesus met Mary, He suddenly appeared to ten of His Apostles who were in a locked room. Jesus commissioned them to their ministry as Foundation Apostles,

---

[20] There are some who mistakenly think Jesus went to Hell after he died on the cross. In fact, He went to Hades which was divided into two compartments: Paradise and Hell. Jesus went into Paradise and showed Himself to the righteous who were waiting for their redemption. He was in Paradise for part of Friday, all of Saturday, and part of Sunday. The story of Lazarus and rich man describes the positional domains between Hell and Paradise where the rich man in Hell called out to Abraham who was in Paradise. Abraham testifies how there was a great gulf between them that no one could cross over. (Luke 16:19-31)

[21] For a complete chronology of Jesus's resurrection as given in the four Gospels, compare Matthew 28:1-0; Mark 16:1-8; Luke 24 (entire chapter); and John 20 (entire chapter).

Jesus Sends the Holy Spirit

including Thomas, who for some reason, was not present. He then explained how their commission was to be carried out.

> "So Jesus said to them again, 'Peace be with you; as the Father has sent Me, I also send you.'" (John 11:21)

How did the Father send Jesus? Obviously, He was not referring to His virgin birth or His sinless state. Nor was He referring to His Jewish orthodox upbringing. He specifically referred to the power of the Holy Spirit. Jesus knew that in order to victoriously stand against Satan and his kingdom, His Apostles had to be armed with the *same power* He possessed in His incarnate state—the power of the Holy Spirit!

> "And Jesus returned to Galilee <u>in the power of the Spirit</u>, and news about Him spread through all the surrounding district. 15 And He began teaching in their synagogues and was praised by all." (Luke 4:14-15. Underline by author for added emphasis.)

(4) He breathed on them and said, "Receive the Holy Spirit." This proves that before He sent the Holy Spirit, Jesus had previously ascended to the Father and was re-glorified (John 7:39).

Jesus breathed on His Apostles and told them to receive the permanent indwelling presence of the Holy Spirit. This was the exact moment when the Apostles were formally commissioned. However, even *after that event*, they were NOT empowered with the Holy Spirit's gift—His Baptism. Their empowerment occurred forty-seven days later on Pentecost. Accordingly, they were to WAIT for the Holy Spirit's power so that their testimony and preaching of Jesus Christ would be authorized with signs, wonders, and miracles!

> "Gathering them together, He commanded them not to leave Jerusalem, but to wait for what the Father had promised, 'Which,' He said, 'you heard of from Me; 5 for John baptized with water, but you will be baptized with the Holy Spirit not many days from now.'" (Acts 1:4-5)

> "And as you go, preach, saying, "The Kingdom of Heaven is at hand.' 8 Heal the sick, raise the dead, cleanse the lepers, cast out demons. Freely you received, freely give." (Matthew 10:7-8)

Jesus Sends the Holy Spirit

The Lord Wanted Us to Know...

The Lord wanted us to know precisely when the Holy Spirit was sent as a permanent indwelling resident. Scripture defines the Holy Spirit's initial permanent indwelling as occurring the instant of one's salvation. It is a separate event from the Holy Spirit giving His gift—the Baptism of power. They are distinctly unique and different events!

Again, to emphasize the point, Jesus *did not* breathe the Baptism of the Holy Spirit upon them. If that were the case, they would not have been instructed to wait in Jerusalem for the promise of the Father that occurred forty-seven days later on Pentecost (Acts 1:4).

If these two events, the Holy Spirit's permanent indwelling presence and His Baptism of power are not properly distinguished, it produces confusion, uncertainty, and ambiguity. However, each event is well defined and documented by Scripture in order to remove all doubt.

Just as the Apostles received the Holy Spirit but were not Baptized *in* power, it explains why Christians today can have the Holy Spirit's permanent indwelling presence, but not be Baptized in His gift that produces power. Thankfully, as the Book of Romans clearly points out, the Holy Spirit permanently indwells every Christian.

> "However, you are not in the flesh but in the Spirit, if indeed the Spirit of God dwells in you. But if anyone does not have the Spirit of Christ, he does not belong to Him."
> (Romans 8:9)

The Baptism of the Holy Spirit (which is the Holy Spirit's gift) is not required for salvation. It is erroneous, therefore, to assert that if one is *not* Baptized in the Holy Spirit, then he or she is unsaved.

Salvation occurs when a person receives Jesus Christ as their Lord and Savior. At that instant, the Holy Spirit assumes permanent residence within the Believer. But...the Baptism of the Holy Spirit, proven by speaking in other **Tongues**, is an absolute proof of salvation. This is because the Holy Spirit's Baptism is only given *if* the Holy Spirit *first* permanently indwells the individual. Therefore, anyone who has the permanent indwelling Holy Spirit is saved.

Three Gifts

According to Scripture, each Person of the Triune Godhead is vital to our salvation and spiritual maturity in God's Kingdom:

Jesus Sends the Holy Spirit

- The Father gave us His gift: Jesus Christ.
- Jesus gave us His gift: The Holy Spirit.
- The Holy Spirit gives us His gift: His Baptism of power.

Those who reject the Baptism of the Holy Spirit are, in fact, rejecting the Holy Spirit's *gift of power.* But to be perfectly clear, those who reject the Holy Spirit's gift are not necessarily rejecting the Holy Spirit.

Conversely, it doesn't mean that those who reject His gift are unsaved. However, they will not operate in His power as compared to those who *do* accept His gift.

If we submit ourselves to the way Jesus wants to use us in power, then we must accept the Holy Spirit's gift. By accepting His gift, we are empowered to be witnesses of Him with attesting signs, wonders, miracles, and...an ever-increasing revelation of His Word.

> "Then He opened their minds to understand the Scriptures." (Luke 24:45)

The inverse is just as obvious: Those who refuse His gift are disadvantaged against the works and power of the enemy.

◆◆◆◆
Key Facts

1. When Mary clung to Jesus at the tomb, He had not yet ascended to His Father to be re-glorified with the glory He had before the world began.

2. On the same day Jesus met Mary at the tomb, later that evening He suddenly appeared to His Apostles. By that time, He was in His re-glorified state upon which He sent the Holy Spirit.

3. After Jesus was re-glorified, (as John 7:38-39 states), Jesus breathed on them to dramatically demonstrate the definitive moment that He sent the Holy Spirit. From that time forward, everyone who receives Jesus Christ instantly receives the permanent indwelling presence of the Holy Spirit.

4. The indwelling presence of the Holy Spirit occurs at the moment of salvation, but His indwelling presence is *not* the Holy Spirit's Baptism.

Jesus Sends the Holy Spirit

5. Those who reject the Holy Spirit's gift of power are not specifically rejecting the Holy Spirit.

6. If we reject the Holy Spirit's Baptism, it does not mean we lose our salvation. Rather, it means we will not walk in power to be an effective witness of Jesus with attesting signs, wonders, and miracles.

The Final Words of Jesus

CHAPTER 17
HIS FINAL WORDS
Key Observation #3

OBJECT SCRIPTURE

"Gathering them together, He commanded them not to leave Jerusalem, but to wait for what the Father had promised, "Which," He said, "you heard of from Me; 5 for John baptized with water, but you will be baptized with the Holy Spirit not many days from now." 8 But you will receive power when the Holy Spirit has come upon you; and you shall be My witnesses both in Jerusalem, and in all Judea and Samaria, and even to the remotest part of the earth." (Acts 1:4-5,8)

◆ ◆ ◆ ◆

In John 20:21-22, Jesus breathed on the Apostles and told them to receive the Holy Spirit. Then, in Acts 1:4-5, they were told not to leave Jerusalem until they were endued with the Holy Spirit's gift of power. By comparing these two events, it is obvious to see that they are separate and distinct from each other.

Before Jesus ascended into Heaven, He spoke important final words to the Apostles. There could have been many things to say. He could have reminisced about their ministry and shared a few touching moments. He could have encouraged them and told them how much He loved them. But, none of those words are recorded. A far weightier impression had to be made. His final words pointed to an important requisite event.

He gave them explicit instructions for the next thing to do: they were to wait in Jerusalem for the Baptism of the Holy Spirit. Even though they had received the Holy Spirit's indwelling presence when Jesus breathed on them (John 20:22), they were *not* to commence their ministry until they were endued with power. This is a point of strong emphasis!

The Final Words of Jesus

If we analyze this according to modern seminary principles, the Apostles were well qualified to *immediately* start their ministry. They had been with Jesus for three and one-half years. They lived with Him. He was the perfect model of ministry, character, and authority. He mentored each of them. He explained all things pertaining to any question they asked (Mark 4:33-34). Furthermore, they had exceptional field experience in preaching the Kingdom with signs, wonders, and miracles. Yet, despite all of that, Jesus told them not to leave Jerusalem *until* they received the Holy Spirit's *power*—the same power Jesus possessed.

Again, when Jesus told them to remain in Jerusalem, they had already received the permanent indwelling presence of the Holy Spirit. This is one of many Scriptural proofs that the Baptism of the Holy Spirit is a separate and distinct work from the initial permanent indwelling presence of the Holy Spirit at the instant of salvation.

◆◆◆◆
Key Facts

1. The final Words of Jesus emphasized the difference between water baptism and the Baptism of the Holy Spirit.

2. The final Words of Jesus restrained the Apostles from going forth into ministry without the power of the Holy Spirit.

3. The final Words of Jesus distinguished the difference between the initial indwelling presence of the Holy Spirit at the moment of salvation as compared to the Baptism of the Holy Spirit. This again proves they are separate and distinct events.

The Promise of the Father

CHAPTER 18
THE PROMISE OF THE SPIRIT'S BAPTISM IS FULFILLED
Key Observation #4

OBJECT SCRIPTURE

"When the day of Pentecost had come, they were all together in one place. 2 And suddenly there came from Heaven a noise like a violent rushing wind, and it filled the whole house where they were sitting. 3 And there appeared to them Tongues as of fire distributing themselves, and they rested on each one of them. 4 And they were all filled with the Holy Spirit and began to speak with other Tongues, as the Spirit was giving them utterance. 5 Now there were Jews living in Jerusalem, devout men from every nation under Heaven. 6 And when this sound occurred, the crowd came together, and were bewildered because each one of them was hearing them speak in his own language. 7 They were amazed and astonished, saying, 'Why, are not all these who are speaking Galileans? 8 And how is it that we each hear them in our own language to which we were born? 9 Parthians and Medes and Elamites, and residents of Mesopotamia, Judea and Cappadocia, Pontus and Asia, 10 Phrygia and Pamphylia, Egypt and the districts of Libya around Cyrene, and visitors from Rome, both Jews and proselytes, 11 Cretans and Arabs–we hear them in our own tongue speaking of the mighty deeds of God.' 12 And they all continued in amazement and great perplexity, saying to one another, 'What does this mean?' 13 But others were mocking and saying, 'They are full of sweet wine.'" (Acts 2:1-13)

♦♦♦♦

Before a person can receive the Holy Spirit's Baptism they must be saved. Furthermore, no one has salvation unless the Holy Spirit permanently indwells them.

> "In Him, you also, after listening to the message of truth, the gospel of your salvation–having also believed, you

The Promise of the Father

were sealed in Him with the Holy Spirit of promise, 14 who is given as a pledge of our inheritance, with a view to the redemption of God's own possession, to the praise of His glory." (Ephesians 1:13-14)

On the day of Pentecost, one hundred twenty Christians were gathered in an upper room. Each of them possessed the permanent indwelling presence of the Holy Spirit who was sent by Jesus only forty-seven days earlier.

The Holy Spirit Cannot Be Seen or Felt

He is not detected by the natural senses. Nor is He recognized in a physical form like Jesus. Therefore, Jesus used the metaphor of wind to describe the Holy Spirit.

Wind cannot be seen, but its effect is evident. So it is with the Holy Spirit. He indwells every Christian and works in their life to produce spiritual maturity.

> "The wind blows where it wishes and you hear the sound of it, but do not know where it comes from and where it is going; so is everyone who is born of the Spirit."(John 3:8)

The Sound of a Violent Rushing Wind

It is interesting that the Greek word for "spirit" is the word "pneuma", meaning air or wind. This is where we get the English word, "pneumatic", such as a pneumatic tire filled with air (wind).

And, it is interesting that on the day of Pentecost, the Holy Spirit came as a mighty rushing *wind* with visible cloven **Tongues of Fire**.

When the Holy Spirit gave His Baptism, suddenly, one hundred twenty Christians in the upper room spoke in **The Gift of Tongues**. This was *before* the Apostles stepped onto the public stage.

The Gift of Tongues is the *only* definitive sign that proves one has received the Baptism of the Holy Spirit. The proof of His Baptism is not the sound of wind, nor the appearance of cloven "Tongues of Fire" that rested on each person.

In Scripture, other instances of wind and fire were as much supernatural as on the day of Pentecost. For example, Elijah prayed, and fire came down from Heaven (2 Kings 1:12). And when the children of Israel

The Promise of the Father

came to the Red Sea, God send a strong wind to dry the ground after He parted the waters (Exodus 14:21).

On the day of Pentecost, the **Tongues** they spoke were *known languages* for a specific purpose. This was because devout Jews from one hundred fifty colonies throughout the Roman Empire were in Jerusalem to celebrate Pentecost. As mentioned in verses 9-11, large numbers of them spoke different dialects. Those who heard the Apostles speaking in various languages by **The Gift of Tongues**, testified to what they were saying:

> "...we hear them in our own tongues [language] speaking of the mighty deeds of God." (Acts 2:11. Square brackets by author for added clarity.)

In chapter twenty-six near the end of this book, the five categories of **Tongues** are detailed. The type of **Tongues** they spoke on the day of Pentecost was the first category: **Tongues for the Unbeliever**. However, it was not the speaking in **Tongues** that initially attracted the people; it was the Holy Spirit coming as a tornadic rushing wind:

> "When this sound occurred, the crowd came together. They were bewildered <u>by the sound</u> because each of them heard his own language as the Apostles spoke in the gift of other Tongues." (Acts 2:6. Underline by author for added emphasis.)

When the crowd gathered to the sound of rushing wind, they heard anointed words of God spoken through the Apostles as the Spirit gave them utterance. These were not complicated words. They were words spoken by the inspiration of the Holy Spirit—words that were supercharged with conviction, power, and authority.

Some, not understanding what was happening, thought the Apostles were drunk at nine o'clock in the morning. To explain the spiritual phenomenon, Peter stepped forward and addressed the crowd:

> "But Peter, taking his stand with the eleven, raised his voice and declared to them: "Men of Judea and all you who live in Jerusalem, let this be known to you and give heed to my words. 15 "For these men are not drunk, as you suppose, for it is only the third hour of the day; 16 but this is what was spoken of through the prophet Joel:

The Promise of the Father

17 "and it shall be in the last days,' God says, "that I will pour forth of My Spirit on all mankind; and your sons and your daughters shall prophesy, and your young men shall see visions, and your old men shall dream dreams; 18 even on My bondslaves, both men and women, I will in those days pour forth of My Spirit and they shall prophesy. 19 "and I will grant wonders in the sky above and signs on the earth below, blood, and fire, and vapor of smoke. 20 "the sun will be turned into darkness and the moon into blood, before the great and glorious day of the Lord shall come. 21 "and it shall be that everyone who calls on the name of the Lord will be saved.'" (Acts 2:14-21)

This event was none other than the Baptism of the Holy Spirit of which Jesus told the Apostles to wait for in Jerusalem—the promise of the Father. This was the power they needed to be witnesses for Him.

Four important observations are to be noted in Peter's address. (1) He quotes the Prophet Joel. Joel references the Baptism of the Holy Spirit as a non-biased out-pouring. No longer were men religiously privileged as compared to women. God's Spirit, through His Baptism, reached both men and women, young and old, and slave and free to accomplish His works.

(2) The Baptism came with **Prophecy**, visions, and night visions (dreams) upon the young and old, and upon men and women.

(3) The dispensation of the Holy Spirit giving His Baptism started on the day of Pentecost which marks the beginning of the *Final Days* according to Joel.

Joel's prophecy says that the Holy Spirit would continue giving His gift to all Christians until the day the Lord returns at the time of the 6th Seal of Revelation. Again, this is proven by Joel's prophecy which cites the same signs of Jesus' return as noted in the Book of Revelation 6:12-17 and Matthew 24:29-31.

> "And I will grant wonders in the sky above and signs on the earth below, blood, and fire, and vapor of smoke. 20 "the sun will be turned into darkness and the moon into blood, before the great and glorious day of the lord shall come."

The Promise of the Father

(4) When Peter quotes Joel's prophecy, **The Gift of Tongues** is not mentioned. The reason is simple: Peter's emphasis was not upon one particular gift of the Holy Spirit. Rather, it was upon the Holy Spirit's Baptism which includes all nine gifts proven by the speaking in **Tongues**.

◆◆◆◆
Key Facts

1. All one hundred twenty people in the upper room received the Baptism of the Holy Spirit. Thus, the outpouring was not restricted to just the twelve Apostles.

2. Only the Apostles spoke in *known languages* by **The Gift of Tongues**. However, one hundred eight others in the upper room also spoke in **Tongues**. There is no record that the **Tongues** they spoke were directed to the crowd outside of the room. Rather, they remained in the upper room out of sight from everyone. Therefore, their **Tongues** were directed to God, not man. This is significant because it destroys the argument that **The Gift of Tongues** was only used to speak in *known languages* so that people could understand what was being spoken.

3. The *phonetics* of speaking in other **Tongues** (by **The Gift of Tongues**) can sound like the babbling of drunken men. This does not demean the gift, but it serves as an appropriate description of how **The Gift of Tongues** can sound.

4. Those who spoke in **The Gift of Tongues** did not know what they were saying. To them, it was an outflow, a gushing by the inspiration of the Holy Spirit through their spirit. Even though the Apostles did not know what they were speaking, others understood their language and testified that they spoke great things of God.

5. The dispensation for the Holy Spirit's Baptism is bracketed by the Prophet Joel. Joel's prophecy says the Holy Spirit's Baptism began on the day of Pentecost and continues to the very day of Christ's return. Therefore, the Baptism of the Holy Spirit cannot be limited to the era of the early church at the time of the original Apostles.

The Spirit's Gift Is For All

CHAPTER 19
THE SPIRIT'S GIFT IS FOR ALL GOD'S CHILDREN
Key Observation #5

OBJECT SCRIPTURE

"Therefore let all the house of Israel know for certain that God has made Him both Lord and Christ–this Jesus whom you crucified.' 37 Now when they heard this they were pierced to the heart, and said to Peter and the rest of the Apostles, 'Brethren, what shall we do?' 38 Peter said to them, '<u>Repent, and each of you be baptized in the name of Jesus Christ for the forgiveness of your sins; and you will receive the gift of the Holy Spirit.</u> 39 '<u>For the promise is for you and your children and for all who are far off, as many as the Lord our God will call to Himself.</u>' 40 And with many other words he solemnly testified and kept on exhorting them, saying, 'Be saved from this perverse generation!' 41 So then, those who had received his word were baptized; and that day there were added about three thousand souls." (Acts 2:36-41; Underline by author for added emphasis.)

♦♦♦♦

On the day of Pentecost, over three thousand people were astonished by the miraculous demonstration of the Holy Spirit's rushing wind and **The Gift of Tongues** spoken through the Apostles. Peter then explained the prophetic implications of what they *heard and saw.*

As he closed his message with strong exhortations, those listening realized their demise. They shockingly learned they had crucified their Messiah! This cut them to the heart. Standing utterly hopeless, they asked what they should do.

What a powerful contrast to the crowd of people that only fifty-four days earlier yelled, "Crucify Him!" And what a contrast in the Apostles. Prior to their Baptism of the Spirit, they hid in fear from the Jews that mobbed together and demanded Jesus' crucifixion. But on the most crucial of all days, the zenith of Jewish Festivals—Pentecost, the once

The Spirit's Gift Is For All

fearful Apostles boldly stepped forward, faced the same crowd, and preached the message of Jesus!

The Promise: What It Is and Who It Is For

To explain why the Apostles were speaking in **Tongues**, Peter specifically points to the Baptism of the Holy Spirit. He calls it *the gift of the Holy Spirit*, which is to say, *the Holy Spirit's gift*—the promise of the Father.

The *promise* of the Father is not the Holy Spirit's permanent indwelling presence that comes with salvation, but rather the Holy Spirit's Baptism of power.

> "Repent and let each one of you be baptized in the name of Jesus Christ for the forgiveness of your sins and you shall receive the gift of the Holy Spirit. <u>For the promise</u> [the Baptism of the Holy Spirit] is for you and your children and all who are far off, as many as the Lord our God shall call to Himself." (Acts 2:38-39, Underline by author for added emphasis.)

> "Therefore having been exalted to the right hand of God, and having received from the Father <u>the promise of the Holy Spirit</u>, He has poured forth this which you both <u>see and hear</u>. (Acts 2:33 Underline by author for added emphasis.)

> "And behold, I am sending forth <u>the promise</u> of My Father upon you; but you are to stay in the city until you are clothed with power from on high." 50 And He led them out as far as Bethany, and He lifted up His hands and blessed them. 51 While He was blessing them, He parted from them and was carried up into Heaven. (Luke 24:49-51, Underline by author for added emphasis.)

Jesus referred to the Holy Spirit's Baptism of power as *the promise of the Father*—exactly what Peter stated when he said, "...you shall receive the gift of the Holy Spirit". Peter said: "For the *promise* is for you and your children, and for all who are far off..."

No one prays for the Holy Spirit to permanently indwell them at the moment of salvation. Peter knew this as well as anyone. This is because the Holy Spirit automatically indwells the Believer at the instant of

The Spirit's Gift Is For All

salvation. Therefore, it is ludicrous to think that Peter referred to the permanent indwelling presence of the Holy Spirit as "the gift".

As Peter attested, the *gift of the Spirit* is for all Christians for all time, for as many as the Lord calls to Himself who desire the Holy Spirit's gift. Again, the Holy Spirit's gift should not be confused with His initial permanent indwelling presence at the moment of salvation.

Whether we realize it or not, the Holy Spirit assumes His permanent indwelling presence at the instant we receive salvation through Jesus Christ. This was quite obvious when Paul discovered twelve disciples of Christ in Acts 19:1-7. They, being Christians, had never heard of the Holy Spirit. Yet, because they were disciples of Jesus they had the Holy Spirit living in them without even knowing it.

After Paul explained certain facts to them about Jesus Christ, they were subsequently water baptized by Paul. After that, Paul prayed for them to receive the Baptism of the Holy Spirit:

> "And when Paul laid his hands on them, the Holy Spirit came on them, and they *began* speaking in [unknown] Tongues [languages] and prophesying." (Acts 19:6. Square brackets by author for added clarity.)

When the twelve men spoke in **Tongues**, their words were not directed to anyone such as on the day of Pentecost. This contradicts the assertion that **Tongues** are only given in order to speak in *"***Known Languages***"* so that others can understand. Yet, in this instance, all twelve men knew each other. Furthermore, no crowd was present to hear the twelve Believers speak in **Tongues**.

Knowing how strongly Jesus emphasized the importance of the Holy Spirit's Baptism, the Apostles defined *normal* Christianity as having the Holy Spirit's gift. They clearly understood that *power* was required to be an effective witness of Jesus Christ—an assignment given to all Christians. And, the only access to this power is through the Baptism of the Holy Spirit.

Moreover, it must be understood that Peter time-brackets the Holy Spirit's Baptism *as a promise* for all Christians throughout time—to as many as the Lord our God calls unto Himself, even to the very day of Jesus' return.

The Spirit's Gift Is For All

Knowing these biblical facts, we must **not** assume that the Holy Spirit's Baptism was only for the early Christians, which thereby disqualifies today's Christians from receiving His power. This popular teaching is a satanic ploy to turn Christians away from God's divine POWER that comes through the Baptism of the Holy Spirit.

◆◆◆◆
Key Facts

1. Peter describes the Baptism of the Holy Spirit *as the gift of the Holy Spirit, or conversely, the Holy Spirit's gift*. He referred to the Holy Spirit's Baptism which the crowd could both <u>see and hear</u>.

2. Peter time-brackets the Baptism of the Holy Spirit as being for all Christians for as many as the Lord calls unto Himself, even to the very day of Jesus' return.

3. The prophet Joel time-brackets the Baptism of the Holy Spirit as *starting* on the day of Pentecost to the very day Jesus returns in the Book of Revelation, specifically the 6th Seal.

4. The Apostles emphasized the Baptism of the Holy Spirit as an important and essential gift in order for each Christian to be a *powerful* witness of Jesus Christ.

Tongues is the Proof

CHAPTER 20
TONGUES IS THE PROOF
Key Observation #6

OBJECT SCRIPTURE

"**Therefore having been exalted to the right hand of God, and having received from the Father the promise of the Holy Spirit, He has poured forth this which you both see and hear.**" (Acts 2:33)

♦ ♦ ♦ ♦

The Holy Spirit's substance is spirit. As such, He is not comprehended through the natural senses of seeing, smelling, tasting, touching, or hearing. When Peter explained the Holy Spirit's Baptism on the day of Pentecost, he referred to **The Gift of Tongues** because it was something never before *seen or heard* in all of Israel.

He could not say, "Look! See the Holy Spirit!", for no one has ever seen His substance. Nor can anyone say, "I both heard and saw Him entering me when I was saved." Therefore, Peter could only refer to the *effects* of the Holy Spirit's Baptism which is evidenced by speaking in other **Tongues**.

When the wind blows, we say, "Look at the wind." But in truth, no one sees the wind; they only see the *effect* of the wind. So it is with the Baptism of the Holy Spirit. According to the consistency of Scripture, **The Gift of Tongues** is *the only definitive proof* that one has received the Holy Spirit's gift—His Baptism.

Miracles do not prove the Baptism of the Spirit. After all, starting from the time of Adam, God has used people for miracles. Mercifully, God works miracles through those who call on His name. Nonetheless, a miracle of itself, is not the sign that one has received the Holy Spirit's Baptism. Uniquely, **Tongues** is the only gift which proves one has received the Holy Spirit's Baptism.

Tongues is the Proof

Jesus said at the closing of Mark's Gospel:

> "These signs will accompany those who have believed: in My name they will cast out demons, they will speak with new Tongues." (Mark 16:17)

The above verse applies to all Christians who desire the Holy Spirit's Baptism throughout the church age; not just those of the early church!

Again, **Tongues** is the consistent and only proof given throughout the New Testament Scriptures that assures one has received the Holy Spirit's gift. Accordingly, when Peter explained what happened, he referred to the *effects* of the Holy Spirit: what they <u>saw</u> and <u>heard</u>. Accordingly, what exactly did they *see and hear*? They saw no miracles such as healing or deliverance, for none are recorded. The only proof they <u>saw</u> was the men speaking in **Tongues** and they <u>*heard*</u> them.

There are some who claim to be Baptized in the Holy Spirit but do not speak in **Tongues**. Yet, Scripture is repetitively clear that those who are Baptized in the Holy Spirit *do* speak in **Tongues**. In another way of stating it, we have no other example in God's Word that affirms a person has received the Baptism of the Holy Spirit other than **The Gift of Tongues** as an accompanying verification.

To emphasize the point, if God can make the rocks cry out (Luke 19:40), and cause a dumb donkey to talk (Numbers 22:28), He can use anyone to minister a miracle. Consequently, if God performs a miracle through a person, it does not prove that he or she is Baptized in the Holy Spirit.

Without the unique proof of speaking in **Tongues**, anyone can claim to be Baptized in the Spirit. Therefore, to eliminate all doubt and ambiguity, God gives one specific standardized proof—**The Gift of Tongues**. Otherwise, if there was no definitive, absolute, and consistent standard of proof, Satan would confuse the Holy Spirit's Baptism to mean anything based on anyone's opinion and definition.

◆◆◆◆
Key Facts

1. The Holy Spirit's *permanent indwelling presence* occurs at the instant of salvation. There is no natural sensory evidence when He comes to permanently indwell the Believer. Nonetheless, based

Tongues is the Proof

upon the Word of God, we know He permanently indwells each Christian.

2. According to Scripture, speaking in **The Gift of Tongues** is the *only* proof that one is Baptized in the Holy Spirit. We have NO OTHER consistent confirming sign to indicate otherwise.

3. Peter said the Baptism of the Holy Spirit was the *promise of the Father.* He referred to what the people *saw and heard* in order to confirm the Baptism of the Holy Spirit.

Salvation Without Power

CHAPTER 21
SALVATION, BUT NO BAPTISM OF THE SPIRIT
Key Observation #7

OBJECT SCRIPTURE

"**Philip went down to the city of Samaria and began proclaiming Christ to them. 6 The crowds with one accord were giving attention to what was said by Philip, as they heard and saw the signs which he was performing. 12 But when they believed Philip preaching the good news about the kingdom of God and the name of Jesus Christ, they were being [water] baptized, men and women alike.**" (Acts 8:5-6,12).

♦ ♦ ♦ ♦

It is plain to see that Philip had a great move of God among the Samaritans. Since water baptism never precedes salvation, verse twelve can only mean that those being water baptized had first received Jesus Christ as their Savior.

Despite Philip's preaching of Jesus (proven by salvation, signs, wonders, and miracle**s**), he failed to tell them the full counsel of God. It was a perfect opportunity to minister the Baptism of the Holy Spirit, especially after they saw the Holy Spirit's power operating in him. All he needed to do was give an invitation to receive the Holy Spirit's gift so that they could have the same power that he had to be a witness of Jesus.

For whatever reason, he didn't minister that vitally important truth to the people. Consequently, the new Samaritan Believers were saved but not empowered as witnesses of Jesus Christ. This is why Jesus was adamant that His Apostles remain in Jerusalem until they were endued with *power.*

Salvation Without Power

Every Christian is a minister of the Gospel, but not every Christian stands in a ministry office. Nonetheless, every Christian can minister in the power of the Holy Spirit *after* they receive His gift.

When ministering the Gospel, the whole counsel of God should be preached: salvation, water baptism, and the Holy Spirit's Baptism. These should be preached as a unit of the Christian faith.

A Holy Spirit Baptized Believer is empowered to effectively testify about the covenant benefits in Jesus Christ. Such words would be charged with a powerful anointing that gets results with signs, wonders, healings, and miracles.

> "Then the disciples went out and preached everywhere, and the Lord worked with them and confirmed His word by the signs that accompanied it." (Mark 16:20)

The Apostle Paul testified of this very thing when he said:

> "And my message and my preaching were not in persuasive words of wisdom, but in demonstration of the Spirit and of power so that your faith would not rest on the wisdom of men [academic knowledge without experience], but on the power of God." (1 Corinthians 2:4-5.)

> "For our gospel did not come to you in word only [mere academic information], but also in power and in the Holy Spirit and with full conviction; just as you know what kind of men we proved to be among you for your sake."
> (1 Thessalonians 1:5. Square brackets by author for added clarity.)

Today, massive numbers of Believers are settled into a word-only testimony of Jesus without any expectation of the supernatural. They expect nothing more of our Heavenly Father than hearing academic information about His historical works. They have an antiquated view of the Father rather than a *right now reality* of His love, power, and presence. For this reason, Paul reminds us that he did not preach the Gospel in "word only" but also in the power of the Holy Spirit. The power of the Holy Spirit was demonstrated by his word having great conviction along with signs, wonders, miracles, deliverance, and the gifts of the Holy Spirit in operation. This was Paul's anticipated and expected mannerism of ministry and those who were with him.

Salvation Without Power

The truth is, Christianity is the only faith in the world that promises eternal life and the demonstration of the supernatural. When the modern church understands the revelation of *that* truth, she will rise to a higher standard of expectation and storm the earth with the testimony of Jesus.

It is a mistake to think that the Lord is only interested in converts. This is merely the first step in the journey of faith. He wants His children to mature in Him—to grow spiritually strong and wise. He wants His Spirit-filled *disciples* armed with His power to storm the darkness and testify of Jesus's victory that results in massive numbers of souls being saved!

◆◆◆◆
Key Facts

1. Philip, having been Baptized in the Holy Spirit, preached Jesus to the Samaritans which resulted in their salvation.

2. He preached with *power* because he was Baptized in the Holy Spirit. Signs, wonders, healings, miracles, and the casting out of devils were proofs of the New Covenant in Christ.

3. Because of the signs, wonders, healings, and miracles that the Samaritans saw, even the most hardened sinners, including Simon the Sorcerer, was converted to Christ.

4. Water baptism was administered to those who received Jesus Christ as their Lord and Savior. This proves that the Samaritans were Christians.

5. As a result of their salvation, those who believed in Jesus Christ received the permanent indwelling presence of the Holy Spirit, but...they were not Baptized in the Holy Spirit's gift.

What Is Normal Christianity?

CHAPTER 22
WHAT IS NORMAL CHRISTIANITY
Key Observation #8

OBJECT SCRIPTURE

"Now when the Apostles in Jerusalem heard that Samaria had received the word of God, they sent them Peter and John, 15 who came down and prayed for them that they might receive the Holy Spirit. 16 For He had not yet fallen upon any of them; they had simply been baptized in the name of the Lord Jesus. 17 Then they began laying their hands on them, and they were receiving the Holy Spirit. 18 Now when Simon saw that the Spirit was bestowed through the laying on of the Apostles' hands, he offered them money..." (Acts 8:14-18)

♦♦♦♦

Obviously, Philip was excited by the great number of souls that received Jesus Christ. They were convinced of his words because of the signs and wonders which God worked through Philip. However, when Philip reported the good news to the Apostles, they very specifically asked if he ministered the Baptism of the Holy Spirit to them.

Samaria was about twenty miles from Jerusalem. Upon hearing that Philip had not told them about the Baptism, the Apostles felt it necessary to go there. Their primary purpose was NOT to preach Jesus; Philip had masterfully accomplished that task. Their motive was singular: to pray for the Samaritans to receive the Baptism of the Holy Spirit. This sizeable effort involved a roundtrip forty-mile foot journey!

Today, some might walk forty miles to minister Jesus, but fewer would walk even five miles to minister the Baptism of the Holy Spirit. If the Apostles considered the Baptism of the Holy Spirit as incidental, nonessential, or merely a formality, they would not have made such a long journey for an unimportant event. Rather, they might have made the

What Is Normal Christianity?

trip at a more convenient time. But, they knew the importance of power in order to be witnesses of Jesus Christ. Furthermore, the Samaritans needed this same power to reach their own people.

The Gospel must be spread by every Believer, and every Believer needs power to get the job done. Without the Holy Spirit's power, the testimony of Jesus' disciples is substantially less effective.

Christianity was never meant to be a *word-only* academic testimony of Jesus. From the beginning of the Ephesian church until today, the standard remains the same. We are to be witnesses of Jesus Christ with proving signs and wonder. But, as Jesus said, we need power to minister with convincing proofs—the same power that Jesus walked in which comes ONLY through the Baptism of the Holy Spirit.

Talking Heads

Why would anyone need power to merely "talk" about Jesus? The truth is, any Christian can speak words about Him, but not every Christian's words are anointed with power and authority that prove what they say.

If the full covenant of Jesus Christ includes healing, salvation, and deliverance, we should expect God's miracle working power to confirm the Words of His promises. Consequently, we need the Holy Spirit's POWER to produce the proof of our testimony. We must, therefore, be more than talking heads and voices without power.

Yet, when Christian leaders reject, stifle, or suppress the Holy Spirit's power and refuse to allow His gifts to operate in the congregation of the Saints, the Gospel message is reduced to an information-based *word-only* format with no provable results. And when Christians reject the Holy Spirit's gift, their faith is little more than a *talk-about* message in the yester-years of ancient history. This does not effectively represent Jesus Christ who is the same yesterday, TODAY, and TOMORROW (Hebrews 13:8). He is our miracle working God that brings us intimately into our Father's presence. And because 64% of the Body of Christ lacks His power[22], 75% of the world remains unsaved! This is not the

---

[22] There is an estimate 2.63 billion people on the earth who claim to be Christian. That number, however, includes the cults such as the Mormons, Jehovah Witness, and any other group saying they are Christian. The actual number that follow the Christian orthodoxy of

What Is Normal Christianity?

fault of Heaven. It is the fault of weak shallow *word-only* preachers that refuse to allow their congregations to receive the Father's power through His Holy Spirit.

To be a witness of Jesus, we must speak from more than intellect. We must speak under the power and anointing of the Holy Spirit. The Baptism of the Holy Spirit is the only prescription that Jesus gave in order to walk in His power. It is this power which proves the present-tense covenant of Jesus where He gives us victory in four domains of life:

> **The material realm**: So that we might have all sufficiency for every good work (2 Corinthians 9:8-9). Jesus destroyed the spirit of poverty.
>
> **The Soul of man:** The mind of Christ was given to us when Jesus shed His blood in the Garden of Gethsemane (Mark 14:34; Luke 22:44). His blood was shed for the mind of man.
>
> **Health for our bodies**: Health and well-being was given to us when Jesus received thirty-nine lashes so that we might walk in strength for all our appointed days on earth (Psalm 139:16; 1 Peter 2:24; 3 John 1:2).
>
> **Our born again spirit**: This was given to us in order to grow in the glory and revelation of our Father through Jesus Christ (Ephesians 1:17-23). Our spirit is made alive to His Spirit.

All needs in life are confined to the above four domains.

The normal standard of Christian life (as emphasized by the Apostles), is having the Baptism of the Holy Spirit. Subnormal Christianity is faith without power. We must, therefore, get back to the original blueprint that Jesus gave the church so that we can fulfill the Great Commission to the entire world.

Yet, without the power of His Holy Spirit, Christians who *refuse* the Holy Spirit's gift are less than equipped to walk in the full potential of

---

scripture is about two billion. And of that number, only six hundred seventy-five million Christian are Baptized in the Holy Spirit.

What Is Normal Christianity?

what Jesus promised. Conversely, how can anyone act on the promise of healing if they do not believe healing is for today's church? How can they pray for miracles if they do not believe miracles are for today's church? However, when one receives the Holy Spirit's Baptism, they are empowered with a confident expectation to believe for signs, wonders, healings, miracles, and powerful salvations.

> "I assure you *and* most solemnly say to you, anyone who believes in Me [as Savior] will also do the things that I do; and he will do even greater things than these [in extent and outreach], because I am going to the Father." (John 14:12)

We may have great means to broadcast the Gospel on TV and the Internet; print literature; produce recordings; and travel from one end of the earth to the other in less than a day. But without the Baptism of the Holy Spirit, metaphorically speaking, we are still farming with archaic horse-drawn plowshares instead of four-wheel drive air-conditioned tractors that turn fifty furrows at a time.

Are we so empty-headed and prideful as to assume we can accomplish the supernatural without the Baptism of the Holy Spirit? Are we to assume that we can be witnesses of Jesus Christ contrary to His instructions for power?

It is no wonder that Holy Spirit-filled Christians are overtaking the enemy. After all, intellectualism and academic presentation is no challenge to Satan at all.

Without the power of the Holy Spirit, there is no global world view. We need the Holy Spirit's Baptism of power to invade towns, cities, regions, and nations; to deliver people who are lost in the darkness; to unchain people that are trapped in addiction; to heal the sick; and unshackle broken souls held by demonic captivity.

STORY:
I was in the region of Sunyani in Ghana, Africa. We had traveled by van for six hours to get to our location. In the back seat of the vehicle, my traveling companion, "Bishop", prayed in **The Gift of Tongues** during the entire journey. As for me, I was sick with an upper respiratory infection and had a fever. I told the devil I would not stop, and that I was going to preach the Gospel to the villages deep in the jungle.

What Is Normal Christianity?

By the time we arrived, the drums had been playing for several hours and the crowd was gathered and waiting.

A small gas generator powered two four-foot long neon bulbs along with a PA system at the location where I was to preach. The moment I took the mic and started speaking, I felt as tall as a building and as strong as a speeding train. The power of the Holy Spirit came upon me and I testified of the amazing love Jesus has for them. I told them of His power to heal, deliver, keep them safe, and give them eternal life. I told them they must no longer submit to the witch-doctors and fetish-doctors—that to serve vain idols and offer sacrifices and libations to idols was no longer required if Jesus was in their lives. I testified how the demons that the witch-doctors served would be cast into the Lake of Fire along with the witch-doctors and fetish-doctors unless they too repented and received Jesus for the forgiveness of their sins. Every word was anointed by the Holy Spirit that went deep into their hearts with conviction and power.

Far beyond the reach of the light, people stood and listened. At any second, I expected arrows or spears to fly at me. I knew I had angered the spirits of darkness that held the villagers hostage to fear for over one hundred fifty years of tradition. By the Holy Spirit's power, I ignored the looming spiritual threats and boldly preached Christ and His promises. I was covered in prayer by my church in the USA, including the six hours of prayer when Bishop prayed in **Tongues**.

What I did not know was that I was standing on the exact spot where human sacrifices were performed in the pagan rites of their juju. When I gave the call to salvation, the village king, queen mother, witch-doctors, fetish-doctors, and the people came forward to receive Jesus Christ!

A woman in the crowd stepped forward amidst the joy of salvation and handed my co-worker the limp body of her baby. My co-worker thought the child was sleeping. Accordingly, she simply placed her hand on the child's forehead, blessed the child, politely smiled, and handed it back to the mother. The mother erupted into near uncontrollable joy. My co-worker did not know that the child was unconscious with fever. When my co-worker, a lady who was Baptized in the Holy Spirit, laid hands on the child, the Lord healed the child even though the co-worker had no idea that the Lord used her so powerfully.

What Is Normal Christianity?

That evening, hundreds were saved, healed, and delivered. Later, they gathered together and started a church. Bishop, my Ghanian friend, helped them find a pastor.

◆◆◆◆

Because the Samaritans were water baptized by Philip, it proves they were Christians and had the permanent indwelling presence of the Holy Spirit in them. But in the next verse of the Object Scripture (verse 17) the Apostles were laying hands on them and they were receiving the Baptism of the Holy Spirit.

To our brethern in Christ who mistakenly oppose the Baptism of the Holy Spirit, this is a major observation of Scripture: what were the Apostles praying for when they laid hands on the Samaritan Christians if the Holy Spirit was already in them at the instant of their salvation?

Moreover, who today, upon receiving Jesus Christ as their Savior, asks for the Holy Spirit to permanently indwell them? No one! So why were the Apostles praying for them to receive the Holy Spirit? It was simply this: they taught the Samaritans about the *Baptism of the Holy Spirit* and then laid hands on them to receive His gift.

Verse seventeen is yet another point of reference. When they placed their hands on them as a point of contact, they were receiving the Holy Spirit.

It has already been pointed out that the Spirit is not a visible person that can be detected by our natural senses. Therefore, the effects of the Holy Spirit's Baptism was *seen* and *heard* in order to prove they were receiving His power.

Simon the Sorcerer saw *something happening* because he offered the Apostles money so that on whomever he laid his hands they too would receive the Holy Spirit. If it was merely laying hands on someone and nothing manifestly occurred, then Simon could have done that quite easily. The truth is, Simon *saw and heard* something happening from the laying on of hands by the Apostles. He knew that power was imparted to those receiving the Holy Spirit's Baptism by the evidence of them speaking in **The Gift of Tongues.**

The implied sense of verse seventeen is that they spoke in **Tongues**. While the Scriptures do not specifically say that, all other examples throughout the New Testament pertaining to the Holy Spirit's

What Is Normal Christianity?

Baptism, both before and after the Samarian campaign, consistently report the speaking in **Tongues**.

◆◆◆◆
Key Facts

1. When Philip ministered to the people of Samaria, they received Jesus as their Savior and were subsequently water baptized.

2. The Apostles understood the importance of the Holy Spirit's Baptism as a necessity to be an effective witness about Jesus. Accordingly, they traveled forty miles on foot (round trip) to minister the Holy Spirit's Baptism to the Samaritans.

3. In the Samaritan campaign, the Baptism of the Holy Spirit came upon them *after* they were water baptized, but not *before* their conversion to Jesus Christ. The Baptism of the Holy Spirit is never given before salvation.

4. When the Apostles ministered the Baptism of the Holy Spirit by the laying on of hands, Simon *saw the results* and wanted the power to do what the Apostles were doing.

The House of Cornelius

CHAPTER 23
THE BAPTISM OF THE HOLY SPIRIT COMES TO CORNELIUS
Key Observation #9

OBJECT VERSE
"While Peter was still speaking these words, the Holy Spirit fell upon all those who were listening to the message. 45 All the circumcised believers who came with Peter were amazed, because the gift of the Holy Spirit had been poured out on the Gentiles also. 46 For they were hearing them speaking with Tongues and exalting God. Then Peter answered, 47 'Surely no one can refuse the water for these to be baptized who have received the Holy Spirit just as we did can he?' 48 And he ordered them to be baptized in the name of Jesus Christ. Then they asked him to stay on for a few days."(Acts 10:44)

◆ ◆ ◆ ◆

Categorically, anyone who is not a Jew by birth is a Gentile. The Jews had a prevailing belief towards Gentiles and did not fellowship them or enter their homes. This was because Gentiles were routinely defiled and ceremonially unclean by eating things which the Jews were prohibited to eat or touch such as pork, shrimp, lobster, clams; or by violating various Jewish laws. Thus, a Jew would be spiritually defiled by being with a Gentile.

Peter, a devout Jew, embraced caution toward the Gentiles and did not keep company with them throughout his life. However, multiple prophecies in the Bible foretold that God would join the Jew and the Gentile into one common salvation. Peter knew this, but he did not know how and when the Lord would accomplish that task.

Just as God chose Peter to open the door of salvation to the Jews on the day of Pentecost, about ten years *after* Pentecost, God again chose him to officially open the door of salvation to the Gentiles. However, to help Peter accept the Gentiles, the Lord first prepared Peter's heart in order to dismantle his mindsets toward the Gentile people.

The House of Cornelius

It happened one day that Peter was in Joppa at Simon the Tanner's house. He had gone up to the flat-top roof to pray (Acts 10: 1-20). During his prayer time, he saw a vision a sheet filled with all types of prohibited foods that was lowered from Heaven. In the vision, the Lord told him to kill and eat. Peter replied that he had never eaten any *unclean* foods. Moreover, he was repulsed by the very thought of it. God corrected him and told him that he should not call *unclean* what the Lord has made clean. This happened three times. Needless to say, Peter was perplexed as to what the vision meant.

Four days before Peter had his vision, an angel appeared to Cornelius, a Roman Centurion. Cornelius lived in Caesarea, a seaport village north of Joppa along the shoreline from where Peter was residing. The angel told Cornelius that his prayers and alms had come before God as a memorial. Then he told him to get Peter who was at Simon the Tanner's house in Joppa.

God's timing was perfect. Cornelius' servants traveled to Joppa, forty miles south from Caesarea, and found Peter at the address they were told.

They knocked at the door just *after* Peter had received his vision. The Gentile travelers informed the people how they knew Peter's location and then asked to see him. Based on the miracle visitation, there was no question in Peter's mind that it was a divine appointment. Moreover, God told Peter to accompany the Gentiles without any misgivings (Acts10:20). Regardless of all things, it was a quantum leap in contrast to Peter's lifelong religious and cultural upbringing.

Peter traveled with the Gentile men on a two-day journey back to Cornelius' house. When he entered the house, the first thing he said to Cornelius was, *"You yourselves know how unlawful it is for a man who is a Jew to associate with a foreigner (Gentile) or to visit him; and yet God has shown me that I should not call any man unholy or unclean. That is why I came without even raising any objection when I was sent for. So, I ask for what reason you have sent for me?"* (Acts 10:28)

Cornelius explained everything to him, including how an angel appeared and gave him Peter's address. From there, Peter explained the truth of Jesus Christ according to the Gospel. Since the Apostles considered the Holy Spirit's Baptism as an essential part of a Christian's life, it is most assured that he made reference to it.

The House of Cornelius

Cornelius was already a God-fearing man. However, he did not have the full knowledge of Jesus Christ until Peter explained everything to him. When that happened, the picture was complete.

There is no record of Peter inviting anyone to receive Jesus as their Lord and Savior. But at some point while Peter was speaking, they believed in Jesus as their Savior and received Him.

But how did Peter know they were saved? Because the Holy Spirit's gift came upon them. This took Peter by surprise because he knew that the Baptism of the Holy Spirit always follows salvation—it never precedes it. Therefore, much to Peter's surprise, he knew they had received Jesus Christ.

While Peter was sharing the good news about Jesus, the Holy Spirit came upon each person in the household and they were Baptized in the Holy Spirit.[23] It was a sovereign work of the Heavenly Father which made the Gentiles as coheirs of salvation with the Jews. This was a "first" in the history of humanity!

But how did Peter know they were Baptized in the Holy Spirit? It was simply this: he heard them speaking with other **Tongues**—the proof of the Holy Spirit's Baptism. Upon seeing this, Peter instructed them to be water baptized.

This is somewhat contrasted with the Samaritans, who, after receiving Jesus Christ, were *first* water baptized by Phillip and *then* Baptized in the Holy Spirit after the Apostles prayed for them by the laying on of hands.

Based on these comparatives, the Baptism of the Holy Spirit can occur *before or after* water baptism. Furthermore, the Baptism of the Holy Spirit can be given with or without anyone laying hands on the receiver. This is not to demean the importance of water baptism, for such is a command of Jesus Christ. But it proves that salvation must occur *before* the Baptism of the Holy Spirit is given and received.

---

[23] As previously stated, no one can receive the Holy Spirit's gift, His Baptism, until they first have His permanent indwelling presence. And no one has the permanent indwelling presence of the Holy Spirit until they first receive Jesus Christ in order for them to be legally cleaned of all their sins.

The House of Cornelius

◆◆◆◆
Key Facts

1. The Baptism of the Holy Spirit can come *before or after* water baptism.

2. The Baptism of the Holy Spirit is never given as a reward for good works. It is a *gift* for anyone in Jesus Christ. Cornelius' house had no opportunity to repent or produce works of any kind while they listened to Peter explain Jesus.

3. After the Samaritans received Jesus Christ, they were water baptized. The Apostles returned to them and instructed them on the Baptism of the Holy Spirit. The Apostles then prayed for them to receive the Holy Spirit's gift. But in Cornelius' house, the Holy Spirit's Baptism came upon them spontaneously without anyone praying for them or laying hands on them.

4. From this example, we see that the Baptism of the Holy Spirit can spontaneously come upon anyone without the detailed knowledge of the Holy Spirit's work.

5. In most cases, the Baptism of the Holy Spirit is taught so that people have an understanding about the Holy Spirit's gift.

6. The Baptism of the Holy Spirit, as evidenced by the speaking in **Tongues**, was proof that God accepted the Gentiles into salvation with the Jews.

7. On the day of Pentecost, our Heavenly Father used **The Gift of Tongues in Known Languages** to speak to men of different dialects. However, that purpose did not apply to the Samaritans or the household of Cornelius: they all spoke the same natural language. The point is this: **The Gift of Tongues** is not always given for the same purpose as on the day of Pentecost.

CHAPTER 24
PETER TESTIFIES OF THE SPIRIT'S BAPTISM
Key Observation #10

OBJECT VERSE

"And as I began to speak, the Holy Spirit fell upon them just as He did upon us at the beginning. 16 And I remembered the word of the Lord, how He used to say, 'John baptized with water, but you will be Baptized with the Holy Spirit.' 17 Therefore if God gave to them the same gift as He gave to us also after believing in the Lord Jesus Christ, who was I that I could stand in God's way?" (Acts 11:15-17)

◆◆◆◆

After Cornelius' household openly received the Baptism of the Holy Spirit, Peter said, *"Surely no one can refuse for these to be water baptized who have received the Holy Spirit just as we did can he? And he ordered them to be water baptized in the name of Jesus Christ."* (Acts 10:47-48)

Peter then traveled to Jerusalem and joyfully shared the account with the Apostles. He specifically described how the Holy Spirit came upon them just as He did the Apostles (Acts 11:1-17).

In verse seventeen, Peter refers to the Baptism of the Holy Spirit as *a gift* proven by the speaking in **Tongues**—the same gift the Apostles received *after* Cornelius' household believed in the Lord Jesus Christ.

This is an important observation. Those who misguidedly oppose the Holy Spirit's gift often misinterpret Cornelius' experience by saying that he simply received the *indwelling presence of the Holy Spirit* incident to their salvation—but not the Baptism of the Holy Spirit. However, the proof that Cornelius' entire household received the Baptism of the Holy Spirit was when they spoke in **Tongues**.

Peter Testifies

The Holy Spirit's Baptism was not given *before* Cornelius' household received salvation, but subsequent to their salvation. His entire household first received the Holy Spirit's permanent indwelling presence at the moment of their salvation. *Then*, they received the Holy Spirit's Baptism immediately *after*, which was proven by them speaking in **Tongues**. Peter attests to that point in Acts 11:15-17.

In Peter's words, he described the event as, *"The Holy Spirit fell upon them, just as He did upon us at the beginning."* (Acts 11:15)

Exactly, what was Peter talking about? It wasn't when Jesus breathed on them in the account of John 20:22. It wasn't the cloven **Tongues** of fire that rested on each of the one hundred twenty individuals in the upper room on the day of Pentecost. It wasn't the sound of rushing wind. It wasn't the crowd of waiting people. It was simply **The Gift of Tongues** that proved they had been Baptized in the Holy Spirit.

> "For they heard them talking in [unknown] tongues languages) and exalting *and* magnifying *and* praising God. Then Peter said, 47 "Can anyone refuse water for these people to be baptized, since they have received the Holy Spirit just as we did?" (Acts 10:46-47)

The setting in Cornelius' house was quiet, focused, confined, and private. Each person knew one another. All the members shared the same language and culture.

There was no fanfare waiting beyond the walls of Cornelius' home for people to hear them speak in known languages as on Pentecost. So what was the purpose of **Tongues**? It was as much for the benefit of Peter as it was for them. **The Gift of Tongues** proved they were Baptized in the Holy Spirit which proved that the Holy Spirit was already in them. This further proved that they had received Jesus Christ as their Lord and Savior which meant that the Gentiles were now coheirs of salvation with the Jews!

Peter, along with the Apostles, needed this evidence to know with all certainty that God included the Gentiles (non-Jewish people) into the promise of eternal life. This made the Gentile people as brothers in the Lord to the Jewish people!

Peter Testifies

♦♦♦♦
Key Facts

1. The **Tongues** used on the day of Pentecost were "**Known Tongues**" and intended for unbelievers from over one hundred fifty Romans provinces that heard them speaking about the great things of God.

2. **The Gift of Tongues** used at Cornelius' house was *not* for unbelievers. All persons in the house were Christians. Everyone knew each other and spoke the same language. Therefore, **The Gift of Tongues** they spoke did not serve the same purpose as **Tongues** on the day of Pentecost. Rather, it was **Tongues** for worship or **Tongues** for personal edification (1 Corinthians 14:4).

3. When Peter described the events that happened in Cornelius' house to the Apostles, he specifically referred to it as "the Baptism of the Holy Spirit".

4. Peter equated the experience of the Holy Spirit's gift in Cornelius' house as the Holy Spirit's Baptism—the same **Gift of Tongues** that the Apostles received on the day of Pentecost.

CHAPTER 25
BELIEVERS IN EPHESUS ARE BAPTIZED IN THE SPIRIT
Key Observation #11

OBJECT VERSE

"It happened that while Apollos was at Corinth, Paul passed through the upper country and came to Ephesus, and found some disciples. 2 He said to them, 'Did you receive the Holy Spirit when you believed?' And they said to him, 'No, we have not even heard whether there is a Holy Spirit.' 3 And he said, 'Into what then were you baptized?' And they said, 'Into John's baptism.' 4 Paul said, 'John baptized with the baptism of repentance, telling the people to believe in Him who was coming after him, that is, in Jesus.' 5 When they heard this, they were baptized in the name of the Lord Jesus. 6 And when Paul had laid his hands upon them, the Holy Spirit came on them, and they began speaking with Tongues and prophesying. 7 There were in all about twelve men.'"(Acts 19:1-7)

◆◆◆◆

This event is comparable to that of Cornelius' house: it was a small group of people—twelve men in all who were individually acquainted with each other and who spoke one common natural language.

In verse one, Paul called them *disciples*, meaning disciples of Jesus Christ. However, they were completely unaware that the Holy Spirit even existed until Paul told them.

Paul would not have asked them about the Baptism of the Holy Spirit if they had not previously received Jesus Christ as their Savior (verse three). He knew that the Holy Spirit's Baptism cannot be received until *after* salvation.

Paul explained the difference between John the Baptist's water baptism and the Holy Spirit's Baptism. He then water baptized them into

Believer's In Ephesus

the name of the Lord Jesus Christ. Subsequent to that, he laid his hands on them and they were Baptized in the Holy Spirit.

When Paul laid his hands on them, what was the proof they had received the Holy Spirit's Baptism? It was the same evidence as all the other incidents: they spoke in **Tongues** and **Prophesied**.

Here again, the purpose for speaking in **Tongues** was uniquely different from the **Tongues** spoken in known languages on the day of Pentecost.

Accordingly, **The Gift of Tongues** among the twelve men; the Samaritans; and Cornelius' house, was different than the **Tongues** spoken on Pentecost. In none of the events after Pentecost was anyone waiting for an interpretation, or for that matter, needed an interpretation. The **Tongues** that were spoken in the gift of the Holy Spirit were directed to God, not to men. Hence, no interpretation was required.

◆◆◆◆
Key Facts

1. As a Christian, one can have the indwelling presence of the Holy Spirit and be totally unaware of Him.

2. Being a Christian does not automatically mean one is Baptized in the Holy Spirit. In some cases, His *gift* must be ministered to the Believer. In whichever manner the Baptism of the Holy Spirit comes to the Christian, the promise is for all Christians if they choose to receive His gift.

3. The Samaritans were water baptized *after* being saved. Then, they received the Baptism of the Holy Spirit *after* being taught about His gift. In Cornelius' household, they were Baptized in the Holy Spirit without such teaching and *before* water baptism. The disciples in Ephesus were water baptized, taught about the Holy Spirit, and then Baptized in the Holy Spirit.

4. Again, the standardized proof that they were Baptized in the Holy Spirit was when they spoke in **The Gift of Tongues**.

5. The purpose for **Tongues** in Samaria; Cornelius' house; or with the believers in Ephesus, was not the same as on the day of Pentecost. In Ephesus, Samaria, and Cornelius' house, they all spoke the same

Believer's In Ephesus

languages. But when they were Baptized in the Holy Spirit, they all spoke in **The Gift of Tongues**.

Five Operations of Tongues

CHAPTER 26
FIVE OPERATIONS OF TONGUES
"The Full Spectrum of the Spirit's Gift"
Key Observation #12

OBJECT VERSE

"For if I pray in an [unknown] tongue, my spirit [by the Holy Spirit within me] prays, but my mind is unproductive–bears no fruit and helps nobody. 15 Then what am I to do? I will pray with my spirit by the Holy Spirit that is within me; but I will also pray intelligently with my mind and understanding; I will sing with my spirit by the Holy Spirit within me; but I will sing (intelligently) with my mind and understanding also." (1 Corinthians 14:14-15, The Amplified Bible.)

◆ ◆ ◆ ◆

The Gift of Tongues is used five different ways in Scripture. By failing to rightly divide God's Word on this issue, heated controversy, bias, confusion, and division often occur.

There is only one **Gift of Tongues**, but according to the Holy Spirit's wisdom, He uses the same gift in a variety of ways. In the same way, there is only one Healer, but His gift of Healing is described as **Gifts of Healing**—in the plural, not singular. (1 Corinthians 12:9)

God allows no one to use His gifts at the whim of their own choosing, time, or setting. One cannot simply choose to heal whenever he wants. Healing comes from the Holy Spirit's power, and the Believer, in every case, must follow the Holy Spirit's wisdom and leading. In the same way, no one can apply **The gift of Tongues** in any manner they choose (with the exception of **Tongues** *for personal edification,* as will be explained).

The Gift of Tongues which were spoken on the day of Pentecost proved that the Holy Spirit gave His power to the disciples which Jesus

Five Operations of Tongues

required they possess *before* commencing their ministry. Moreover, the type of **Tongues** used on Pentecost was not the Holy Spirit's only application of **Tongues**. When this model is used at the exclusion of the other accounts, wrong conclusions are easily assumed.

Many Christians mistakenly claim that the **Tongues** spoken on Pentecost were restricted to *known languages* so that those to whom it was spoken could understand what was being said. They erroneously use the Baptism that occurred on Pentecost, a unique isolated event, as a universal standard for all applications of **Tongues**.

However, on Pentecost *only* the Apostles came forward in front of the public to speak in *known languages*. Of the one hundred twenty people in the upper room, the remaining one hundred eight stayed out of sight, presumably in the upper room of the house where they were meeting. Since the Scriptures do not mention them after the **Tongues of Fire** was seen on their heads, then to whom were they speaking in the upper room? Accordingly, two different types of **Tongues** were spoken on the Day of Pentecost.

The **Tongues** spoken by the one hundred eight persons was a different type of **Tongues** than the **Tongues** which the Apostles spoke in *known languages* that were directed to the gathering crowd.

Oppositionists to the Holy Spirit's Baptism mistakenly claim that if anyone were to speak in **Tongues** today, they would be speaking gibberish because the event on Pentecost will not be repeated. Thus, in their lack of understanding, they invalidate **Tongues** for the modern church. They concede, however, by asserting a restrictive clause, that *if* **Tongues** were spoken today like on Pentecost, (which they do not believe the Holy Spirit will do) then the **Tongues** would have to be *known languages* directed to those who understand what was being spoken.

Added to this presumption, they mistakenly believe that because we now have the printed Bible, it invalidates the gift of **Tongues. Using** their logic-driven deduction, they believe that (1) the Bible is now printed in all major languages, and (2) God's Written Word is sufficient as His final communication. Thus, **Tongues** is not needed.

Here is the problem with their reasoning: (1) The Scriptures do not support their logic-driven assessment. (2) The Baptism of the Holy Spirit, (proven by speaking in other **Tongues**), does not invalidate the

Five Operations of Tongues

printed Bible. Rather, it confirms it. The functional purpose of the Holy Spirit's Baptism *confirms* the Written Word. Those testifying about the Lord Jesus, speak of those things found *in* the Bible.

> "And they went out and preached everywhere, the Lord working with them and confirming the word [they preached] through the accompanying signs. Amen." (Mark 16:20. Square brackets by author for added clarity.)

Words are only words unless there is power and authority behind them. Accordingly, when people testify, preach, or teach according to the Written Word, the Holy Spirit confirms their words with proving signs, wonders, miracles, healing, deliverances, and salvation. This PROVES the Written Word of God. Accordingly, the Holy Spirit's power (which comes through the Holy Spirit's Baptism) authenticates the Written Word. The printed Bible does not, therefore, cancel the purpose of the Baptism of the Spirit, nor does the Baptism of the Spirit supplant the Written Word.

(3) Since the Baptism of the Spirit is valid for today, **Tongues** are valid for today as well. To prove this point, Joel's prophecy (Joel 2:28-31) time-brackets the Holy Spirit's gift as starting on Pentecost at 32 AD, forty-seven days after Jesus was resurrected, to the very day of Jesus' return (See Chapter 33 on the Last Days.).

> "And it shall come to pass in the last days, says God, that I will pour out of My Spirit on all flesh; your sons and your daughters shall prophesy, your young men shall see visions, your old men shall dream dreams. 18 And on My menservants and on My maidservants I will pour out My Spirit in those days; and they shall prophesy. 19 And I will shew wonders in heaven above, and signs in the earth beneath; blood, and fire, and vapor of smoke. 20 The sun shall be turned into darkness, and the moon into blood, before the coming of the great and awesome day of the LORD. (Acts 2:17-21. Underline by author for added emphasis.)

(4) The Holy Spirit's Baptism comes with the nine gifts, seven of which do not involve speaking in **Tongues**. The Holy Spirit's gifts are inseparable with His Baptism and cannot be line-item selected. They stand as a collective with His Baptism of power. By His wisdom, He bestows His gifts on whomever He chooses for whatever purpose.

Five Operations of Tongues

(5) The printing press was not invented until 1450 AD during the time of the Renaissance. This leaves a gap of 1,350 years *before* the Bible was first produced by the printing press. And even though the Bible has been translated in all "major" languages of today, there remains 6,000 languages currently not translated into a printed Bible. Aside from that, what do we do with over a thousand three hundred years *before* the Bible was canonized and printed if **Tongues** were no longer valid after the last Foundation Apostle died?

(6) Fourteen years *after* Pentecost, persecution struck the New Testament church in about 44 AD. The Apostle's scattered throughout the Gentile nations where the languages of Jews was *not* spoken. Consequently, the Baptism of the Spirit was needed as much in those regions as it was in Israel.

Those that do not believe the Holy Spirit's gift is for the modern church, are cultured by generations of fallacious doctrine linked in a series of wrong conclusions through misassociation of unrelated factors.

In Calvin's day, the world had 94.7% fewer people than today. His logic-based theology did not consider the nations of people yet to be discovered. He had no idea that the population of mankind would be more than nineteen times larger than in his day.

The answer to the rhetorical question is obvious: do we still need power to testify of Jesus where six billion out of eight billion three hundred million people have not received Jesus?

Consider the fact that North America was discovered on Wednesday, October 12, 1492 when a sailor aboard the Pinta, one of Columbus' three ships, spotted land. Sixteen years and nine months later, John Calvin was born on Saturday, July 10, 1509. He would receive his Masters of Theology at the age of eighteen and then a law degree.

Calvin's world was confined to Europe. Lands across the oceans were as yet undiscovered while he was earning his Master's Degree. Accordingly, his Christian perspective was essentially centered on the European and Middle East populace of his day. He could not possibly have envisioned a global population that would be over nineteen times larger which included nations yet to be found. These unexplored areas would have to be won by the Gospel. Consequently, the Holy Spirit's Baptism of power remains critically essential.

Five Operations of Tongues

Modern oppositionists cannot ignore the overabundant references regarding the Holy Spirit's gifts throughout the entire New Testament. Consequently, the subject is impossible to avoid. Therefore, they are obligated to give answers. This puts them in a conundrum between what the Bible says in a network of examples and teaching as contrasted against their logic-based Cessationist doctrines.

In order to protect their Reformational doctrines, those who oppose the Baptism of the Holy Spirit and the speaking in **Tongues**, must "redefine" the Holy Spirit's gifts. Thus, they claim **The Gift of Tongues** is an ability to quickly learn known languages for Bible translations. This far-reaching and very desperate attempt to explain what they do not understand relegates **Tongues** as being nothing more than an intellectual ability rather than by the Holy Spirit's power and gifting.

In consideration of all the above, and to avoid a great deal of confusion on the issue of **Tongues**, let us now consider how the Holy Spirit applies His **Gift of Tongues** in five different ways.

#1
THE GIFT OF TONGUES FOR THE UNBELIEVER

This is when a Christian speaks in **Tongues** by the Holy Spirit to others in *known languages* so that the message is understood as to what is spoken. However, the Christian speaking in such **Tongues** does not know what he or she is saying. Rather, they are being led by the Holy Spirit to speak in a foreign language by **The Gift of Tongues**.

> "And they were all filled with the Holy Spirit and began to speak with other tongues, as the Spirit was giving them utterance." (Acts 2:4)

> "They were amazed and astonished, saying, 'Why, are not all these who are speaking Galileans? 8 And how is it that we each hear them in our own language to which we were born?'" (Acts 2:7-8)

Missionaries have occasionally spoken in unknown **Tongues** when their interpreter, for one reason or another, could no longer continue. In other cases, someone sitting in a church might hear **Tongues** spoken in a language which they perfectly understood. Perhaps they are not saved and as a result they give their life to Christ, or they might confirm the **Tongue** as a testimony to those listening.

Five Operations of Tongues

But to be perfectly clear, when someone speaks in **Tongues**, they have no idea what they are saying. The Bible is very clear about that:

> "For if I pray in a tongue, my spirit prays, but my mind is unfruitful." (1 Corinthians 14:14)

Of the one hundred twenty people that spoke in **Tongues** on the day of Pentecost, not one of them intelligently comprehended the language they spoke.

#2
THE GIFT OF TONGUES FOR INTERCESSION

Tongues for Intercession is no less supernatural than speaking in **Tongues** for the unbeliever. The reference to this is found in the Book of Romans:

> "In the same way the Spirit also helps our weakness; for we do not know how to pray as we should, but the Spirit Himself intercedes for us with groanings too deep for words; 27 and He who searches the hearts knows what the mind of the Spirit is, because He intercedes for the saints according to the will of God." (Romans 8:26-27)

At times, we do not know how to pray according to the will of God. And even when we do pray, our human understanding is limited. Sometimes, certain facts or issues are hidden from our knowledge. But God, in His mercy, does not leave us helpless. As we yield to the Holy Spirit, He makes intercession for us. In such instances as we pray in **Tongues**, His Spirit prays through our spirit. God desires our prayers, both from the spirit and the soul—the spiritual prayer and the natural prayer.

> "Then what am I to do? I will pray with my spirit [by the Holy Spirit that is within me] and I will pray with my mind [using words I understand]; I will sing with my spirit [by the Holy Spirit that is within me] and I will sing with my mind [using words I understand]." (1 Corinthians 14:15. The Amplified Bible. Square brackets inserted by the Bible publisher for clarity.)

It must be understood that no one speaking in **The Gift of Tongues** can, of their own choosing, specifically target their prayer. Rather, the

Five Operations of Tongues

Holy Spirit leads the Believer to pray "in the Spirit" upon which the Holy Spirit makes intercession for us through the prayer language He gives.

How then does one know he is praying in **Tongues** for intercession? Simply this: after pouring out his heart in his natural language, the Holy Spirit seamlessly transitions us into intercession by using **Tongues**. Thus, our prayers are directed by Him in **Tongues** as He prays through our spirit. Furthermore, we have confidence that the Holy Spirit's prayer is received because the Holy Spirit always prays the perfect will of God.

During the times we pray through the Holy Spirit, the Holy Spirit reveals God's will to us. We know what the next step is by His leading, impressions, and spiritual communication. This is parallel with **The Gift of Interpretation**.

#3
THE GIFT OF TONGUES FOR PROPHECY

In its basic form, **Prophecy** is to exhort, edify, and comfort (1 Corinthians 14:3). At times during spiritual gatherings, the Holy Spirit will prompt someone to speak in **Tongues** which is directed to the church or to a gathering of people. When that happens, the Holy Spirit will prompt someone, or even the one speaking in Tongues, to interpret the **Tongue** by **The Gift of Interpretation**.

An **Interpretation of Tongues** is not a transliteration. By definition, a transliteration is a word-by-word interpretation. Accordingly, the gift of **Interpreting Tongues** is a summary explanation of what the Holy Spirit said as He spoke through the person that is speaking in **Tongues**.

The **Interpretation of Tongues** renders the same benefit as one speaking by **Prophecy** in his or her *known language* so that everyone understands what was said.

Thus, speaking in **Tongues**, combined with its **Interpretation**, is equal to the same effect or benefit as **Prophecy** spoken in the natural language.

Paul is not saying that **Prophecy** is greater than **Tongues**. Each gift stands unique in its own purpose. Rather, he emphasizes the importance of other people's *edification*. **Prophecy**, spoken in a *known*

Five Operations of Tongues

language, benefits those listening more than **Tongues** spoken *without* an **Interpretation**.

Therefore, when **Tongues** is directed to people, it must be interpreted. When that happens, it is classified as **Tongues for Prophecy**. But when **Tongues** is directed to God as in the case of prayer or worship, then no interpretation is required.

#4
THE GIFT OF TONGUES FOR PERSONAL EDIFICATION

One who is Baptized in the Holy Spirit can speak in **Tongues** for personal edification *at any time*. This is one of the greatest blessings of the Holy Spirit's Baptism.

> "For one who speaks in a tongue does not speak to men but to God; for no one understands, but in his spirit he speaks mysteries." (1Corinthians 14:2)

> "One who speaks in a tongue edifies himself; but one who prophesies edifies the church." (1 Corinthians 14:4)

There are two aspects to this mode of personal edification: (1) When the Believer prays in **Tongues,** the Holy Spirit intercedes for them. The Holy Spirit prays the perfect will of God *through and for* the Believer, even though the Believer may not know what the Holy Spirit is praying. However, the spiritual effect of the Holy Spirit's prayer builds up the Believer according to the wisdom of the Lord.

> "But you, beloved, building yourselves up on your most holy faith, praying in the Holy Spirit." (Jude 1:20)

(2) As one prays in the Holy Spirit, the Holy Spirit reveals what He is saying to the spirit of the one praying. This form of edification renders the same effect as **The Interpretation of Tongues**.

> "The Spirit Himself testifies and confirms together with our spirit [assuring us] that we [believers] are children of God." (Romans 8:16)

This is incredibly valuable. By praying in the Holy Spirit, sensitivity to the Holy Spirit's voice is developed. Praying in **Tongues** for personal edification teaches us, by repetitive experience, how to recognize the Holy Spirit's impressions, leadings, and spiritual communications to

Five Operations of Tongues

our spirit. Through repetitive exposure, our spirit grows in understanding, recognition, and sensitivity to the Holy Spirit's voice, impressions, and leading. This is essential. Learning to spiritually recognize His voice, leading, and impressions is also required in the other gifts such as **Healing** and **Miracles**.

When one speaks in **Tongues** for personal edification, he enters into the supernatural realm where the Holy Spirit builds him up on his faith (Jude 1:20). In such cases, **Tongues for Personal Edification** are not directed to man, but to God. Accordingly, no **Interpretation** is required because God knows what is being said. Yet, to the one speaking in **Tongues**, the Holy Spirit reveals what He is praying to them.

During the church service, however, praying in **Tongues for Personal Edification** serves no benefit to others. This is not to say one cannot pray silently in **Tongues** if no one hears or is distracted. But, it would be out of order if it drew people's attention away from the emphasis of what God is doing.

It is interesting to note that Jesus, our High Priest, continually makes intercession for us. The Holy Spirit, in like manner, makes intercession for us as we pray through the Holy Spirit by **The Gift of Tongues** used for personal edification.

Scripture exhorts us to pray at all times with all manner of prayer by praying through the Holy Spirit. This exhortation is not given to just a few select Christians. It is directed to all Christians throughout time until Jesus returns. But how shall *all* obey His Word unless *all* are Baptized in the Holy Spirit?

> "Pray at all times (on every occasion, in every season) <u>in the Spirit</u>, with all [manner of] prayer and entreaty. To that end keep alert and watch with strong purpose and perseverance, interceding in behalf of all the saints (God's consecrated people)." (Ephesians 6:18. The Amplified Bible. Underline by author for added emphasis.)

The above verse of Scripture is one Word to all Christians, not select Christians. (Acts 2:33-43 with special emphasis to verse 38-39). In order to obey God's exhortation, it is implied that all Christians, if they choose, can be Baptized in the Holy Spirit.

Five Operations of Tongues

"Then Peter said to them, "Repent, and let every one of you be baptized in the name of Jesus Christ for the remission of sins; and you shall receive <u>the gift of the Holy Spirit</u>. 39 For the promise is to you and to your children, and to all who are afar off, as many as the Lord our God will call." (Acts 2:38-39. Underline by author for added emphasis..)

"But you, beloved, building yourselves up on your most holy faith, <u>praying in the Holy Spirit</u>." (Jude 1:20. Underline by author for added emphasis.)

Some Christians mistakenly interpret "praying in the Spirit" as praying with fervency and zeal. Such rendering is a self-serving definition designed to fit their doctrine rather than adjusting their doctrine to fit God's immutable Word.

Paul's definition of "praying in the Spirit" is crystal-clear. He explains **The Gift of Tongues** in 1 Corinthians 14:16 where it says:

"Otherwise if you <u>bless [pray] in the Spirit</u> only, how will the one who fills the place of the ungifted say the "Amen" at your giving of thanks, since he does not know what you are saying?" (Underline and square brackets by author for added emphasis and clarity.)

If praying in the Spirit, or stated in another way, *blessing in the Spirit,* means fervently praying in the natural language, then anyone listening would naturally understand what is spoken. But Paul says that blessing *in* the Spirit cannot be understood because it is speaking in **Tongues**. Therefore, the term "praying *in* the Spirit" means praying in **Tongues**.

How shall those who are not Baptized in the Holy Spirit obey the instruction to pray *in* the Spirit? What shall be done with the various Scriptures admonishing us to do so? Remember, God's Word regarding the Baptism of the Holy Spirit is one Word to ALL Christians, not just to select Believers. Consequently, we are left with only two choices. First, those who do not believe that the Holy Spirit's Baptism is a promise for all in Christ, by default, must twist God's Word and change it to fit their doctrinal perspective.

Second, if the Scripture is taken in its plain and customary meaning (as consistently used throughout the Bible), no other conclusion can

Five Operations of Tongues

be reached than to admit that all Christians can be Baptized in the Holy Spirit.

One group of oppositionists, very particularly Cessationists, want people to believe that not all should speak in **Tongues**. While it is true that not all Christians speak in **Tongues**, it is also true that all Christians, if they so desire, can be Baptized in the Holy Spirit with the evidence of speaking in **Tongues**. After all, the gift is for every Believer without bias.

Paul said:

> "Now I wish that you all spoke in tongues, but even more that you would prophesy; and greater [in benefit to the congregation for edification] is one who prophesies than one who speaks in tongues, unless he interprets, so that the church may receive edifying." (1 Corinthians 14:5)

If the Lord did not provide for all Christians to be Baptized in the Holy Spirit, why would Paul wish for something contrary to God's will? Why would he exhort Christians in general to "pray in the Spirit"? The answer is simple: if anyone desires to be Baptized in the Holy Spirit, the Lord promises to give them the Holy Spirit's gift and they will speak in **Tongues**.

Explaining Paul's Comparatives

> "Are not Apostles, are they? All are not prophets, are they? All are not teachers, are they? All are not workers of miracles, are they? All do not have gifts of healings, do they? All do not speak with other tongues, do they? All do not interpret, do they?" (1 Corinthians 12:29-30)

In the above verses of Scripture, Paul explains the proper order in the church service. In his explanation, he uses an expanded picture of the "Body of Christ" to show that the Lord diversifies His ministry offices among various people. Not all are Apostles, or prophets, or teachers. Then, in a parallel example, in the same way he shows that God diversifies the Holy Spirit's gifts uniquely in each service: not all are workers of **Miracles** in every service; not all are used in **Healings** in every service; not all **Speak in Tongues** in every service that are directed to the congregation; not all **Interpret** such **Tongues** in every service which is directed to the congregation. The Holy Spirit diversifies the operation of the gifts at any given moment based on the needs present.

Five Operations of Tongues

Accordingly, the Lord uses people differently in each service. He uses one person for healing in a particular service as the Holy Spirit wills, and another person for something else, as the Holy Spirit wills.

The next time the church meets, the person whom the Lord previously used in **Healing** might be used to speak in **Tongues**, or the Lord might use him or her in any one of the other nine gifts: **Miracles, Healings, Word of Wisdom, Word of Knowledge, Prophecy, Faith, Discernment of Spirits, The Gift of Tongues, or The Interpretation of Tongues**. Accordingly, the Holy Spirit, by His wisdom, diversifies His gifts according to the needs present.

Paul never says that only *select* Christians can be Holy Spirit Baptized. The Holy Spirit's gift is for all Christians, for all time, until Jesus returns. Unfortunately, certain groups of Christians take 1 Corinthians 12:29-30 out of context and falsely teach that not all Christians can be Baptized in the Holy Spirit. But, again, a careful study of Scripture in its proper context shows that Paul was teaching on the diversity of gifts in any given church service. He was not saying that some are selected to be Baptized in the Holy Spirit and others are not.

#5
THE GIFT OF TONGUES FOR WORSHIP

> "All the circumcised believers who came with Peter were amazed, because the gift of the Holy Spirit had been poured out on the Gentiles also. 46 For they were hearing them speaking with Tongues and exalting God." (Acts 10:45-46)

> "…we hear them in our own Tongues speaking of the mighty deeds of God." (Acts 2:11)

> "What is the outcome then? I will pray with the spirit and I will pray with the mind also; I will sing with the spirit and I will sing with the mind also." (1 Corinthians 14:15)

Worship is an integral part of the Christian faith. We worship what we love. Therefore, we worship our Heavenly Father because we love Him. Scripture repetitively admonishes us throughout the Bible to worship our Father. In fact, because worship is *communication and fellowship with Him*, it is a form of prayer.

Five Operations of Tongues

When our Father's presence manifests during worship, human words cannot express the intensity that draws us deeper into Him. As we worship our Heavenly Father, we are drawn deeper by singing and praying in **The Gift of Tongues**. This is where the Holy Spirit comes alongside us.

> "But You are holy, You who inhabit the praises of Israel."
> (Psalms 22:3. New Heart English Bible)

By the Holy Spirit's gift of **Tongues**, worship ascends into a deeper spiritual realm. He perfectly directs our **Tongues** as our spiritual words ascend before our Father's throne. This delights the Holy Spirit:

> "But when He, the Spirit of truth, comes, He will guide you into all the truth; for He will not speak on His own initiative, but whatever He hears, He will speak; and He will disclose to you what is to come. 14 <u>He will glorify Me</u>, for He will take of Mine and will disclose it to you. 15 All things that the Father has are Mine; therefore I said that He takes of Mine and will disclose it to you." (John 16:13-15. Underline by author for added emphasis.)

During times of worship, **Tongues** can either be spoken or offered in singing. This is often considered as **Tongues for Intercession** because the Holy Spirit aides us in worship in order to take us beyond the limits of our own language or ability.

Typically, we think of intercession as being associated with times of crisis or difficulty. However, in worship, we need His assistance for deeper spiritual interactions of worship.

When Jesus spoke to the woman at the well, He told her that the hour was coming when worship will go beyond the limits of the human soul and reach into the spiritual dimension of truth. That hour came on the day of Pentecost when the Holy Spirit Baptized one hundred twenty people in the upper room. Furthermore, it continues to this very day.

> "But an hour is coming, and now is, when the true worshipers will worship the Father in [the dimension of the] spirit and truth; for such people the Father seeks to be His worshipers." (John 4:23. Square brackets by author for added clarity.)

Five Operations of Tongues

When worship reaches the level of profound depth, the effect is similar to what the priests experienced after Solomon finished the temple.

> "It happened that when the priests came from the holy place, the cloud filled the house of the LORD, 11 so that the priests could not stand to minister because of the cloud, for the glory of the LORD filled the house of the LORD." (1 King 8:10-11)

Spirit-Baptized Christians enjoy unique intensities in worship as compared to those that reject the Holy Spirit's Baptism. This is because having the Holy Spirit's Baptism of power provides deeper access into the spiritual dimension by the purity of the Holy Spirit's truth.

Spirit-Baptized Believers are able to reach beyond the limits of their soul and transition their worship into greater dimensions by the ushering of the Holy Spirit. Accordingly, on the principles of spiritual depth and comprehension, Scripture tells us:

> "We also speak of these things, not in words taught *or* supplied by human wisdom, but in those taught by the Spirit, combining *and* interpreting spiritual *thoughts* with spiritual *words* [for those being guided by the Holy Spirit]. 14 But the natural [unbelieving] man does not accept the things [the teachings and revelations] of the Spirit of God, for they are foolishness [absurd and illogical] to him; and he is incapable of understanding them, because they are spiritually discerned *and* appreciated, [and he is unqualified to judge spiritual matters].15 But the spiritual man [who understand revelation by the Spirit] judges all things [questions, examines and applies what the Holy Spirit reveals], yet is himself judged by no one [because the unbeliever is not qualified to judge and understand the believer's spiritual nature]. 16 For who has known the mind *and* purposes of the Lord, so as to instruct Him? But we have the mind of Christ [to be guided by the Spirit's thoughts and purposes]." (1 Corinthians 2:13-16. Amplified Bible. Square brackets by author for added clarity.)

Again, worship through the Holy Spirit's power reaches beyond human ability. Conversely, worship expressed through the limits of the soul (which can sometimes be a delight before the heart of God), is comparatively limited.

Five Operations of Tongues

Non-spiritual worship originates from the soul. It is frequently academic. This is not to suggest that worship from the soul is refused by our Heavenly Father. Rather, it is characteristically limited without the Holy Spirit who escorts us by His power into the secret places of the Lord.

> "<u>Bless the LORD, O my soul: and all that is within me, bless His holy name.</u> 2 Bless the LORD, O my soul, and forget not all his benefits: 3 Who forgives all your iniquities, Who heals all your diseases, 4 Who redeems your life from destruction, Who crowns you with lovingkindness and tender mercies, 5 Who satisfies your mouth with good *things, So that* your youth is renewed like the eagle's." (Psalm 103:1-5. Underline by author for added emphasis.)

Those that do not believe in the Holy Spirit's Baptism claim that Spirit-filled Christians are too emotional and that their worship is fleshly. But at football games, the same critics stand up, wave their arms, scream, shout, cheer, dress in ridiculous costumes, and paint their face to glorify their team. No one criticizes them for such zeal!

We easily get excited over temporal vanities while at the same time withhold unlimited expressions of praise and worship to our Heavenly Father. Religiously, we strip worship of its passion and suppress any manifestation of emotion.

Emotions are powerful tools of communications! Imagine loving your spouse or children without the display of emotions. They would feel unloved, disliked, or even despised. In the same principle, why do we treat our Heavenly Father with clinical cold methodologies, controlled religious restraints, and traditionally mandated behavior?

Cynics claim that Spirit-filled worship is indecent and out of order. They claim it is irreverent and insulting to the holiness of God. But by whose standard? Whose doctrine? Theirs? In fact, Scripture encourages us in the liberty of worship!

> "Now the Lord is the Spirit, and where the Spirit of the Lord is, there is liberty." (2 Corinthians 3:17)

Our Father desires us to be free and expressive in our worship. We are individually known by our Heavenly Father and He desires our individual uniqueness in worship. Unfortunately, controlled non-expressive worship is little more than form-cut cookies on a conveyor belt.

Yes, there are abuses and works of the flesh in worship just as there are in every aspect of the Christian faith. Such extremes, however, are easily corrected. Balance is the key of life in all things. Therefore, let us not disqualify freedom in worship by fear.

When we yield to the Holy Spirit, everything is conducted decently and in order. He takes us deep into the heart of our Heavenly Father. Instinctively, naturally, we lift our hands heavenward. This is the unscripted universal expression of worship from culture to culture, nation to nation, and people to people throughout time.

> "Therefore I want the men in every place to pray, lifting up holy hands, without anger and disputing *or* quarreling *or* doubt [in their mind]. (1 Timothy 2:8. The Amplified Bible. Square brackets by publisher for added clarity.)

Tightly formatted religion with all its protocols restrict both personal and corporate expressions of love and worship toward our Heavenly Father. This is evident in many churches where those who raise hands in worship are often reprimanded. And singing in the Spirit, as Paul instructed, is ruthlessly forbidden.

> "But it was because of the false brethren secretly brought in, who had sneaked in to spy out our liberty which we have in Christ Jesus, in order to bring us into bondage." (Galatians 2:4)

Worship is never dispensational. Accordingly, David's instructions on the subject of worship were written under the inspiration of the Holy Spirit. And yet, while multiple denominations proudly claim to be devoted followers of God's Word, at the same time they completely disregard the admonitions of Scripture pertaining to worship as noted below in various admonitions of Scripture (Underline and square brackets by author for added emphasis.):

Psalm 2:11 "Worship the LORD with <u>reverence and rejoice with trembling</u>."

Five Operations of Tongues

Psalm 95:6 "Come, let us <u>worship and bow down</u>, <u>let us kneel</u> before the LORD our maker."

Psalm 33:3 "<u>Sing to Him a new song</u> [born fresh out of the spirit of the Christian]; play skillfully with <u>a shout of joy</u>."

Psalm 71:23 "<u>My lips will shout for joy</u> when I sing praises to you; and my soul, which you have redeemed."

Psalm 84:2 "<u>My heart and my flesh sing for joy</u> to the living God."

Psalm 87:7. "Then those who sing as well as those <u>who play the flutes</u> shall say 'All my springs of joy are in you.'"

Psalm 98:4-6 "<u>*Shout joyfully*</u> to the LORD, all the earth; break forth and sing for joy and sing praises. Sing praises to the LORD with the *lyre,* with the lyre and the sound of melody. <u>*With trumpets*</u> and the <u>sound of the horn</u> <u>shout joyfully</u> before the King, the LORD."

Psalm 63:4So "I will bless you as long as I live; <u>I will lift up my hands</u> in Your Name."

Psalm 150:5 "Praise Him with <u>loud cymbals</u>; praise Him with <u>resounding cymbals</u>."

2 Samuel 6:5 "Meanwhile, David and all the house of Israel were celebrating before the LORD *with all kinds of instruments* made of fir wood, and with <u>lyres, harps, tambourines, castanets and cymbals</u>."

1 Chronicles 13:8 "David and all Israel were <u>celebrating before God with all their might</u>, even with songs and with <u>lyres, harps, tambourines, cymbals and with trumpets.</u>"

Spirit-filled worship is robust with the presence of the Lord. Liberty in Christ releases heartfelt expressions such as kneeling, standing, raising of the hands, shouting unto God with a voice of triumph, making a joyful sound, etc.

A garden without variety is like worship without expression. The Garden of the Lord's worship is composed of many colors, races, tongues, emotions, and varieties of sounds. Deep in the African jungle, it is the beating of drums with dancing; in China it is the chorus of voices singing by acappella; among the Pigmies it is sounds and voices among the trees; among the Khoisan people in Southwest Africa, it is the vocal sounds with the "clicking" of the tongue.

Fearless worship is expressive worship. But those who mistakenly think the Holy Spirit's Baptism is no longer for Christendom today, are the ones that suppress worship by wrong doctrine, fear, and blind tradition. They withhold rightful worship due our Heavenly Father by restricting Scripturally endorsed expressions with doctrinal chains. This is one of the most heinous crimes of all: restricting worship justly due our gracious Father in Heaven.

CHAPTER 27
THE UNREGENERATED SOUL
"Why Our Intellect Rejects the Holy Spirit's Gift"

The controversy about the Holy Spirit's Baptism is popularized by those, who, for the lack of revelation and illumination in God's Word, reject His Baptism. Consequently, such Christians, sincere as they are in wanting the truth, do not realize they are refusing the promise of our Heavenly Father.

Jesus said the truth would set us free. The implied reverse is equally as true: in the absence of truth, bondage remains. Mistakes have consequences. We saw this in John's Calvin's life. He adamantly preached against the gifts of healing and miracles by telling his students that such things were only for the early church. As a consequence, when he, his wife, and their children encountered sickness and disease, they had no recourse. Instead, the entire family died of various diseases: first the children, then his wife, and finally himself. This was not God's will.

Under the pretext of love, a new class of emergent preachers faddishly embrace every developing social trend. Wanting to appease their congregations and make the Gospel relevant and appealing to their culture, they characteristically remove the urgency for conformity to righteousness. They wink at non-marital co-habitation; are non-confronting on gender identity issues including LGBTQ lifestyles, abortion, or anything that offends its attendees. Their doctrinal standard suppresses the truth—hoping, of course, to win souls, but at the expense of truth.

To mitigate those members who are easily offended, seeker-sensitive churches conciliate the impact of truth. As a result, their preaching is filled with metaphorical candy, ice cream, and soda pop. This gives their members the sensation of fullness, but contributes nothing toward spiritual nutrition that leads to healthy spiritual maturity.

The Unregenerated Soul

> "You're going to find that there will be times when people will have no stomach for solid teaching, but will fill up on spiritual junk food–catchy opinions that tickle their fancy. They'll turn their backs on truth and chase mirages." (2 Timothy 4:3-5. The Message Bible.)

A perfect paradigm of spiritual immaturity is illustrated by the child and a candy bar: Set a candy bar and the title-deed to a half-million dollar home in front of a child. The child will reach for the candy bar. In the same way, untaught, carnal, and imperceptive Christians rooted in seeker-friendly perspectives always gravitate toward that which makes them feel good while avoiding or dismissing Christ-likeness. Such churches foolishly play on God's mercy in the name of love.

Typically, seeker-friendly churches are well known for their social benefits and programs, such as sending Christmas boxes overseas, school backpack kits, various social assistance, and even missionary outreaches. But when such works are fronted as righteous endorsements, Heaven sees them as filthy rags. Conversely, good works are little more than a false front for righteousness where repentance is ignored.

One particular pastor, Paul Carter, ultimately abandoned the Seeker-Friendly church model and described it this way:

> *"The basic logic of the seeker sensitive movement was that we would get people in the door by playing contemporary music, singing contemporary songs, speaking contemporary jargon and addressing contemporary issues. Then at some unspecified point in the future, we would transition into more meaty and substantial things.*
>
> *It was your basic bait and switch operation, and as you might imagine, it never really worked out in practice.*
>
> *The bottom line is that what you win people with is what you have to keep people with. If you market yourself as a church for people who don't like church, then you can't do churchy things without expecting significant pushback.*
>
> *This is why most seeker churches never managed to exit the theological merge lane. If you sell them on Christianity Lite then you need to continue to offer Christianity Lite*

> *week after week after week. The logic of seeker church traps you in a spiritual reenactment...*[24]

The greatest majority of seeker-friendly churches are found in first world countries such as America, Canada, Australia, and Great Britain. These are nations that have the least amount of lack. As compared to the rest of the world, the general population of such nations minimally experience serious conflict, suffering, and hardship. As a result, their churches draw unneedy Christians in great numbers. However, the spiritual depth and strength of its members remains to be seen (Matthew 13:21). This is because they have little dependence upon God for their needs. Consequently, their Gospel is designed to accommodate trendy ideologies (2 Timothy 4:3). Very little demand is placed on conformity to the standard of Jesus (Hebrews 12:14). For this reason, Jesus said:

> "Again I say to you, it is easier for a camel to go through the eye of a needle, than for a rich man to enter the kingdom of God." (Matthew 19:24)

The core philosophy of their preaching is comparable to a Bible-Story-time-hour. They are best described as information-based churches lacking the revelation and inspiration of the Holy Spirit. It is an empty Gospel that fills the head but wanes the spirit. Those accustomed to such messages unwittingly think all is well. They assume it is the "normal relevant" message of the Gospel fitted to modern society. Largely, such congregants are untested in their faith and predictably form the rank and file of those in the coming great apostasy:

> "Let no one in any way deceive or entrap you, for that day will not come unless the apostasy comes first [that is, the great rebellion, the abandonment of the faith by professed Christians], and the man of lawlessness is revealed, the son of destruction [the Antichrist, the one who is destined to be destroyed]." (2Thessalonians 2:3, Amplified Bible. Square brackets by author for added clarity.)

In tandem with the above prophecy, Paul warns by the Holy Spirit:

---

[24] https://ca.thegospelcoalition.org/columns/ad-fontes/abandoned-seeker-church/

The Unregenerated Soul

"For the time will come when they will not endure sound doctrine; but wanting to have their ears tickled, they will accumulate for themselves teachers in accordance to their own desires, 4 and will turn away their ears from the truth and will turn aside to myths. 5 But you, be sober in all things, endure hardship, do the work of an evangelist, fulfill your ministry." (2 Timothy 4:3-5)

Paul's prophetic insights speak directly to our day. They are precisely on point with this generation, a generation ignorantly fading into an ever worsening darkness.

૱

Thanks be to our Heavenly Father's great love!
He has not abandoned us in our ignorance.
In these final days, the glory of the Triumphant Holy Spirit
will shine the revelation of Jesus onto the hearts
of all who seek truth.

૱

Man—A Tri-Part Being

Man is a tri-part being. He is spirit, soul, and body. While the spirit and soul are eternally bonded, the body, upon physical death, returns to the earth.

The soul is the mind, emotions, will, and intellect. The body animates the dictates of the soul: laughter, anger, fright, joy, peace, etc. The spirit is that which gives the body its life. When the body dies, the spirit and soul are released from its corporal form.

At the moment of physical death, a Christian's spirit and soul return to the Lord. But for those who rejected Jesus, their spirit and soul is eternally banished. They are sent to Hell and remain there until Jesus conducts the White Throne judgment which occurs after His 1,000-year rule on earth. At that time, their eternal torment is metered according to their deeds and they are cast into the Lake of Fire.

Because the spirit and soul are inseparable, those living in Hell, which are later cast into the Lake of Fire, exist in a continual loop of recall, feelings, emotions, regret, sadness, grief, and pain. But those in Heaven are healed of all negative emotions and memories.

The Unregenerated Soul

Even though salvation gives us a *new nature* in Christ, we still have an *unregenerated mind*. Regarding that, the Scriptures give us clear instructions:

> "And that you be renewed in the spirit of your mind, 24 and put on the new self, which in the likeness of God has been created in righteousness and holiness of the truth." (Ephesians 4:23-24)

> "And do not be conformed to this world, but be transformed by the renewing of your mind, so that you may prove what the will of God is, that which is good and acceptable and perfect." (Romans 12:2)

The progressive renewal of our mind occurs by the washing of our Father's Word as we cooperate with the Holy Spirit. It is an ongoing unending process on this side of Heaven. The Holy Spirit is the voice of conscience and the standard of conviction that leads and guides every Believer.

The renewal of our mind is a process through regeneration. Pride, fear, doubt, unbelief, inordinate desires, and sensuality, for example, is enthroned in that area of our unrenewed soul. Therefore, we must humble ourselves under the Holy Spirit's leading; walk in the power of His truths that make us free; and consciously subject every thought, word, and deed to the Holy Spirit's scrutiny. The access to this is through humility. This is why Jesus said:

> "Truly I say to you, whoever does not receive the kingdom of God like a child will not enter it at all." (Mark 10:15)

The Necessity of Humility

Humility is required throughout the transformational process. We must listen to the Holy Spirit and yield to Him. We must be humble, approachable, and teachable. This is the only way to enter the renewal of our minds through God's Word.

> "But to this one I will look, to him who is humble and contrite of spirit, and who trembles at My word." (Isaiah 66:2)

With all certainty, the Holy Spirit's Baptism offends the dignity of our unregenerated soul. Why? Because the soul does not approve what it cannot comprehend or understand. With an air of sophistication, it rejects what is spiritual and illogical.

The Religious Pride of Man

Immature Christians equate humility as being gullible. For this very reason, they also consider the Holy Spirit's Baptism as a freak demonstration. Their doctrines shape their belief and they cannot receive His gift. They do not believe one can suddenly speak in an unknown language. They do not believe God's Spirit speaks through man's spirit. They do not understand the Holy Spirit whom they cannot see. As a consequence, being natural minded rather than spiritually minded, they reject or minimize the supernatural realm.

> "We also speak of these things, not in words taught or supplied by human wisdom, but in those <u>taught by the Spirit</u>, combining and interpreting spiritual thoughts with spiritual words [for those being guided by the Holy Spirit]." (1 Corinthians 2:13. Underline by author for added emphasis.)

> "But <u>a natural man does not accept the things of the Spirit of God</u>, for they are foolishness to him; and he cannot understand them, because they are spiritually appraised. 15 But he who is spiritual appraises all things, yet he himself is appraised by no one." (1 Corinthians 2:14-15. Underline by author for added emphasis.)

> "<u>The Spirit Himself testifies with our spirit</u> that we are children of God." (Romans 8:16)

Those who academically analyze the Holy Spirit's Baptism cannot see the truth of His gift. They need the revelation of His insights which He gladly supplies if they would receive them. By default, they filter His works through pattern reflexive mindsets, unbelief, and the grid of their Cessationist doctrines.

Again, the soul is not where the Holy Spirit resides. The prayer language that one receives by the Holy Spirit's Baptism originates within a person's spirit where the Spirit of God dwells.

> "For if I pray in an [unknown] tongue, my spirit [by the Holy Spirit within me] prays, but my mind is unproductive bears no fruit and helps nobody. 15 Then what am I

The Unregenerated Soul

to do? I will pray with my spirit by the Holy Spirit that is within me; but I will also pray intelligently with my mind and understanding; I will sing with my spirit by the Holy Spirit within me; but I will sing (intelligently) with my mind and understanding also." (1 Corinthians 14:14-15, The Amplified Bible. Square brackets by publisher for added clarity.)

The Holy Spirit's Gentle Approach

The Holy Spirit never violates a person's will. In love, He solicits our cooperation as He forms our character and gives us His gifts. He offers His love to all who receive Him. He does not force Himself into anyone's life. His gift, the Baptism, is for anyone willing to receive it. And whether or not a person accepts or refuses His gift, our Father's love never changes toward them.

Being Spirit-Baptized is always a collaboration between the Believer and the Holy Spirit. Accordingly, the Holy Spirit's gift does not come upon a person and overtake their will. If the Believer speaks in **The Gift of Tongues**, it is because he yields and cooperates with the Holy Spirit.

CHAPTER 28
THE CORINTHIAN CHURCH CONFUSION
"The Holy Spirit's Instruction"

The church at Corinth was established as a Spirit-filled church by Paul. However, they did not have the centralized writings of the Bible that we have today. Accordingly, they needed instruction concerning the Holy Spirit's gifts in their services. Fortunately for us, their instruction is our guideline as well.

When trying to understand the issues of the Corinthian Church, it is helpful to know something about their metro society. Its similarity to Las Vegas is nearly parallel. It had a population of about 700,000 people and was commonly known for its tourism and vice. It was also a hub of pagan religions where over 1,200 temple prostitutes[25] offered themselves in free service to the sexual rites of pagan worship. As such, the Corinthians, having been saved out of a rather sordid society, were less pious in their ways.

There were problems in relationships within the church and a lot of confusion in their meetings. Schisms, factions, personalities, economic inequalities—you name it, it operated in the congregation. Despite all of that, Paul said they were not lacking any gifts of the Holy Spirit (1 Corinthians 1:7).

> "Therefore you do not lack any spiritual gift as you eagerly wait for our Lord Jesus Christ to be revealed."

Most everyone in the church spoke in **Tongues** and **Prophesied**, but there was no order in the delivery. Consequently, the congregation

---

[25] The phone book in Las Vegas, Nevada, has over 700 pages in the Yellow Pages listing sex workers of various kinds, including transportation services to and from the brothels outside of county borders of Las Vegas.

did not benefit from the Holy Spirit's gifts. Confusion stood to the forefront of the services and the people received very little. The problem, however, was not the gifts, but their improper use of them.

The truth is, without biblical instructions, any church could make the same mistake. In that regard, Paul addressed multiple issues within the church and graciously showed them how to correct the problem pertaining to the utterance gifts, particularly the gifts of **Tongues** and **Prophecy**.

Despite the Corinthian's passionate use of the Holy Spirit's gifts, they did not know how to properly use **Tongues** or **Prophecy** *to edify* one another. Chapters 12 through 14 of 1st Corinthians is devoted to Paul's instructions regarding such gifts. Context and balance is key. Sadly, when oppositionists remove Paul's instructions from its context, confusion results.

Because **Tongues** fundamentally builds people up in their holy faith, Paul does not discourage them from speaking in the gift. In fact, the use of **Tongues** in personal prayer is encouraged in Jude 1:20 and Ephesian 6:18. However, during the church service, **Tongues for Personal Edification** should *not* be openly used if it brings distraction of confusion.

The Tongues of Men and of Angels

Paul makes reference to two categories of **Tongues**: earthly and Heavenly. He says it is possible to speak in either one.

> "If I speak with Tongues of men and of angels, but do not have love, I have become a noisy gong or a clanging cymbal." (1 Corinthians 13:1)

> "There are, perhaps, a great many kinds of languages in the world, and no kind is without meaning." (1 Corinthians 14:10)

The various languages of mankind include forgotten languages, including languages as from hidden tribes. It could also be *known languages*, or variations of the same language such as Chinese that has hundreds of different dialects.

Since we have no specific knowledge of the language of angels, they cannot be readily identified. Nonetheless, Paul says they are Heavenly in origin.

The Corinthian Confusion

The Holy Spirit's gifts which are listed in 1st Corinthians 12:1-11, are generally categorized in three groups of three:

POWER GIFTS
Miracles
Gifts of Healing
Faith

REVELATIONAL GIFTS
Word of Knowledge
Word of Wisdom
Discerning of Spirits

UTTERANCE GIFTS
The Gift of Tongues
Interpreting Tongues
Prophecy

Specifically, the utterance gifts is where the confusion was centered. Based on that, Paul gives his instructions.

The Gifts In The Believers

Anyone Baptized in the Holy Spirit can be used in any of the nine gifts. This is different from the "ministry office gifts" of the apostle, prophet, evangelist, pastor, and teacher.

If the Holy Spirit appoints someone to a particular ministry office, one, two, and sometimes three gifts of the Holy Spirit are more dominant in his or her ministry than the other gifts. For instance, the power gifts are typically displayed through the offices of the evangelist and prophet more than the pastor or teacher. Of course, this is a general assumption, and sometimes pastors operate in the realm of miracles, but not nearly as common as evangelists or prophets.

Anyone can **Prophesy,** just as anyone can be used in any of the nine gifts.

> "For you can all prophesy one by one, so that all may learn and all may be exhorted." (1 Corinthians 14:31)

The Holy Spirit might use a person more consistently in one gift than another. For instance, someone might flow in the gift of **Prophecy** more confidently than the **Interpretation of Tongues**. Perhaps in the gift of **Prophecy** they are better acquainted with how the Holy Spirit

The Corinthian Confusion

speaks through them. They have developed sensitivity to His voice, leading, and impressions with greater accuracy.

However, just because someone frequently prophesies, it does not mean they are a prophet any more than preaching makes one a pastor. Accordingly, the Holy Spirit can use any Holy Spirit-Baptized Believer in any gift at any moment.

> "But one and the same Spirit works all these things, distributing to each one individually just as He wills." (1 Corinthians 12:11)

Another point of consideration is this: simply because the Holy Spirit uses a person in one particular gift during a church service, it does not mean He will use them the same way in the next service. In one service, the Holy Spirit might prompt someone to speak in **Tongues**. In the next service, the same person might be used by the Holy Spirit to speak a **Word of Knowledge**. It all depends on the Holy Spirit's choice according to His wisdom.

In the Corinthian church, it would have been unusual if someone was not Baptized in the Holy Spirit. After all, it was Paul who founded the church. As a Foundation Apostle, he emphasized the importance of the Holy Spirit's Baptism. Throughout his ministry, he customarily emphasized the Holy Spirit's Baptism with the same earnestness that he ministered to the twelve men of Ephesus (Acts 19).

With this being the consistent pattern of his ministry, it is reasonable to assume that nearly everyone in the Corinthian church spoke in **Tongues** with the exception, perhaps, of those who recently came into salvation.

With so many congregation members being Baptized in the Holy Spirit, Paul instructs his church on three specific gifts: **Tongues, Interpretation of Tongues**, and **Prophecy**. Accordingly, when the Holy Spirit directs a person to speak in **Tongues** to the congregation, an **Interpretation** is required so that the congregation can benefit from what the Holy Spirit said through **The Gift of Tongues**. The **Interpretation** can come from the person who initially spoke the **Tongue**, or from someone else.

The Corinthian Confusion

> "Therefore let one who speaks in a tongue pray that he may [be gifted to] translate or explain [what he says]."
> (1 Corinthians 14:13. Square brackets by author for added clarity.)

When An Interpretation Is <u>Not</u> Needed

Many people mistakenly claim that any time **Tongues** is spoken in the church, an **Interpretation** is required. This is *limitedly* true. Unfortunately, those who make such claims often take the following Scripture out of context and misapply its usage:

> "Therefore if the whole church assembles together and all speak in Tongues, and ungifted men or unbelievers enter, will they not say that you are mad?" (1 Corinthians 14:23)

The above Scripture refers to an out-of-order chattering of **Tongues**. However, the same Scripture *would not apply* when the entire congregation sings in the Holy Spirit during worship unto God. In *that* case, **Tongues** is directed to God and not man. Therefore, God, who understands what is being said, does not require an **Interpretation**.

There is only one context when God requires **Tongues** to be **Interpreted**: it is when the Holy Spirit directs the **Tongues** to a person or congregation.

When **Tongues** are spoken in worship, it is directed to God. No Interpretation is required.

When **Tongues** are spoken privately for *personal* edification, it is directed to God. No Interpretation is required. (1 Corinthians 14:4)

When **Tongues** are privately spoken for intercession, it is directed to God. No Interpretation is required. (1 Corinthians 14:14; Romans 8:26-27)

In the church, the usage of **Tongues** must be properly understood in their context of setting. If the use and context is not considered, lesser informed people automatically assume an interpretation is required in every instance.

If speaking in **Tongues** is categorically prohibited in the church, those who prohibit such activity are in direct violation of God's Word.

The Corinthian Confusion

> "Therefore, my brethren, desire earnestly to prophecy, and <u>do not forbid to speak in Tongues</u>. 40 But all things must be done properly and in an orderly manner." (1 Corinthians 14:39-40. Underline by author for added emphasis.)

Proper order is required when **Tongues** and **Prophecy** are spoken. If **Prophecy** is spontaneously spoken, it must be done in such a way that there is clear distinction between each **Prophecy**. No one is to shout or assert over another. Nor are they to compete for the opportunity to speak.

> "Let two or three prophets speak, and let the others pass judgment. 30 But if a revelation is made to another who is seated, the first one must keep silent. 31 For you can all prophesy one by one, so that all may learn and all may be exhorted; 32 and the spirits of prophets are subject to prophets; 33 for God is not a God of confusion but of peace, as in all the churches of the saints." (1 Corinthians 14:29-33)

The same rule applies to those speaking in **Tongues** to the church and its **Interpretation**:

> "If anyone speaks in a tongue, it should be by two or at the most three [at a time], and each in turn, and one must interpret [in correlation to each tongue spoken]; 28 but if there is no interpreter, he must keep silent in the church; and let him speak to himself and to God." (1 Corinthians 14:27-28. Square brackets by author for added clarity.)

As described above, in both applications, **Prophecy** and **Tongues** is directed to men. And, as required, there is order, clarity, and understanding for each message given.

But if the congregation speaks in **Tongues** at the same time *when it is not directed to God*, no one is edified. It is therefore out of order and produces confusion.

The corporate weight of Scripture in its many repetitive references abundantly supports the Baptism of the Holy Spirit as relevant and essential for all Christians throughout the entire church age, even up to the time of Jesus' return. Therefore, let us not withdraw from the

The Corinthian Confusion

Holy Spirit's gifts, nor suppress His works. Rather, let us use His gifts decently and in order according to the instructions in God's Word.

CHAPTER 29
HOW TO RECEIVE THE BAPTISM OF THE HOLY SPIRIT
"Eliminating Presumption and Confusion"

There is no standardized method for receiving the Baptism of the Holy Spirit. In fact, throughout the New Testament, there are various examples where He bestows His gift in different ways.

On the day of Pentecost, He suddenly baptized one hundred twenty people at the same time. On this particular occasion, the appearance of fire (looking like cloven tongues) appeared on their heads and they began speaking in **The Gift of Tongues**.

My good friend, Mel Tari, whom the Lord used mightily in the Indonesian revival of the early 70s and continues to this very day, saw the dead raised along with regeneration miracles where food multiplied. He walked on water to get to a remote hidden village, saw water changed to wine on six occasions where they wanted to share in the Holy Communion, and hosts of other such miracles as recorded in the Bible.[26] He told me that the revival began in his nation exactly as the Holy Spirit showed Himself on the day of Pentecost. Mel told me that a mighty wind came into their church and cloven tongues of fire rested upon those who were praying for revival in their nation. I would not be surprised if the Holy Spirit does the same again in various places throughout the world in the coming world-wide revival.

After explaining the Baptism of the Holy Spirit in Samaria, (Acts 8:5-17) Peter and John laid hands on the Samaritans and the Samaritans received His gift.

At Cornelius' house, Peter was telling them about Jesus (Acts 10:44). while he was speaking, the Holy Spirit imparted His gift to them

---

[26] Tari, Mel. 1972. *Like a Mighty Wind*. Creation House.

How To Receive His Gift

without anyone laying hands on them or explaining the Baptism. They suddenly began speaking in **The Gift of Tongues** and **Prophesying**.

Paul discovered twelve disciples in Ephesus (Acts 19:1-7) who never heard that the Holy Spirit even existed. Since they never heard of Him when Paul mentioned it, it is implied that Paul explained the Holy Spirit's gift to them.

After Paul water baptized them into Jesus, he laid his hands on them and they received the Baptism of the Holy Spirit. Paul heard them speaking in **The Gift of Tongues** and **Prophesying**. In fact, this was similar to the Samaritans receiving the Holy Spirit's Baptism: they were first taught, and then they received the Holy Spirit's gift by the laying on of hands.

I have been in meetings in Africa where I have seen hundreds of people receive the Baptism of the Holy Spirit at the same time without anyone laying hands on them.

Water Baptism
In two accounts (Samaria and the twelve disciples in Ephesus), water baptism was given *before* the Baptism of the Holy Spirit. At Cornelius' house, water baptism was given *after* the Baptism of the Holy Spirit. Accordingly, there is no specific order of what comes first: water baptism or the Holy Spirit's Baptism. His Baptism can be given before or after water baptism, but NEVER before salvation.

Laying on of Hands
There is no specific method to receive the Holy Spirit's Baptism, whether by the laying on of hands, or simply praying for His gift to come upon a person. In Samaria, Peter and John laid hands on them; in Cornelius' house, no one laid hands on them.

A Gift Cannot Be Earned
On the day of Pentecost, Peter explained to thousands of people standing before him that the Baptism of the Holy Spirit was a gift:

> "And Peter said to them, "Repent [change your old way of thinking, turn from your sinful ways, accept and follow Jesus as the Messiah] and be baptized, each of you, in the name of Jesus Christ because of the forgiveness of your sins; and you will receive the gift of the Holy Spirit." (Acts 2:38. Square brackets by author for added clarity.)

How To Receive His Gift

Let's Make This Personal

A gift cannot be earned, nor is it rewarded for the performance of good behavior. As such, if you feel you must *earn* His Gift in any way at all, or meet a list of "pre-qualifiers" other than salvation, immediately abandon that idea.

There is no record of anyone having to confess their sins before the Holy Spirit bestowed His gift upon them. And while it is true that each of us need to live a life of holiness, the truth is, no one has ever fully confessed all their sins even when they try to do so. Accordingly, when receiving the Baptism of the Spirit, you must receive His gift on the credibility of the cleansing blood of Jesus—nothing else. Only His blood makes you a clean and holy vessel unto the Father. Nothing more is required.

It is *only* by the power of Jesus' cleansing blood that the Holy Spirit dwells in you. If the blood of Christ did not COMPLETELY and CONTINUALLY cleanse you, the Holy Spirit could not permanently remain in you.

Except You Are As a Child

Unlike most adults, a child easily believes and receives without the struggle of pride, analysis, and unbelief. Children are simplistic in their beliefs and they easily receive the truth. In all things pertaining to God's Kingdom, in whatever you seek, you must approach the Lord in humility and trust. On this cause, Jesus said:

> "I assure you and most solemnly say to you, whoever does not receive and welcome the kingdom of God like a child will not enter it at all." (Mark 10:15)

Again, when asking for the Baptism of the Holy Spirit, ask in humility. Trust Him that He will do exactly what He promised in His Word. In other words, simply receive.

Settle the fact that the Blood of Christ has purified you. Then, by faith in God's Word, know that in your Father's eyes you are completely clean. After that, simply receive the Holy Spirit's gift without any conditions attached to the receiving.

Peter instructed the Jews that were gathered on the day of Pentecost to repent. *Repent*, in this context, was to turn to Jesus and be forgiven of their sins. In fact, the word repent means to *stop and turn the other*

How To Receive His Gift

way. Unless they received Jesus as their Savior, they could not receive the Holy Spirit's gift. Cleansing by the blood of Jesus had to occur first.

> "Peter replied, "Repent and be baptized, every one of you, in the name of Jesus Christ for the forgiveness of your sins. And you will receive the gift of the Holy Spirit. 39 For the promise is for you and your children and for all who are far off, as many as the Lord our God will call to Himself." (Acts 2:38-39)

Yielding to the Holy Spirit

Frequently, I meet people that have *preconceived ideas* as to how the Holy Spirit will impart His gift. Some think His power will overcome them and they will fall to the ground and suddenly start speaking in **Tongues**. This is not how the Holy Spirit operates! In any case, eliminate all presumption and preset opinions as to how the Holy Spirit will impart His gift to you and simply receive. In most cases, it is somewhat uneventful, but nonetheless, joyous.

Your Body

You are the steward of your body, but you are not the owner. God made you. All souls belong to Him (Ezekiel 18:4). But not until you receive Jesus as your Savior are you the Heavenly Father's covenant <u>child</u>. Once you receive Jesus Christ, the Blood of Jesus cleanses you and your body becomes the Holy Spirit's temple.

> "Do you not know that your body is a temple of the Holy Spirit who is within you, whom you have [received as a gift] from God, and that you are not your own [property]?" (1 Corinthians 6:19. Square brackets by author for added clarity.)

Your personal "will" is sacred to the Holy Spirit. As such, He will not overpower you. A demon, however routinely violates the will of its host.

Some people that ask for the Holy Spirit's Baptism assume He will come upon them with an overwhelming force, take over their tongue, and they will suddenly start speaking as if they have no control. We see this disgusting effect in the occult, but this is NOT the conduct of the Holy Spirit.

How To Receive His Gift

In order for you to receive the Holy Spirit's Baptism with the proof of speaking in **Tongues**, you must yield to Him. The same bodily functions that are used to speak in your natural language, is the same function that the Holy Spirit uses to speak in **Tongues** through you.

To speak, the Holy Spirit uses your lips, tongue, vocal cords, and air in your lungs. There is one difference, however: When you speak in **Tongues**, the Spirit speaks *through* your spirit, not your soul (the mind, emotions, will, and intelligence). For this reason, your mind will most generally reject your **Tongues** because it makes no sense to your intellect.

There are actual electroencephalograph readings (EEG) of the brain's activity that shows people praying in their natural language as compared to their prayers spoken in **Tongues** by the Holy Spirit. When praying natural prayers, the area of the brain used to speak shows normal activity. But when the same person speaks in **Tongues**, scientists were baffled as to the brain's activity![27] We know by Scripture that **Tongues** comes through the spirit of the person *by the Holy Spirit in them*.

When wanting to receive the Holy Spirit's Baptism, people often close their mouth because they assume He will come upon them and suddenly they will start talking in **Tongues**. Nothing is further from the truth. The Holy Spirit respects your will. Accordingly, He requires your cooperation by yielding to Him when speaking in **Tongues**.

Fear

Satan uses fear-based tactics to turn people away from the Holy Spirit's Baptism. One such ploy is the despicable idea that a person speaking in **Tongues** could be the voice of a demon. This hideous tactic is commonly promoted by those who oppose the Holy Spirit's Baptism. To this presumption, the Lord gives us a promise in His Word:

> "What father among you, if his son asks for a fish, will give him a snake instead of a fish? 12 Or if he asks for an egg, will give him a scorpion? 13 If you, then, being evil [that is, sinful by nature], know how to give good gifts to your children, how much more will your Heavenly Father

---

[27] https://www.nytimes.com/2006/11/07/health/07brain.html

How To Receive His Gift

give the Holy Spirit to those who ask and continue to ask Him!" (Luke 11:11-13. Square brackets by author for added clarity.)

The Heavenly Father assures you in His Word that no foul spirit can supplant the Holy Spirit. Those who suggest that a demon spirit could come upon a Christian that is seeking the Holy Spirit's gift, offends the integrity of our Heavenly Father and His faithful love for us. His promise is for all Christians to be given power through the Baptism of the Holy Spirit—if they will ask of Him.

One Prayer at a Time

When people ask for the Holy Spirit's Baptism, they pray in their natural language. And while praying, they presume that the Holy Spirit will interrupt their natural prayer language and suddenly they will speak in **Tongues**.

There is nothing wrong with initially praying in one's natural prayer language when starting out. However, there comes the moment when speaking in the natural language must stop and speaking the spiritual language begins. In other words, you cannot speak in your natural prayer language and your spiritual language (**The Gift of Tongues**) at the same time. No. You must yield to the gentleness of the Holy Spirit who respects your will. You must choose to stop praying in your natural language in order to speak in **Tongues**.

What Will The Gift of Tongues Sound Like?

There are many languages in the world. One thing common to ALL languages is this: they are composed of syllables, accents, tones, vowels, and in some instances, such as the language of the Khoisan people in Southwest Africa, non-verbal clicking sounds.

On the day of Pentecost, some thought the Apostles were babbling drunk men until Peter explained what was happening. Obviously, the Jews from various regions heard their own language being spoken, but they also heard the Apostles speak other languages of which the same onlookers did not understand. For that reason, to those who did not understand them, it sounded like babbling.

Of no surprise, your soul contributes *nothing* when you speak in the supernatural language of **Tongues**. Therefore, the soul cannot comprehend what is being said because **The Gift of Tongues** is not formulated through the natural process of thought and articulation. Accordingly, the soul reacts with unbelief!

How To Receive His Gift

An important key to receiving the Baptism of the Holy Spirit with the proof of speaking in **Tongues**, is to let the syllables, accents, tones, and sounds simply flow from your mouth. These are words formed by the Holy Spirit according to the language He gives you. It is that simple—like a child. Furthermore, when you first start speaking in **Tongues**, it seems as nothing more than babbling.

It reminds me of the tongue-twister games I often played with my children when they were young and started pronouncing words and holding conversation. I would tell them to say, "aluminum, molybdenum, and feminine"—all in one sentence. It was quite comical to hear them mumble-the-jungle of approximate syllables and vowels.

Well, **The Gift of Tongues** can initially sound just as strange. Immediately, your dignified soul rushes to the analysis and tells you it is NOT from the Holy Spirit. If you yield to such uncertainty through doubt and fear, it will divert you from receiving the Holy Spirit's gift. I encourage you, therefore, to continue praying in your new language until it flows by the Holy Spirit's leading.

In My Private Space

Sometimes when well-meaning Christians are praying for a person to be Baptized in the Holy Spirit, the one being prayed for can feel overwhelmed and ganged upon. When this happens, I often take the brother or sister aside and tell them to relax. The Holy Spirit never pressures anyone to receive His gift. Conversely, this is not a test of one's faith, or a test of Christian character. It is simply receiving His gift in faith.

In that regard, people sometimes need to be ALONE with the Lord in order to receive from Him. I personally know many Christians who received the Holy Spirit's gift while at home without the distractions, pressure, or being spotlighted to receive.

If that scenario applies to you, then when you are alone with no one around, ask for His gift. Simply open your mouth, and in faith let the syllables of your prayer language flow. He is there giving you His gift.

STORY:
I was teaching a School of Ministry for pastors and church leaders in Monrovia, Liberia in the West Africa region. Two hundred fifteen pastors from various denominations were present, including many mainline church leaders. I was teaching a specific type of prayer for

How To Receive His Gift

breaking demonic strongholds. This type of prayer emphasizes **The Gift of Tongues** which is key in breaking the control of spiritual forces that spans across multiple generations, particularly the dark powers used by witch-doctors that hold entire villages and regions in fear.

I explained the vital importance of God's power when dealing with demonic spirits that influence regions and territories. After completing this part of the lesson, I asked how many pastors were Baptized in the Holy Spirit.

Nearly two hundred pastors had NEVER received the Baptism of the Spirit, and 100% of the twelve Spirit-filled pastors were ignorant as to how the gifts of the Holy Spirit operated. Consequently, it was futile to move forward with my teaching on the subject of breaking demonic strongholds. I stopped and taught on the Scriptural proof of this vital necessity for power.

I explained the truth according to Scripture and then asked them if they wanted this power. They unanimously agreed. Keep in mind, many of the pastors were graduates from formal seminaries and had their various levels of degrees, some of them with PhDs.

I then explained how to receive the Holy Spirit's gift. I asked those who were Baptized in the Spirit to gather around those seeking His gift and pray for them. After an intense but brief time of fervent prayer, EVERYONE received the Baptism of the Holy Spirit and the entire place exploded in joyous praises.

♦ ♦ ♦ ♦

Exercise the Gift!

After you receive the Baptism of the Spirit with the evidence of speaking in **Tongues**, you must FREQUENTLY use the gift for personal edification as explained in 1st Corinthians 14:2-4 and Jude 1:20. It is very important that you acquaint yourself with His gift as soon as possible in order to know how the Holy Spirit speaks through your spirit.

Satan Changes Strategies

Remember, Satan has only three agendas: to kill, STEAL, and destroy. Since he could not stop you from receiving the Baptism of the Holy Spirit, he then changes strategies *after* you receive it. Satan needs to keep you from using it through apathy, complacency, and lethargy. Don't let him steal this from you by such tactics. Do not set the gift

How To Receive His Gift

aside. You need to experience the Holy Spirit's gift and how you can witness about Jesus by the power through His gift.

Charismatic Christians / Spirit-filled Christians

As previously explained, Neo-Pentecostal churches are the gathering places of Charismatic Christians. Additionally, Charismatic Christians are in every mainline denomination throughout the world. Therefore, we need to know what defines a Charismatic Christian.

The phrase "Charismatic Christian" is not a term found in Scripture. Nonetheless, it is commonly used as a description for the sake of clarity. The term defines those who received the Baptism of the Holy Spirit but have little or nothing to do with the power that He gave them.

Charismatic Christians are typically indifferent to the Holy Spirit's gifts. They are content to remain in churches that prohibit or altogether suppress the works of the Holy Spirit.

Typically, Charismatic Christians have no stewardship of the gift which the Lord gave them.

> "Just as each one of you has received a special gift [a spiritual talent, an ability graciously given by God], <u>employ it in serving one another as [is appropriate for] good stewards</u> of God's multi-faceted grace [faithfully using the diverse, varied gifts and abilities granted to Christians by God's unmerited favor]." (1 Peter 4:10, Amplified Bible. Square brackets and underline by author for added clarity.)

Charismatic Christians seldom ever, or never, speak in **The Gift of Tongues** to build themselves up on their most holy faith (Jude 1:20). Through ignorance, indifference, apathy, and complacency, they remain largely unacquainted with the Holy Spirit's leading, impressions, and operations.

> "With all prayer and petition pray [with specific requests] at all times [on every occasion and in every season] in the Spirit, and with this in view, stay alert with all perseverance and petition [interceding in prayer] for all God's people." (Ephesians 6:18, Amplified Bible. Square brackets by author for added clarity.)

How To Receive His Gift

Charismatic Christians are completely indifferent about the Lord's power. They choose to remain in churches that oppose or suppress the Holy Spirit's outward manifestations. Consequently, they are little more than non-enthusiastic listeners of God's Word according to the parable of the three types of stewards:

"For it is just like a man about to go on a journey, who called his own slaves and entrusted his possessions to them. 15 To one he gave five talents, to another, two, and to another, one, each according to his own ability; and he went on his journey. 16 The one who had received the five talents immediately went and did business with them, and earned five more talents. 17 In the same way the one who had received the two talents earned two more. 18 But he who received the one talent went away and dug a hole in the ground, and hid his master's money. 19 Now after a long time the master of those slaves came and settled accounts with them. 20 The one who had received the five talents came up and brought five more talents, saying, 'Master, you entrusted five talents to me. See, I have earned five more talents.' 21 His master said to him, 'Well done, good and faithful slave. You were faithful with a few things, I will put you in charge of many things; enter the joy of your master.' 22 Also the one who had received the two talents came up and said, 'Master, you entrusted two talents to me. See, I have earned two more talents.' 23 His master said to him, 'Well done, good and faithful slave. You were faithful with a few things, I will put you in charge of many things; enter the joy of your master.' 24 Now the one who had received the one talent also came up and said, 'Master, I knew you to be a hard man, reaping where you did not sow, and gathering where you did not scatter seed. 25 And I was afraid, so I went away and hid your talent in the ground. See, you still have what is yours.' 26 But his master answered and said to him, 'You worthless, lazy slave! Did you know that I reap where I did not sow, and gather where I did not scatter seed? 27 Then you ought to have put my money in the bank, and upon my arrival I would have received my money back with interest. 28 Therefore: take the talent away from him, and give it to the one who has the ten talents.' 29 For to everyone who has, more shall be given, and he will have an abundance; but from the one who does not have, even what he does have shall be taken away. 30 And throw the worthless slave into the outer darkness; in that place there will be weeping and gnashing of teeth."

It is wise to remember that the Baptism of the Holy Spirit is given to Believers for three primary purposes:

(1) To build up and edify the Body of Christ (1 Corinthians 14:12).
(2) To build up and edify one's personal faith (Jude 1:20).
(3) To evangelize the world by the power of His Spirit with signs, wonders, and miracles (Mark16:20).

To Whom Much is Given, Much is Required

In whatever the Lord gives, He requires stewardship. Accordingly, the Baptism of the Holy Spirit is not simply a novel experience with the Lord. The Holy Spirit's gift comes with accountability.

> "From everyone who has been given much, much will be required; and to whom they entrusted much, of him they will ask all the more." (Luke 12:48b)

> "As each one has received a special gift, employ it in serving one another as good stewards of the manifold grace of God." (1 Peter 4:10)

A significant difference between Spirit-filled Christians that attend Spirit-filled churches, and Charismatic Christians that attend non-Spirit-filled churches, is one's sense of personal responsibility toward the Gospel.

Spirit-filled congregations expect the Holy Spirit to operate through any Spirit-filled Believer for the good of all. By earnest expectation, He performs His works, be they **Healing**, **Prophecy**, **Words of Knowledge**, **Words of Wisdom**, or any of the nine gifts of the Holy Spirit.

In non-Spirit-filled churches, there is no expectation for any individual to be used of God. Nor is any person permitted to be used by the Holy Spirit except those who are assigned to specific duties such as ushering, maintenance, etc.

How To Receive His Gift

Christians of non-Spirit-filled churches merely sit and listen with no expectation of the Lord doing anything in the supernatural. Such types of churches are pulpit-focused where the emphasis is centered exclusively on the pastor and his personality. It is a powerless academic word-only teaching that is often skewed with error. This is NOT the model which the Holy Spirit instructed us through the Apostle Paul:

> "And there are varieties of effects, but the same God who works all things in all persons. But to each one is given the manifestation of the Spirit for the common good (1 Corinthians 12:6-7).
>
> For you can all prophesy one by one, so that all may learn and all may be exhorted." (1 Corinthians 14:31).

The most powerful churches are those that operate in *body ministry* rather than pastor-pulpit-focused ministry. This is not to suggest that the pastor is minimized or that he should not preach from the pulpit. Rather, a Spirit-filled pastor will recognize and yield to the spontaneous unction of the Holy Spirit as God moves throughout the congregation.

A body-ministry church is what the early church modeled. In such types of churches, the members understand how the Holy Spirit uniquely distributes His gifts among them from one service to the next. In this manner, each service is freshly anointed according to how the Holy Spirit leads. This is what makes church exciting, powerful, and fresh. It is when man and his traditions get out of the way. Thus, when the people yield to the Holy Spirit according to what He is doing at any given moment, His manifest glory produces salvations, healings, miracles, deliverances, and encouragement.

His Nine Gifts

CHAPTER 30
THE GIFTS OF THE HOLY SPIRIT
"What They Are and What They Are Not"

"There are varieties of effects, but the same God who works all things in all persons. 7 But to each one is given the manifestation of the Spirit for the common good. 8 For to one is given the word of wisdom through the Spirit, and to another the word of knowledge according to the same Spirit; 9 to another faith by the same Spirit, and to another gifts of Healing by the one Spirit, 10 and to another the effecting of Miracles, and to another prophecy, and to another the discerning of spirits, to another various kinds of Tongues, and to another the interpretation of Tongues." (1 Corinthians 12:6-10)

♦♦♦♦

As noted above, there are nine gifts of the Holy Spirit listed in 1 Corinthians 12: 6-10. In this chapter, I will list the gifts and define each one according to Scripture. In contrast, I will also show how those who oppose the Baptism of the Holy Spirit must change the Scriptural definition to fit their Cessationist doctrine.

It is important to note that even among the Cessationists, there is no standardized definition of the Holy Spirit's gifts. Cessationist Theology ranges from the total denial of the gifts altogether, to a modified version in Scripture, depending on who is doing the preaching.

The gifts of the Holy Spirit are succinctly demonstrated by Jesus and the Apostles throughout the New Testament. This leave Cessationists and Neo-Pentecostals in a conundrum. If Cessationists and Neo-Pentecostals follow the model of Scripture, they must admit their doctrines are wrong. This, in turn, blows holes through their Cessationist Theology.

Realizing that their doctrine is more important to them than the immutable Word of God, they must define the Holy Spirit's gifts to meet the standard of their philosophy and logic-based reasonings. Despite the straining and often absurd definitions, their modified explanation is like driving square pegs into round holes. Try as they will, the network of Scripture simply does not support their claims.

For example, when Jesus spoke to the woman at the well, He told her she had five husbands, and that the one she was currently living with was not her husband (John 4:18). Jesus knew this by **The Word of Knowledge**.

Second, **Healings**, **Miracles**, and deliverances abounded in Jesus' ministry and those of the Apostles. **Prophecy** is mentioned with Phillip's seven daughters as well as others who were Baptized in the Spirit such as the twelve men in Ephesus that spoke in **Tongues** and **Prophesied** (Acts 19:6).

Paul spoke by **Prophecy** concerning the Endtimes. Agabus was considered a prophet who warned Paul not to enter Jerusalem, and Peter spoke by prophecy about the end of the age, not to mention the Apostle John's entire Book of Revelation.

Tongues and **The Interpretation of Tongues** was common *in* the church of Corinth as in other churches. **The Discerning of Spirits** is mentioned in the lives of Paul, John, and Peter, as well as those having visions and dreams as recorded in Joel's prophecy.

The point is this: Those who object or stifle the Holy Spirit's gifts, have no specific bright line; no specific event of demarcation; and nothing to definitively stand on as to when, in their minds, the Holy Spirit's gifts ceased operating. By misassociation and mispairing of unrelated factors and nonrelevant issues apart from Scripture, their error is based on three false premises: (1) the church is now established; (2) the death of the last Apostle; and (3) the Bible now printed in most major languages.

The church was fully established by 100 AD; John died in 100 AD; and the printing press was invented in 1450 AD. None of these factors have any association whatsoever to the Holy Spirit's gifts for the modern church. Accordingly, the entire platform of Cessationist Theology is based on man's *natural logic-based* reasoning as strained through Calvin's subjective experiences for which there is no Scriptural support.

His Nine Gifts

Starting from John Calvin, Cessationist Theology teaches a network of erroneous beliefs regarding the Holy Spirit's gifts. Such beliefs have been repetitively spoken from generation to generation until it is accepted as truth.

As compared to the Foundation Apostle's doctrines, Calvin's theology is relatively new to the Body of Christ. His *opinions* was birthed during the Sardis Church which was approximately four hundred sixty years ago. This leaves Calvinism as a relatively new and different belief as compared to the over one thousand five hundred years of the Apostle's teachings which were fully established before John died of natural causes.

Cessationist Theology teaches a distorted version of Paul's instructions regarding the Holy Spirit's gifts. This requires that they altogether ignore the demonstrations of the Holy Spirits gifts found in Scripture, and then apply a new and different definition to them. This is nothing less than dark logic, a doctrine of demons that oversteps the Scripture.

Paul promoted the Baptism of the Holy Spirit, but Calvin opposed it. Calvin taught that the Baptism of the Holy Spirit was no longer given by God after the death of the Apostle John.

What should have Calvin done with the detailed explanations of Paul's writing regarding the Holy Spirit's gifts? He should have taught them according to Scripture. Instead, Calvin distorted them to fit the scheme of his theology.

Imagine an unsaved person trying to explain salvation while rejecting Jesus Christ. In the same way, Calvin's rejection of the Holy Spirit's Baptism is defined according to his personal experience and his logic-based reasonings. His writings modified the Scriptures to fit his Cessationist doctrines. Consequently, Calvin's *intellectual and analytical view* about the Holy Spirit's Baptism is a desperate far reaching attempt to establish what Scripture cannot support. The danger of his theology is that it appeals to the reason and logic of uninformed people.

The Nine Gifts of the Holy Spirit

The Holy Spirit's gifts, according to their precise description in Scripture, is found in 1st Corinthians 12:8-10 as follows:

His Nine Gifts

The Word of Wisdom
The Word of Knowledge
Faith
Gifts of Healing
Miracles
Prophecy
Discerning of Spirits
The Gift of Tongues
Interpretation of Tongues

Lesser informed people claim that the Holy Spirit's gifts are listed in the order of importance and prestige. Each gift, as previously stated, stands in its unique purpose and use. However, nothing in scripture supports this assumption. Nonetheless, I have listed them according to how they are listed in Scripture. It is important, therefore, that careful consideration is applied to the precise wording of Paul's instructions which were given to him by the Holy Spirit.

Contrasting Definitions of the Holy Spirit's Gifts

The Gift of Wisdom

AN OPPOSITIONIST'S FALSE DEFINITION: This gift gives one the ability to make choices and assign leadership according to God's will. Individuals with this gift have the ability to make wise decisions and to advise others similarly.

THE SCRIPTURAL DEFINITION: Many call it the "gift" of wisdom. This is improper. Scripture describes this gift as *The **WORD** of* **Wisdom**.

The Word of Wisdom is when the Holy Spirit reveals something that will occur in the future involving a person's life. It is similar, in a sense, to **Prophecy** in foretelling, but this gift is almost always paired with **The Word of Knowledge** where **Prophecy** generally stands alone.

An example of this gift is when Agabus told the Apostle Paul what would become of him if he set foot in Jerusalem (Acts 21:4 and Acts 21:10-13).

The Gift of Knowledge

AN OPPOSITIONIST'S FALSE DEFINITION: This is the Spirit's gift that gives a person the ability to comprehensively understand a spiritual issue or circumstance. People with this gift have a greater understanding of God's will and ways, both personally and through Scripture.

Supernaturally, they can discern truths about spiritual matters in order to teach or direct the church.

THE SCRIPTURAL DEFINITION: This is not properly called the "Gift" of Knowledge. It is called, **The <u>WORD</u> of Knowledge**. The false definition implies that one is given the ability by *learning* God's will.

The truth is, **The WORD of Knowledge** is when a person, (operating under the influence of this gift), speaks what God has shown them concerning facts or circumstances that are past or present in a person's life. The person speaking by the Holy Spirit's inspiration would have no previous natural knowledge of what is being said.

For instance, we see Jesus operating in this gift when He encountered the woman at the well (John 4:1-44). He told her to go and get her husband:

> "Jesus said to her, "Go call your husband and come back." 17 The woman answered and said to him, "I do not have a husband." Jesus answered her, "You are right in saying, 'I do not have a husband.' 18 For you have had five husbands, and the one you have now is not your husband. What you have said is true." (John 4:16-18)

Jesus spoke by the Holy Spirit according to **The Word of Knowledge** when He told her the exact status of her relationship, both in her past and her present. When He spoke such to her, she was convinced Jesus was operating by the Spirit of God.

EXAMPLE:
I was speaking in church one time when the Lord stopped me cold and focused my attention on a young man at the back of the church. I said to him, "If you don't stop doing what you are doing right now, you are going to get your mail at a different address for a long time."

A month later he was arrested by federal DEA agents for dealing heavy narcotic drugs. He was ultimately sentenced to ten years in federal prison. As of the date of this book, the young man just got out of prison after ten years.

When I spoke the word to him, it was by **The Word of Knowledge**. This proved to him that God was warning him about his drug dealing and He wanted to spare him the agony of its consequences if he would repent. The two gifts coupled: **The Word of Knowledge** and **The Word of Wisdom**.

The Word of Knowledge addressed the current issue in his life, and **The Word of Wisdom** told him the future consequence if he didn't repent. Both gifts blended as one word to him.

The Gift of Faith

AN OPPOSITIONIST'S FALSE DEFINITION: This is the gift to trust God and inspire others to trust God, no matter the conditions.

THE SCRIPTURAL DEFINITION: The Scripture simply lists this as **Faith,** nonetheless it is aptly named **The Gift of Faith**. The Holy Spirit gives the substance of faith as an added *special endowment* that is joined to one's resident faith that he or she already possesses (Romans 12:3). When this gift is joined to one's *resident faith*, it gives him or her the ability to do what the Lord instructs to be done for a specific event or purpose, especially during ministry operations.

In Matthew 14:22-33, Peter sees Jesus walking on the water. Peter calls out to Him and says, "Lord, if it is You, command me to come to You on the water."

Peter was an experienced fisherman and knew the temperament of the sea. But when Jesus sent him a personal Word (Rhema) to come to Him by walking on the water, **The Gift of Faith** joined with Peter's resident faith. Suddenly, an endowment of **Faith** was given to him by the Holy Spirit. This displaced Peter's natural knowledge, logic, and common sense with a supernatural confidence of knowing that he could do the impossible. He climbed over the boat, in the night, in the storm, and walked on the water.

At one point while he was walking, he looked around. Suddenly, he reembraced his natural mindset. As a result, logic and fear displaced the operation of **Faith**. In brief, he changed from the supernatural operation of **Faith** to a natural mindset and began sinking. However, the Lord was right there to rescue him and together they walked back to the boat.

As shown in Peter's example, the special endowment of **Faith** is also displayed when Jesus sent the disciples to raise the dead, cleanse the lepers, heal the sick, preach the kingdom, and cast out demons. They were endowed with added **Faith** for a specific time and function to perform **Healings** and **Miracles**. This was made possible when the Holy Spirit's endowment of **Faith** was added to their faith and they performed the works of the Father's Kingdom.

The Gift of Healing

AN OPPOSITIONIST'S FALSE DEFINITION: This gift is the wondrous gift to use God's healing power to cure a person who is ill, wounded, or suffering. God works through a person with this gift to heal and restore people's bodies, minds, and emotions. This person has a level of faith to believe God for healing in any situation and is willing to try even non-conventional methods if God so leads.

THE SCRIPTURAL DEFINITION: While the false definition says "Gift of Healing", the actual reading in Scripture says, **Gifts of Healing**, which is in the plural, not the singular. **Healing** can occur in various ways. However, this gift differs in that it is specific to **Healing**. Even though **The Gift of Miracles** can include **Healing**, it is not limited to **Healing** alone.

Using the plural form of **Gifts Of Healing**, we see various means of **Healing** such as cloths anointed with oil which were sent to the sick and the demon possessed. Those who received them were healed and demons left their bodies (Acts 19:11-12). In other instances, Peter's shadow passed across people and they were healed (Acts 5:15). In James 5:14-15, the sick are anointed with oil, their sins are forgiven, and they are healed. Further, Jesus applied various means for healing: using only His spoken Word; the use of mud; and even touching a man's tongue with (Jesus') saliva.

In consideration of the various ways and means that **Healings** occur, the sense of this comes in two forms: some people are healed over the process of time; others are healed instantly. Instant **Healings** can be considered as **Miracles** just as gradual **Healings** can be considered as **Miracles**.

The Gift of Miracles

AN OPPOSITIONIST'S FALSE DEFINITION: This is the gift to display signs and miracles that give credibility. A person with this gift can be used by God to do any type of creative miracle, from using physical strength to picking up a car, to regenerating a body part, to affecting the weather. There is no limit to what God can do, and the person with this spiritual gift has the faith to believe God for anything.

His Nine Gifts

THE SCRIPTURAL DEFINITION: This gift is described simply as **Miracles**. It is incorrect to assume that a person *possesses any gift* of the Holy Spirit to use at their own will. Rather, the Holy Spirit uses a Believer *at any given moment for a purpose* to work His gift through them. **Miracles**, in this sense, is expressed through the vessel that the Holy Spirit uses for that particular occasion or purpose. Coupled with this gift is **The Gift of Faith**. In fact, **The Gift of Faith** is commonly coupled with the other gifts.

When the **Miracle** is completed, the person whom the Lord used simply continues on without necessarily retaining the gift in its operation. In other words, no one continually possesses any gift of the Spirit to use at their own choosing except **Tongues for Personal Edification**. For example, there is only one occasion when Peter walked on water. Scripture never records that miracle happening with him anytime later in his life.

The Gift of Prophecy

AN OPPOSITIONIST'S FALSE DEFINITION: This is the gift to declare a message from God. Believers with the **Gift Of Prophecy** do not necessarily tell the future as much as they build up, encourage, and direct the church body. They help the church understand the heart and desires of God, and urge the church to wholeheartedly pursue Him and His righteousness.

THE SCRIPTURAL DEFINITION[28]: Contrary to the oppositionist's false definition of this gift, **Prophecy** is commonly used to call out events in the future, and or, speak the present-tense mind of God. As such, there are two different applications of **The Gift of Prophecy**: (1) forthtelling and (2) foretelling.

Prophecy by *Forthtelling* is speaking by the present tense mind of the Lord under the Holy Spirit's inspiration. We see this type of **Prophecy** when a person speaks a message in church...IF...they are speaking under the Rhema inspiration of the Holy Spirit, that is, speaking under the mantle of **Prophecy** according to the present-tense mind of the Lord. (I explain the Rhema starting on page 202.)

---

[28] Prophesy, prophecy, and prophesying: To prophesy is to speak the prophecy. Prophesying is the present tense act of speaking prophecy.

His Nine Gifts

Prophecy by *foretelling* is declaring events that yet to occur in the future. This can be directed to an individual or in reference to any event. Agabus, for example, was a prophet in the New Testament who foretold of a famine that would occur in that area of the world (Acts 11:28).

Another form of **Prophecy**, especially when one speaks in the present-tense of God's mind, is to edify (build-up); exhort (prompt to do something); and comfort (by giving assurance).

People often confuse **The Gift of Prophecy** with two similar gifts: **The Word of Knowledge** and **The Word of Wisdom**. Usually, **The Word of Knowledge** and **The Word of Wisdom** is directed toward individuals. By contrast, **The Gift of Prophecy** is generally, but not exclusively, directed to people or events in general.

The Gift of Discerning Spirits

AN OPPOSITIONIST'S FALSE DEFINITION: This is the gift to recognize whether or not something is truly from God or in accordance with righteousness. This gift is also referred to as the ability to *distinguish between spirits*. People with this gift have the ability to discern whether a situation, person, or event is good or evil, right or wrong, Heavenly or demonic. This gift is important because it can help protect God's people and lead them in the right direction.

THE SCRIPTURAL DEFINITION: **The Gift of Discerning of Spirits** is *not* human intuition, nor is it something like a feeling, or a sense of uneasiness. In other words, it is not when a person senses something is wrong, or when they sense a person has a wrong spirit. That type of uneasiness might be when the Holy Spirit witnesses to our spirit that something is not right, but it is NOT **The Discerning of Spirits**.

The Discerning of Spirits is when the Holy Spirit enables a person to hear or see into the spiritual realm so vividly that it seems it is the natural realm. In such instances, people might see angels, or demonic spirits, or hear something, even the audible voice of the Lord, or an angel. At the same time, others around them will see nothing or hear nothing.

When people operate in this gift, momentarily as it might seem, they are *in the spiritual dimension* and actually see appearances of things that are impossible to see using the natural senses.

His Nine Gifts

Often times, when the Holy Spirit brings a person into this gift, what they see is so tangible and real that they wonder if they are dreaming or if they are actually experiencing the event.

When a person experiences an "eyes-open-vision" it is actually the operation of **The Discerning of Spirits**. Two such incidents happened to Peter. One incident was when he was in prison and an angel appeared to him. The angel woke him up, instructed him to put on his cloak, and then follow him out of the prison (Acts 12:5-17).

What happened to Peter was so vivid, real, and supernatural that at first he was unsure if he was dreaming. The locked gates of the prison automatically opened as Peter and the angel approached them. Moreover, they walked past the guards who saw nothing at all.

Paul's experience, by his own description, tells how **The Discerning of Spirits** operated in his life when he was taken to Heaven:

> "And I know how such a man--whether in the body or apart from the body I do not know, God knows-,4 was caught up into Paradise and heard inexpressible words, which a man is not permitted to speak."
> (2 Corinthians 12:3-4)

Peter's second event occurred at Simon the Tanner's house in Joppa (Acts 10:13). Peter saw a blanket lowered from Heaven that was filled with unclean food and he heard a voice saying, "Get up Peter, kill and eat." This happened three times and Peter replied that he had never eaten anything unclean. Finally, the Lord said to him, "What God has cleansed, no longer consider unholy."

Regarding Peter's two events, he saw into the supernatural and heard the voice of an angel. In the second event, He heard the voice of God. No one else heard or saw anything. This was by **The Gift of Discerning of Spirits**—the ability to see into the 4th dimension beyond the ability of his natural senses.

Again, this is not when a person claims to know or sense what is operating in a person, or if a person is deceived or is troubled. That would be what we humorously describe as the gift of suspicion.

Specific to this gift, faith is not required. It is the only gift whereby a person suddenly experiences the spiritual realm as if being ushered into it. The Apostle John wrote the entire Book of Revelation under the operation of this gift. Five times he said he was in the Spirit...or conversely, the **Discerning of Spirits** was in operation which enabled him to hear and see what he wrote down.

The Gift of Tongues

AN OPPOSITIONIST'S FALSE DEFINITION: This is the ability to quickly learn a foreign language for Bible translations, or to quickly understand and speak multiple known languages.

THE SCRIPTURAL DEFINITION: Paul said there are the **Tongues** of men and angels (1 Corinthians 13:1). As to **The Gift of Tongues**, there are languages that have long been forgotten; some that have never been heard by modern man; various known dialects; and then there are languages that angels speak for which we know nothing about except they are mentioned in Scripture.

When an individual speaks in **The Gift of Tongues**, the Holy Spirit actually speaks through the person's spirit. In this manner, it is not a prayer offered in the faith by the speaker, rather it is the Holy Spirit speaking through the person's spirit.

> "Then what am I to do? I will pray with [my] the spirit [by the Holy Spirit that is within me] and I will pray with the [my] mind [using words I understand]; I will sing with the [my] spirit [by the Holy Spirit that is within me] and I will sing with the [my] mind [using words I understand]." (1 Corinthians 14:15 Amplified Bible. Square brackets by author for added clarity.)

The Gift of Tongues can be used five different ways, but it is the same gift. (This is explained in Chapter 26.)

The Gift of Interpreting Tongues

AN OPPOSITIONIST'S FALSE DEFINITION: This is the gift to interpret the speech and writings of different languages and translate them back to others.

THE SCRIPTURAL DEFINITION: **The Gift of Interpreting Tongues** is when a person speaks by the unction of the Holy Spirit and tells what the **Tongues** mean that were spoken. It is wise to remember that this

His Nine Gifts

is not a gift of *transliteration*. In other words, it is not a word-by-word interpretation. Rather it is a truthful conveyance of what was spoken.

I have used translators for over thirty years throughout various nations. The use of certain words and phrases often lose their meaning when translated word-by-word from one language to another. Accordingly, to accurately translate from one language to another, compatible words of any given culture are used to render a clear understanding—words that were not necessarily spoken in the original **Tongue**.

For instance, in the English language, a person's passion is often described as, *with the whole heart*. Thus, in the English we say, "Love the Lord with all your heart." But in certain Pacific island villages, using that term would be confusing. For them, the seat of passion is the throat. Hence, the interpreter would say, "Love the Lord with all your throat."

A good translator understands the language and then speaks the interpretation in the context of culture. Accordingly, the Holy Spirit takes the **Tongue** that was spoken and interprets it in the context of the intended culture, or, very specifically, as it impacts the person to whom it is intended. When **The Gift of Tongues** are thus interpreted, it renders the same benefit as **Prophecy** that is spoken in the natural understandable language of the people present.

CHAPTER 31
THE GIFT OF TONGUES
"The Key To Hearing God's Voice"

How many times have you said or heard someone say, "I wish I could hear God's voice?" Or, "I can't hear the Lord."

Naturally, we're not speaking of hearing His audible voice, unless, by **The Gift of the Discerning of Spirits** we are brought into the spiritual realm and hear Him as if it is the natural realm. Accordingly, in most cases when we use the phrase of *hearing His voice,* it is knowing His will, wisdom, and insight.

Communication Then and Now

When Jesus was physically present on the earth, the mode of communication was natural—face to face. God, as Jesus Christ, was in their presence and He explained all things to His disciples (Mark 4:34). They only needed to ask. As instantly as they asked, He gave them the exact and precise answer. There was never an instance when Jesus said, "I don't know the answer", or "Let Me pray about that."

After Jesus ascended into Heaven, the mode of communication changed from the natural to the spiritual. Accordingly, the spiritual is *now* the mode of communication through which we must learn to understand our Heavenly Father's voice, leading, impressions, and communication—through our spirit. This type of communication is emphasized in the following verses:

> "The Spirit Himself testifies and confirms together with our spirit [assuring us] that we [believers] are children of God." (Romans 8:16. The Amplified Bible. Square brackets by publisher for added clarity.)

> "We also speak of these things [God's truths], not in words taught or supplied by human wisdom, but in those taught by the Spirit, combining and interpreting spiritual

Learning By The Gift of Tongues

thoughts with spiritual words [for those being guided by the Holy Spirit]." (1 Corinthians 2:13. The Amplified Bible. Square brackets by publisher for added clarity.)

"Now the mind of the flesh is death [both now and forever–because it pursues sin]; but the mind of the Spirit is life and peace [the spiritual well-being that comes from walking with God–both now and forever]." (Romans 8:6. The Amplified Bible. Square brackets by publisher for added clarity.)

"For all who are being led by the Spirit of God, these are sons of God." (Romans 8:14)

"But when He, the Spirit of truth, comes, He will guide you into all the truth; for He will not speak on His own initiative, but whatever He hears, He will speak; and He will disclose to you what is to come." (John 16:13)

Our walk and communication with our Heavenly Father is 4th dimensional, that is, His spirit to our spirit. The Holy Spirit communicates through our spirit the words and leading of our Heavenly Father.

Our born-again-spirit is made alive in Christ and able to receive our Heavenly Father's leading. It is responsive to the life of His Word. The faith which He gave us to believe (Ephesians 2:8) connects with everything our Heavenly Father discloses to us in His Written Word and by the leading of His Holy Spirit.

At the same time, hearing God's voice, that is, knowing His leading, communication, and impressions, is not automatic any more than a baby learning to walk or run. Being born again is the *beginning* of learning to understand the voice of our Heavenly Father's Kingdom including His spiritual-based communications.

Develop Sensitivity in Your Spirit

One of the most powerful ways to develop sensitivity to the Holy Spirit is by praying in **The Gift of Tongues**. In this mode of communication, the Holy Spirit prays the perfect will of God through your spirit. To that cause, we are told in three areas of Scriptures what praying in other **Tongues** does:

"One who speaks in a tongue edifies himself; but one who prophesies edifies the church [promotes growth in spiritual wisdom, devotion, holiness, and joy]." (1 Corinthians 14:4. Square brackets by author for added clarity.)

"But you, beloved, build yourselves up on [the foundation of] your most holy faith [continually progress, rise like an edifice higher and higher], pray in the Holy Spirit." (Jude 1:20. Square brackets by author for added clarity.)

"With all prayer and petition pray [with specific requests] at all times [on every occasion and in every season] in the Spirit, and with this in view, stay alert with all perseverance and petition [interceding in prayer] for all God's people." (Ephesians 6:18. Square brackets by author for added clarity.)

In 1st Corinthians chapter fourteen, Paul stresses the importance of building up the church. He tells us that speaking in **The Gift of Tongues** during the church service does not benefit the people unless they understand what is being said. For that reason, Paul stresses **Prophecy** spoken in the natural language as more beneficial for edifying the congregation than **The Gift of Tongues**, *unless* **The Gift of Tongues** is followed with its interpretation. When **Tongues** is interpreted, it is equal to the same effect as **Prophecy**.

According to the same *principle* of edification, when you privately pray in **The Gift of Tongues**, it edifies *you*. But how? Praying in the spirit, that is, praying in **The Gift of Tongues** by the Holy Spirit, builds you up on your most holy faith (Jude 1:20).

It builds you up in two ways: (1) The Holy Spirit intercedes for you according to the perfect will of the Father (Romans 8:26). And, (2) as you pray in the Spirit, the Holy Spirit reveals what He is praying *through* you.

The training ground of experience is learning to understand His voice, leading, and impressions. It is here that you fast-track with the Holy Spirit in learning His voice by developing spiritual sensitivity.

STORY:
I was speaking at a conference one time and a gentleman that sat in a front-row seat got up three times during my message to go to the bathroom. Each time he crossed directly in front of the TV cameras. I wondered why he simply didn't stand up, turn, and walk toward the back of the large room and cross over.

Learning By The Gift of Tongues

After the third time, as he sat down I looked at him and then looked at my Bible which was open to the verse I was speaking on. Suddenly, I was lost. I had no idea what I was talking about; I had no idea what my last words were. I looked down at the Bible and said, "Hmm." I then looked up and again noticed the man sitting there.

When I looked at him, suddenly I received a **Word of Knowledge** and a **Word of Wisdom** for him. I said, "Sir. You, from Georgia, (that was all I knew of the man). The Lord said to tell you that He loves you and that He has a wonderful plan for your life."

That was it. There was nothing amazing about it. I could have said that to anyone. It seemed as no great headline or revelation. In fact, I felt a little embarrassed. Of course God loved Him. And of course God had a plan for his life. Doesn't He love everyone? And doesn't He have plans for all His people?

The man, however, looked dumfounded. I again looked at my Bible and suddenly I knew exactly where I had left off. I dismissed the moment and went on with my message.

Several days later, I received a phone call from him. He asked me to come to his house because he wanted to show me something. When I came to visit him, he heartily greeted me and invited me to his living room. He then played a DVD of the service on his TV set.

He asked me if I remembered that moment. I quickly affirmed that I did, and then told him how awkward it seemed, including the word I gave him.

What he explained to me was amazing: After the third time he sat down, he leaned over to his wife and whispered to her, "I am so sick I don't think I can make it through the service." Then he leaned forward, placed his face into the palms of his hands, and said, "Lord, you know I love you. If you love me, have that preacher stop the service and tell me."

That's exactly what happened. But then something else happened as well. The man was suffering from a hiatal hernia and he was instantly healed. He was so incredibly thrilled that our Heavenly Father would do for him what he had prayed only a few seconds earlier. He realized for the first time that he was known by his Heavenly Father; that he was an individual before Him; and that his life mattered.

Learning By The Gift of Tongues

The effect of his Heavenly Father's personal touch lingered over his life for weeks. It so impressed him that it became a reference marker for his life from that point forward.

After he came home from the service that night, an interesting event took place that was equally as impressive. With great excitement, he called a friend that was bedridden and completely paralyzed. Sadly, the doctors did not know the cause. He told his friend about the miracle of God affirming His love. As he told his friend the story, the paralyzed man was instantly healed.

I was concerned. Not at the testimony, but at how gently the Holy Spirit prompted me to speak the word. It was nearly imperceptible to my spirit. And then I realized something even more disturbing: I wondered how many times the Lord had spoken to me in the past when I was too insensitive to hear.

I realized an important lesson: I had to keep myself in laser alignment with the Lord and be in readiness at all times. I needed to be able to hear, know, and understand the promptings of the Holy Spirit at any given moment.

◆ ◆ ◆ ◆

Aligning with the Spirit

Jesus lived His life in unremitting sensitivity to the Holy Spirit. Never, in a single moment in all His earthly sojourn was He ever misaligned or less than sensitive to the voice of His Father.

Unfortunately, in contrast to Jesus who did not have a sin nature, we were born with a sin nature. But when we are born again, our spirit is changed, made alive, and set in alignment with the Holy Spirit. When we sin, we sin from that domain of our unregenerated soul. For this reason, we are told:

> "If in fact you have [really] heard Him and have been taught by Him, just as truth is in Jesus [revealed in His life and personified in Him], 22 that, regarding your previous way of life, you put off your old self [completely discard your former nature], which is being corrupted through deceitful desires, 23 <u>and be continually renewed in the spirit of your mind</u> [having a fresh, untarnished mental and spiritual attitude], 24 and put on the new self [the regenerated and renewed nature], created in God's

image, [godlike] in the righteousness and holiness of the truth [living in a way that expresses to God your gratitude for your salvation]." (Ephesians 4:21-24, Amplified Bible. Square brackets by publisher for added clarity. Underline by author for added emphasis.)

Before you were born again, your spirit was dead to God and you lived a self-serving soul-driven life. But when you accepted Jesus Christ, your spirit was born again and made alive to our Heavenly Father. From that moment forward, you were given a new nature, a nature compatible with the Holy Spirit. You are now able to believe your Heavenly Father, including His Word, leading, directions, impressions, principles, Kingdom authority, and everything He discloses to you about your new life in Jesus Christ. All of this is taught by the Holy Spirit and made known to you in your spirit as He communicates to you.

Spirit, Soul, and Body

At the time you were saved, your soul was not completed in the same way as your spirit. Consequently, your soul is currently being renewed. Thus, we see three things: (1) your spirit is fully born again; (2) your soul is in the process of being renewed; and (3) your body will one day be perfect—specifically on the day of the Rapture when you are given a timeless eternal glorified body and a fully completed and fully regenerated mind.

At the time of the Lord's return, which is the Rapture, our body and soul will be instantly completed and we will have the full "Mind of Christ". Our bodies will instantly be in a glorified condition, fully restored to perfection and never again subject to aging, sickness, or disease. Our spirit will remain in its fully saved condition and filled with the ever-expanding revelation of our Heavenly Father.

If you are born again, you are to be spirit-driven and no longer dominated by that part of your unregenerated soul which is shaped by the lusts of your former life. You have the Holy Spirit's power within you to follow Him. Conversely, you are no longer captive to your soul along with its former patterns of lusts and unclean desires.

The process of your soul's renewal starts with the submission of your spirit to the Word of God. In so doing, your inner person, that is, your spirit, is strengthened to lead the soul instead of the soul leading your spirit. As the Holy Spirit teaches you, that is, His Spirit to your spirit, your soul is in a continuous renewal by God's Word. This process is

Learning By The Gift of Tongues

called *sanctification*, that is, your life changing and being more and more obedient to the Holy Spirit's leading. This is the maturity process in Jesus Christ—the standard for which we are to reach.

> "Whoever says he lives in Christ [that is, whoever says he has accepted Him as God and Savior] ought [as a moral obligation] to walk and conduct himself just as He walked and conducted Himself." (1 John. 2:6. Square brackets by author for added clarity.)

The key to a *power-walk* in Jesus is keeping the dictates of your soul in submission to God's Word where your spirit is already aligned. The soul, which is your emotions, mind, will, and intelligence, must be trained to submit to the Lord as you continually surrender to the Holy Spirit in your spirit. But if you allow yourself to be led by that part of your old nature from the domain of your unregenerated soul, then you will serve the dictates and ambitions of the flesh—the very thing the Lord delivered you from *before* you were born again.

ଓଞ୍ଚ

The Triumphant Holy Spirit, the illuminator and revelator of our Father's Word, will, in these last days, open our eyes and give us revelational understanding of truth. No longer will we struggle over doctrines, division, and differences of beliefs. We will all be as one voice, one heart, under one Father, and serving Jesus in the majesty of His glorious truth in agreement and power.

ଓଞ୍ଚ

In view of this, you must be Holy Spirit-led and stay in laser alignment with Him in everything He tells you and leads you to do.

When you sense the slightest degree of drifting from the intimate fellowship of the Holy Spirit, even small, almost imperceptible degrees, STOP and realign with Him.

Of no surprise, every person is subject to the complications of this present life. For that reason, we must continually feed ourselves with God's Living Word, pray in the Holy Spirit, and remain tenderly sensitive to His presence. As you pray in the Holy Spirit by **The Gift of Tongues**, your spirit is edified, built up, empowered, and strengthened against the demands of your unregenerated soul.

The Doorway to Eight Gifts

CHAPTER 32
THE DOORWAY TO EIGHT GIFTS
"Knowing His Voice in the Leading"

The previous chapter addressed the need to sensitize your spirit to the Lord's Spirit so that you can recognize His impressions, leading, and communications. Further, it is to be noted that the Holy Spirit is permanently present in your life; constantly leading you; and constantly speaking to your spirit. His voice is continually active. If you listen to Him, you can be led by Him. Jesus described the Holy Spirit's assignment in your life as follows:

> "But when He, the Spirit of Truth, comes, He will guide you into all the truth [full and complete truth]. For He will not speak on His own initiative, but He will speak whatever He hears [from the Father–the message regarding the Son], and He will disclose to you what is to come [in the future]. 14 He will glorify *and* honor Me, because He (the Holy Spirit) will take from what is Mine and will disclose it to you. 15 All things that the Father has are Mine. Because of this I said that He [the Spirit] will take from what is Mine and will reveal it to you." (John 16:14-15. Square brackets by author for added clarity.)

The Holy Spirit guides you, second by second; He speaks to you; He discloses deep revelations concerning Jesus; He advances knowledge to you concerning things to come in your life and what you should do or be doing; He takes the truths of Jesus and reveals them so that you can have a deeper revelational understanding of your Heavenly Father.

> "And [I, Paul, pray] that the eyes of your heart [the very center and core of your being] may be enlightened [flooded with light and revelation by the Holy Spirit], so that you will know *and* cherish the hope [the divine guarantee, the confident expectation] to which He has called

you, the riches of His glorious inheritance in the saints [God's people], 19 and [so that you will begin to know by revelation of the Holy Spirit] what the immeasurable *and* unlimited *and* surpassing greatness of His [active, spiritual] power that is in us who believe. These are in accordance with the working of His mighty strength 20 which He produced in Christ when He raised Him from the dead and seated Him at His own right hand in the heavenly *places* 21 far above all rule and authority and power and dominion [whether angelic or human], and [far above] every name that is named [above every title that can be conferred], not only in this age *and* world but also in the one to come. "(Ephesians 1:18-21. Square brackets by author for added clarity.)

As previously mentioned, one of the most powerful tools for sensitizing your spirit to the Lord's Spirit is praying in **The Gift of Tongues**. Paul told the Corinthian church that he spoke in **Tongues** more than all of them (1 Corinthians 14:18).

And of course, as mentioned several times, Jude, the half-brother of Jesus, tells you by the inspiration of the Holy Spirit that you should strengthen yourself upon your most holy faith by praying in the Holy Spirit (Jude 1:20) which is through **The Gift of Tongues.**

The Interplay of The Gift of Tongues

It surprises many Christians that **The Gift of Tongues** is a powerful interplay in eight of the nine gifts of the Holy Spirit. The one gift which is not influenced by **The Gift of Tongues** is **The Discerning of Spirits**. Of this particular gift, it appears that God brings the Believer into it without any contribution or instrumentation of the Believer.

The Apostle John experienced the sudden effect of this gift on several occasions when he memorialized what he heard and saw in the Book of Revelation. Each time, there was no warning or preparation. He described the operation of this gift as happening suddenly and instantaneously when he was ushered into the spiritual realm. This is seen multiple times throughout the Book of Revelation.

Other people in the Bible record the same experience. Paul spoke of his experience in 2nd Corinthians 12:1-4 when he was in the spiritual domain and shown things by **The Discerning of Spirits**. It was so vivid

The Doorway to Eight Gifts

that he did not know whether he was physically there or just his spirit was there.

Of the remaining eight gifts of the Holy Spirit, you, as a Believer, must recognize the Holy Spirit's leading in order to do what He tells you, whether by speaking as in the case of **Tongues**, **Prophecy**, **Interpretation of Tongues**, **Word of Wisdom**, **Word of Knowledge**, laying hands on someone for **Healing**, or in the working of **Miracles**. In each case, He leads you exactly what to say and or do. But this is not how **The Discerning of Spirits** operate.

The Rhema Word of God

Briefly stated, the "Rhema Word of God" is when God speaks or makes something known to you. For instance, when a person gives their life to Jesus Christ, they did so because the Heavenly Father gave them a Rhema Word. His truths were personally revealed to them by the Holy Spirit. They knew they needed their sins forgiven and that Jesus Christ was the answer. They came to know this truth because the Holy Spirit made it personally known to them. This is what is called a "Rhema Word".

His Rhema Word is different than His Written Word which is called the "Logos". The Rhema is God's Word which is personally revealed to you by His Holy Spirit. The Logos is the same Word to all people, i.e., the Bible. Both His Rhema and His Logos are powerful, living, and alive (Hebrews 4:12).

When you read the Bible, the Holy Spirit takes God's Written Word and makes it personal to you. It comes alive to your spirit and you feel the conviction of His Words. They are moral guidance, instruction, power, and wisdom for your daily life.

The Rhema Compared to the Logos

Many times people fail to understand God's leading by His Rhema or when He instructs by His Logos. Both are living Words. Both come from the Lord. In whatever format the Word comes to you, the Rhema and the Logos never contradict each other. For this reason, the established unchangeable Written Word of God, the Bible, (which is the Logos), is the unchanging standard that verifies God's Rhema voice.

For example, if someone says, "That person's spouse needs to marry me", then we know their so-called Rhema is not from God because it contradicts God's Written Word on the sanctity of marriage.

The Doorway to Eight Gifts

Jesus fulfilled over three hundred written prophecies about His life including His place of birth; the tribe He came from; what He would do; where He would go; how He would die; the Words He would speak, etc. But...His daily moment-by-moment walk was lived in the Rhema—the micro-detailed leading of the Holy Spirit who guided Him at all times, in every situation, in every second, throughout all His earthly sojourn.

Every miracle Jesus performed was directly given by the Rhema leading of our Father's Spirit. Jesus knew what to do, what to say, and where to go at any moment because He was led by the Rhema-voice of His Father.

> "For all who are being led by the Spirit of God, these are sons of God." (Romans 8:14)

A Spirit-led life is a described as a "Rhema-led life". As you obey the Holy Spirit, you grow in the knowledge, wisdom, and understanding of the Logos—the Written Word of God.

The Logos (the Bible) is an *information-based truth*. But the Holy Spirit takes the information of His Written Word and transform it into a *revelation of His Word*. This becomes Rhema to the reader.

It is the revelation of our Heavenly Father's Word that changes your life! This is why we MUST develop sensitivity to the voice of the Holy Spirit. By knowing our Heavenly Father's Written Word, when the enemy masquerades as God's voice, we can quickly tell it is not of our Heavenly Father. Again, His Rhema Word and His Written Word never contradict each other.

> "But Jesus answered and said, "It is written, 'Man shall not live by bread alone, but by every word [Rhema] that proceeds from the mouth of God.'" (Matthew 4:4. Square brackets by author for added clarity.)

> "So then faith comes by hearing, and hearing by the word [Rhema] of God." (Romans 10:17. Square brackets by author for added clarity.)

> "For the word [Logos] of God is quick, and powerful, and sharper than any two-edged sword, piercing even to the dividing asunder of soul and spirit, and of the joints and

The Doorway to Eight Gifts

marrow, and is a discerner of the thoughts and intents of the heart." (Hebrew 4:12. Square brackets by author for added clarity.)

By sensitizing your spirit to the Holy Spirit, you can quickly respond to His leading—specifically His Rhema. He always speaks to your spirit and leads you to say or do something.

In fact, every gift of the Holy Spirit is exercised by His Rhema-leading. You speak His Word in **Prophecy**; you speak His **Word of Knowledge**; you speak His **Word of Wisdom**; you lay hands on the sick and they are healed—whichever gift He uses you in, it will come by the leading of the Rhema—His God-breathed Word that directs you. When you feel His unction, when you understand His leading—obey! This is His Rhema for you to do something or say something.

STORY:
A young man went to his pastor and said he felt the Lord told him to stand on his head at a certain intersection on a certain day at 11:30 AM. It seemed rather foolish and mysterious that such a word would come from God, however, the sense of urgency did not go away. Accordingly, the young man went to the assigned location at 11:30 AM and stood on his head on the exact day he felt he was being told to do so.

While the young man was standing on his head, a car was traveling down the street from a distance away. The driver was telling his passenger about salvation in Jesus Christ when the passenger said, "Unless I see a guy standing on his head at an intersection, I will not believe."

Within seconds of that statement, the driver of the car passed the young man standing on his head and the passenger gave his life to Christ. As it turned out, the driver knew the young man as a member of his church.

This was a Rhema Word that the young man received from the Lord.

◆◆◆◆

The Holy Spirit understands the complexity of your soul and how you are wondrously made. When you partner with Him in a few very basic things, He enables you to consistently hear His Rhema.

The Doorway to Eight Gifts

The Word of God, that is, the Written Word of God (Logos), the Bible, is living (Hebrews 4:12). God's Words, (Rhema or Logos), never die. And because the Written Word of God came through the inspiration of the Holy Spirit as He moved upon and guided those who wrote His Word, the Holy Spirit teaches us the *intended truths* according to His inspiration. In that regard, when you read the Bible, you are reading a supernatural Living Word of God—the Logos. It is here that the Holy Spirit comes alongside you and teaches you all things in their proper context and order.

By having a well-rounded and deep understanding of God's Word, you will amass an inventory of powerful truths by which you can know and understand His spiritual guidance. This means that if someone or even another spirit speaks to you, you will recognize whether it is the voice of the Holy Spirit, or another voice masquerading as if it is the Lord.

Your confidence is this: God NEVER contradicts Himself, and the Holy Spirit NEVER speaks or leads you contrary to God's Written Word.

As you read and study God's Written Word, His Word comes to you in the format of *information*. This is the starting point. The Holy Spirit then takes His Written Word and unlocks the depths of His truths which become *revelation*—Rhema to you. This is when His Word makes you free and changes your life. It is an ongoing process.

To accelerate that effect, you must consistently pray in the Holy Spirit by **The Gift of Tongues** for dedicated periods of time, even intermittently throughout the day. Keep your spirit tuned and sensitive to the Holy Spirit. Praying in **The Gift of Tongues** is a powerful tool that feeds your spirit as the Holy Spirit prays through you.

Life-styling the righteous standard of God's Word keeps you from *grieving* the Holy Spirit or quenching His voice (Ephesians 4:30; 1 Thessalonians 5:19). Therefore, separate from anything contrary to the Word of God and follow the Holy Spirit's leading.

Each of us stand before our Heavenly Father according to how He leads us by the Holy Spirit. Nonetheless, our Father never violates His established Written Word.

Let me offer an example of personal influence by the Holy Spirit as it differs from one person to the next: When the angel Gabriel

The Doorway to Eight Gifts

announced John the Baptist's coming birth, he told John's father that John was not permitted to drink anything from the vine, even fresh squeezed juice from the vine, nor any alcoholic beverage (Luke 1:15).

Typically, grape juice starts fermenting within a week after it is placed in a non-refrigerated container. In the era of Jesus, avoiding varying degrees of alcohol in the commonly served grape juice was nearly impossible except for fresh squeezed juice from the vine. Even so, we know that Jesus was NEVER intoxicated.

In contrast to John, Jesus, the sinless and spotless unique Son of God, drank juice that came from the vine. Because there was no refrigeration, after the grape juice was stored, from one container to the other it had varying degrees of alcohol.

John was the greatest prophet of the Old Testament. He was led by the Holy Spirit to refuse anything of the vine in order to avoid alcohol in ANY degree. By comparison, Jesus, who was sinless, was permitted to drink from the vine; but John, who was NOT sinless, was not permitted to drink from the vine.

Both individuals were holy and obedient before the Father; and both individuals were led by the Holy Spirit according to the Father's unique plan in each of their lives.

The point is this: *holiness* is simply defined as obeying the Holy Spirit's leading. It is not a formula where one size fits all. The Holy Spirit never leads you into any sin; nor does He entrap you by legalism; nor does He EVER contradict the Written Word of God. Each person's life, therefore, is unique before our Heavenly Father as to how He leads and uses a person. And always remember: the Holy Spirit never leads anyone contrary to the established Written Word of God.

By practicing these three things: (1) the study of God's Word; (2) praying in the Holy Spirit; and (3) obeying His leading, you will develop an ever increasing sensitivity to His voice. Of course, added to these is the continual fellowship we have with the Believers in church, and the power of worship—both personal and corporate in the Body of Christ. (These need no elaboration to explain them.)

Every gift is launched by the impression and leading of the Holy Spirit. This is His Rhema voice to you. Obedience to the Holy Spirit is being led by His unction—the impression of what He tells us to do at any given moment.

The Doorway to Eight Gifts

Prophecy, **The Word of Knowledge**, **The Word of Wisdom**, and **The Gift of Tongues** are gifts that are spoken through people by the Holy Spirit. Further, **The Interpretations of Tongues** is also directed to people. In each case, it requires that you speak in representation to the Holy Spirit's voice and leading.

First, however, before you can operate in those gifts, you must recognize the Holy Spirit's prompting. After recognizing His voice, you must know whether He wants you to *immediately* speak or *wait* for the proper timing, or in some cases, it might be an insight only for you to know.

God does everything decently and in order. For instance, during worship, the Holy Spirit might give you a word to speak. He never interrupts worship to our Father or hinders the flow of worship. Therefore, the proper time to speak an *utterance-gift*, is when He creates a moment for it to be given. It might be during a lull between songs, or even at the end of the worship. In all cases, however, no one can truthfully say that the Holy Spirit came upon them with such power that they had no control of their will.

> "For the [personal] spirit of the prophet is subject to the prophet [the prophecy is under the speaker's control, and he can stop speaking according to his own will]." (1 Corinthians 14:32. Square brackets by author for added clarity.)

Fear and intimidation produces hesitation which becomes a refusal to speak out. For this reason, during private times when you pray in **The Gift of Tongues** for personal edification, it is an opportunity to recognize the Holy Spirit's voice speaking to your spirit, that is, the interpretation of what He is praying through you. By recognizing His voice/leading in the exercise of **The Gift of Tongues**, you will grow in greater accuracy of what He is saying and how He is leading.

Many times, when the Holy Spirit prompts a person to speak, he or she might only receive a beginning impression of just a few words or insights. This is the key that opens the door. Start with this leading, obey the Holy Spirit, and release His word by speaking forth. The flow will surge as you step out in faith.

Many times when people come to me for prayer, particularly during the moment of an altar call, I place my hands on them and pray in **The Gift of Tongues** until I hear what the Holy Spirit says to me. In this

The Doorway to Eight Gifts

way, **Prophecy**, **The Word of Knowledge**, and **The Word of Wisdom** is accurately given according to how the Holy Spirit leads.

Non-Utterance Gifts

With regard to **Healing** and **Miracles**, these also require His leading. Specifically with **The Gifts Of Healing**, two other gifts might join with it: **The Word of Knowledge** and **The Gift of Faith**. The story of the woman who had the issue of blood for twelve years (Luke 8:43-44) is a prime example. She was led by the Holy Spirit to touch the hem of Jesus' garment. When she did, she was instantly healed. Even though Jesus was in a crowd of people that were pressing all about Him, Jesus, operating in **The Word of Knowledge**, asked who touched Him. Being sensitive to the Holy Spirit, He felt virtue leave His body.

In other instances of **Healing**, even today, especially among evangelists and those speaking in crusades, the Holy Spirit might give the speaker a **Word of Knowledge** and he or she will call out specific sicknesses or conditions. He or she will then speak **The Word of Knowledge** for them to be **Healed**. Often, **Miracles** are performed in this same manner.

In some cases, the Holy Spirit will move among the crowd at a crusade as He heals without anyone calling out sicknesses that are present. Demonic spirits will leave people's bodies. I have personally seen this in our crusades in Africa.

Again, being sensitive to the Holy Spirit's leading, the speaker knows by the Holy Spirit's prompting as to when He shifts direction or purpose in any given meeting.

As you can see, there is no set formula, no particular pattern, no cookie-cutter exact way in which the Holy Spirit does something. For this reason, we must stay tenderly sensitive to His leading and surrender ourselves to His wisdom at any given moment.

The Last Days Are Now

Chapter 33
The Last Days
"The Last Days Are Now"

Object Scripture

"And it shall come to pass in the last days, says God, that I will pour out of My Spirit on all flesh; your sons and your daughters shall prophesy, your young men shall see visions, your old men shall dream dreams. 18 And on My menservants and on My maidservants I will pour out My Spirit in those days; and they shall prophesy. 19 And I will shew wonders in heaven above, and signs in the earth beneath; blood, and fire, and vapor of smoke. 20 The sun shall be turned into darkness, and the moon into blood, before the coming of the great and awesome day of the LORD." (Acts 2:17-21)

♦ ♦ ♦ ♦

Without any doubt, we are in the throes of the last seconds of the final days. Given the context of this book, one might ask what any of that has to do with the Triumphant Holy Spirit. In brief: EVERYTHING! We are the generation of humanity's darkest hour and the greatest time of the church's triumph. Our Father is sending us as His ambassadors of Jesus Christ to carry the final testimony to a world of lost souls that is twenty times larger than the world population in the day of Jesus Christ.

> "And it shall come to pass in the last days, saith God, I will pour out of my Spirit upon all flesh: and your sons and your daughters shall prophesy, and your young men shall see visions, and your old men shall dream dreams: 18 And on My menservants and on My maidservants I will pour out My Spirit in those days; And they shall prophesy. (Acts 2:17-18)

The bracket of time known as "Last Days" began on the day of Pentecost in 32 AD—the same year Jesus was crucified. According to fulfilled

The Last Days Are Now

prophecy, we are now in the last moments of the "Last Days" which is shortly before the Book of Revelation opens with (1) the coming of Antichrist, (2) the return of Jesus Christ, and (3) God's wrath being poured out upon the wicked masses.

Currently, there are just over eight billion three hundred million people on the earth. Every second, more than four people are born.
Over six billion people are on the roles of the eternally damned. Reaching these souls before the wrath of God begins in the Book of Revelation is a top priority of our Heavenly Father.

There is now a fresh resurgence of voices saying, "Jesus is coming." And while we must avoid the same error as generations before us that claimed to know the exact date of His return, the truth is, we have ample fulfilled prophecy that shows we are the Exit Generation. As described below, based on three key events, it can be affirmatively stated that the preliminary steps for the coming Antichrist Beast Empire have already begun:

#1
Before Antichrist's 8th Beast Empire can come, the 7th Beast Empire had to expire.

The only place in the Bible where the 7th Beast Empire is mentioned is found in Revelation 17:8-10.

> **The Beast** [Antichrist] **that you saw was** [one of the seven leaders of the seven Beast Empires], **and is not** [because he is still yet to come in the future on Monday, January 30, 1933], **and is about to come up out of the Abyss** [Bottomless Pit] **and go to destruction** [when he is killed at the Battle of Armageddon of the 7th Bowl Judgment]. **And those who dwell on the earth, whose name has not been written in the book of life from the foundation of the world, will wonder** [be amazed] **when they see the Beast** [Antichrist], **that he was** [one of the leaders of the seven Beast Empires] **and is not** [because he is still yet to come in the future] **and will come** [again as the leader of the 8th Beast Empire]. 9 **Here is the mind which has wisdom. The seven heads** [seven Beast Empires] **are seven mountains** [the world dominions of the previous Beast Empires] **on which the woman** [the Harlot] **sits,** 10 **and they are seven kings; five have fallen** [Egypt, Assyria, Babylon, Medo-Persia, and Greece], **one**

is [the Roman Empire at the time John was shown the Revelation], **the other** [Hitler's 3rd Reich] **has not yet come; and when he** [Hitler] **comes** [on Monday January 30, 1933], **he must remain a little while** [until Monday, April 30, 1945]. 11 **The Beast which was** [a leader of one of the previous seven Beast Empires] **and is not** [for he is yet to come at the time of John's writing], **is himself also** [the leader of] an eighth [Antichrist's 10-Nation Confederation] **and is one of the seven, and he goes to destruction** [at the Battle of Armageddon at the time of the 7th Bowl Judgment]. (Revelation 17:8-11; Square brackets inserted by author to give clarity and understanding.)

When the Apostle John penned The Book of Revelation in 96 AD, 1,837 years would pass before the 7th Beast Empire arrived which was Nazi Germany. It arose under Adolph Hitler on Monday, January 30, 1933. Hitler came into power and remained so for twelve years. Then, on Monday, April 30, 1945 as the Allied Forces were closing in and Germany lost the war, Hitler killed himself with a gunshot to the head.

Since the time of the Roman 6th Beast Empire, the only nation to arise with a resolute organized determination to completely annihilate the Jewish people was Nazi Germany. Thus, Hitler killed more Jews in twelve years than the ten consecutive Roman Emperors starting from 100 AD to 215 AD. When the Roman Emperor, Constantine, converted to Christianity, it put an end to Rome's persecution of the Jews and Christians.

#2
Even though the Jews were scattered across the globe and dissolved as a nationality of people starting in 70 AD, Israel had to become a sovereign nation once more.

Even though most of the Jews lived in Israel at the time of Jesus, they did not independently govern their land. They were under the dominion of the 6th Beast Empire—the Roman government. Exactly as Jesus prophesied,[29] they fled their homeland in 70 AD after Titus' army invaded Jerusalem, slaughtered the Jews, and leveled the temple. From that point until Friday, May 14, 1948, a total of 1,878 years, the Jews remained scattered across the face of the earth!

---

[29] Jesus foretold of the destruction of the temple and the slaughter of the Jews on April 6 and 7, 32 A.D. (Luke 19:41 - 44 and Matthew 24:2)

The Last Days Are Now

"When He approached [Jerusalem on Sunday, April 6, 32 AD] He saw the city and wept over it, 42 saying, 'If you had known in this day, even you, the things which make for peace! But now they have been hidden from your eyes. 43 For the days will come upon you [in 70 AD] when your enemies will throw up a barricade against you, and surround you and hem you in on every side, 44 and they will level you to the ground and your children within you, and they will not leave in you one stone upon another, <u>because you did not recognize the time of your visitation</u>."
(Luke 19:41-44. Square brackets by author for added clarity.)

Not until Friday, May 14, 1948 was Israel again recognized as a sovereign nation in the land of her historic boundaries. This event was fulfilled by US President Truman who signed a declaration recognizing the Jews in the land of Palestine as the new Jewish Nation. The decree also fulfilled Ezekiel's vision of the valley of dry bones (Ezekiel 37:3-14).

"Therefore prophesy and say to them, "Thus says the Lord GOD, Behold, I will open your graves and cause you to come up out of your graves, My people; and I will bring you into the land of Israel." (Ezekiel 37:12)

#3
Israel had to be in possession of Jerusalem:

Daniel's famous 70-Week Prophecy (Daniel 9:24) implied that Jerusalem belongs exclusively to the Jews, not the Muslims, Palestinians, nor any other ethnic or national group of people. Prophecy said that the Jews had to again be in possession and control of *their* Holy City before the 8th Beast Empire could arrive. Nonetheless, when Israel became a nation again in 1948, she did not have possession of Jerusalem. The city remained under the dominion and control of the Gentiles, specifically the Islamic people. In order for key Endtimes prophecies of Daniel to be fulfilled, Jerusalem had to be back in the possession of the Jews. The fulfillment of this prophecy took place on Wednesday, June 7, 1967 after a brief war that lasted only six days.

"Seventy weeks have been decreed for your people and <u>your</u> Holy City, to finish the transgression, to make an end of sin, to make atonement for iniquity, to bring in everlasting righteousness, to seal up vision and prophecy and to anoint the most holy place." Daniel 9:24 (Underline by author for added emphasis.)

Prior to 1967, no generation but ours saw the fulfillment of these three significant prophecies—prophecies that directly precede the coming of Antichrist's 8th Beast Empire. Accordingly, the next event to happen, the event that starts the Period of Revelation, is NOT the Rapture of the Church. Rather, it is the forming of a 3-Nation Coalition headed up by a man posing as a benevolent world leader. He will come to Israel at a time she is in great trouble, specifically when she is at war with Iran. Israel will attack Iran because of Iran's viable threat to wipe Israel off the map with nuclear weapons. Contingencies are already in place for this attack.

Soon after Israel initiates the attack, she will be overwhelmed with forces greater than she can handle. For some reason, the United States will not or cannot offer her adequate protection. Consequently, the leader of a three-nation coalition, Antichrist, most likely coming out of Russia, will offer a 7-Year Peace Pact with Israel. He will ensure his promise on the credibility of the military and economic power at his disposal. At the precise moment Israel signs the Peace Pact, the 1st Seal of Revelation opens. From that instant forward, prophecy tells us there are precisely 1,261 days before the 4th Seal of Revelation begins. The 4th Seal opens with the False Prophet's global mandate to receive the Mark of the Beast under penalty of death for refusing.

At the risk of this writer sounding arrogant, I confidently assert that those who are wise and understanding of biblical prophecy will know the precise signs leading to this 4th Seal event as detailed in God's Word.

Going Back to the 1st Seal

When the 1st Seal opens, Antichrist is disguised as a powerful and benevolent man of global peace. However, it is a false peace and prosperity that lasts precisely 1,260 days from Seals 1 through 3.

The world will be at relative ease during this period. But after 3.5 lunar years,[30] Antichrist breaks his 7-Year Peace Pact with Israel and invades Jerusalem with his army. It is sudden, surprising, and effective. As he

---

[30] Times in the Book of Revelation and in Daniel are figured on a lunar calendar of 360 days, not a solar calendar of 365 days. As such, 3.5 lunar years is 1,260 on the lunar calendar. On the solar calendar, 3.5 lunar years is 1,277.5 days.

plows his way through Jerusalem, two out of three Jews living in Israel will be killed. He then strolls into the newly built temple that the Jews constructed in worship to God. Antichrist takes his seat, audaciously claims he is God, and demands global worship. Those who refuse to accept him are killed. This juncture is commonly known as the Midpoint of Antichrist's 7-Year Peace Pact.

However, the total number of days pertaining to the Endtimes starting from the 1st Seal to the final 7th Bowl Judgment is 2,595 days. In that regard, the midpoint refers to Antichrist's 7-year Peace Pact, not the overall schematic of the Endtime outlay.

The 4th Seal opens with a swift global persecution upon the Righteous in what Jesus called, "The Great Tribulation". Within the span of anywhere from 1.5 to 2 lunar years (540 to 720 days),[31] slightly over two billion (2,000,000,000) people will be martyred before the Rapture occurs.

During the global slaughter, the 5th Seal opens and the prayers of those martyred up to that point resounds throughout the Kingdom of Heaven as they petition the Heavenly Father for His judgments upon those who shed their blood. They are told to wait until an appointed moment. According to Scripture, this happens at the time of the 6th Seal which leads to the Rapture event.

Keep your eyes on Israel! She is the trigger that starts everything into motion. It may surprise the reader to know that we are but two steps from the 1st Seal opening: war with Iran and the signing of a 7-Year Peace Pact.

Former President Obama, in his arrogant, discordant, and unChristian practices and policies, was unknowingly used to facilitate key prophecies by acting on his personal repugnance against Israel. His administration created a plethora of antagonistic policies against God's chosen nation. He is the first President of the United States to stand contrary to Israel while at the same time strongly favoring the Islamic nations—Israel's enemies. His presidency, without doubt, is completely dissimilar to the traditions of America's standing with Israel and the

---

[31] This is an estimated period of time based on the opinion of this writer. The figure is derived from various judgments and the periods of regrowth pertaining to the trees and grass which have replenished from the Trumpet Judgments.

entirety of our America's Judeo/Christian traditions. His deceptive claims of being a Christian were fronted to serve his political ambitions. But in reality, Obama's choice of religion is Islam. He is secretly a practicing Muslim.

Obama's nuclear deal which Iran signed on August 5th, 2015 paved the way toward the 1st Seal of Revelation. The substance of Obama's deal drastically destabilized the Middle East by ultimately enabling Iran's goal to possess nuclear energy. On the merits of this deal, the energy rods used in the nuclear power plants are the by-product used to develop fission material (heavy plutonium) that Iran needs for her nuclear weapons.

Iran is known for one consistent characteristic: she cannot be trusted. She has never honored any formal international agreement. She routinely breaks all compacts based on her Islamic belief that lying is acceptable insofar as it serves the ultimate objective. Consequently, Iran's hatred for Israel leads to one final conclusion. It is simply this: Israel, out of defensive necessity, must attack Iran.

When that happens, a simmering period commences as the Islamic nations gather in force against Israel. How long before Israel reaches the point where she cannot defend herself is difficult to know. However, it will eventually (and quickly) reach a point where Israel will be overwhelmed and require help. This leads her to call out to the international theater of nations for a rescue.

The lead nation of a 3-Nation Coalition will step in and offer to help her with a 7-year Peace Pact. When Israel signs the contract, as the pen lifts from the signature line of agreement, the 1st Seal of Revelation opens. Thus, we are currently two singular steps from that event right now.

We are racing in a compression of time. God's people MUST possess the power of the Holy Spirit to reach over six billion lost souls that are soon to receive the Mark of the Beast. Once this mark is received, it is an unforgiveable sin. Therefore, God, in His mercy, is poised to pour out the power of His Holy Spirit upon all who are in Jesus Christ for a final magnificent sweep of souls. This Endtime army of Christian ambassadors that span across the entire spectrum of Christendom will be fearless. They no longer count their lives dear unto themselves. Rather, they live for one purpose and motivation: to be used of the Holy Spirit for the salvation of souls. Their rewards for such service is exactly as Daniel says:

> "Those who have insight will shine brightly like the brightness of the expanse of heaven, and those who lead the many to righteousness, like the stars forever and ever." (Daniel 12:3)

The magnitude of the Holy Spirit's outpouring upon His people cannot be quantified. They will move as a single army through every religious, political, and social barrier to evangelize the world with signs, wonders, miracles, salvations, and deliverances. It is incomparable to ANYTHING like it in the history of mankind. It is so prolific that it reaches the entire world population in a short compression of time.

Over six billion souls have no idea what lies before them. Moreover, God has chosen YOU to be part of this great Endtime move of His Holy Spirit.

I pray that you will be Baptized in the Holy Spirit in order to walk with the power that produces signs, wonders, miracles, healings, deliverance, and salvation.

Over 6,000,000,000 (six billion) people need Jesus, and you are assigned to this task.

Made in the USA
Middletown, DE
27 July 2024

57973353R00132